TAKING STOCK
THE THEATRE OF MAX STAFFORD-CLARK

MAX STAFFORD-CLARK

Max Stafford-Clark co-founded Joint Stock Theatre group in 1974, following his Artistic Directorship of The Traverse Theatre, Edinburgh. From 1979 to 1993 he was Artistic Director of the Royal Court Theatre, moving on to found the touring company, Out of Joint, in 1993.

His work as a director has overwhelmingly been with new writing, having commissioned and directed first productions by many of the country's leading writers, including Caryl Churchill, David Hare, Timberlake Wertenbaker, Mark Ravenhill, Sebastian Barry, April De Angelis, Sue Townsend, Stephen Jeffreys and Alistair Beaton.

He also has directed debuts from several first-time writers, such as Simon Bennett, Stella Feehily and the late Andrea Dunbar.

In addition he has directed revivals of classic plays for the Royal Court, The Royal Shakespeare Company and Out of Joint. He has also directed for Sydney Theatre Company, the Abbey Theatre, Dublin and Joseph Papp's Public Theatre, New York.

Academic credits include honorary doctorates from Warwick and Oxford Brookes Universities and Visiting Professorships at the Universities of York and Hertfordshire. His first book, *Letters to George* (Nick Hern Books), was published in 1989.

PHILIP ROBERTS

Philip Roberts is Emeritus Professor of Theatre Studies in the University of Leeds. He is the author of *The Royal Court Theatre, 1965–1972* (Routledge) and *The Royal Court Theatre and the Modern Stage* (Cambridge University Press). He is currently engaged on a study of the work of Caryl Churchill for Faber and Faber.

TAKING STOCK

The Theatre of Max Stafford-Clark

PHILIP ROBERTS
AND
MAX STAFFORD-CLARK

With photos by John Haynes

NICK HERN BOOKS

London

www.nickhernbooks.co.uk

Taking Stock
The Theatre of Max Stafford-Clark
first published in Great Britain in 2007
as a paperback original
by Nick Hern Books Limited,
14 Larden Road, London W3 7ST

Copyright © 2007 Philip Roberts and Max Stafford-Clark
All photos (including front cover) copyright © John Haynes

Cover designed by Ned Hoste, 2H

Typset by Country Setting, Kingsdown, Kent, CT14 8ES
Printed and bound in Great Britain by Biddles, King's Lynn

A CIP catalogue record for this book
is available from the British Library

ISBN-13   978 1 85459 840 0

To William Gaskill,

the admiral in whose fleet we have all sailed

To Marilyn

With much thanks and best wishes,

Jax.

Contents

Illustrations

Preface

This book began its life in the late 1990s when Philip Roberts approached Max Stafford-Clark to ask if he could look at Max's fabled Diaries with a view to producing an edition of them. At this point, Max was in denial that any Diaries existed, and little headway was made.

Two years later, Philip took possession of six large carrier bags, which contained Diaries covering the years since 1974. These were read, a lot of material transcribed, and a narrative excavated in order to try to tell an extraordinary story. It was at this stage that the joint decision was taken to develop a series of case studies of important productions. What emerged were three groups of three, relating to Joint Stock, the Royal Court, and Out of Joint.

Given that Max has, at the time of writing, directed over one hundred and thirty plays, it is inevitable that a good deal has necessarily been omitted from this account. Yet the plays chosen here show the development of a life in directing, as well as the evolution of some of our most important writers.

Philip interviewed actors and writers from the whole span of the Diaries. He transcribed and edited them. He is also responsible for the Introduction, the section entitled 'Prelude: the Traverse Theatre, 1966–72', and the Introductions to each of the three parts.

Max, apart from writing the Diaries themselves, then wrote the narrative of each of the nine case studies, both placing them in context and adding a retrospective and contemporary commentary. Overall, we hope that the book offers unusual, if not unique, insights into the rehearsal processes of some of the most important plays of the second half of the twentieth century. We also hope that this collaborative effort illuminates the working life of a theatre director, and also throws some light on the development of British text-based theatre since the sixties.

PHILIP ROBERTS and MAX STAFFORD-CLARK
November 2006

Acknowledgements

We are most grateful to the following for agreeing to be interviewed: April De Angelis; Stuart Burge; Ron Cook; Graham Cowley; Stephen Daldry; Matthew Evans; Sonia Friedman; William Gaskill; Lloyd Hutchinson; Stephen Jeffreys; Tricia Kelly; Lesley Manville; Mark Ravenhill; Ian Redford; Rob Ritchie; Nigel Terry; Timberlake Wertenbaker.

The authors are obliged to Methuen Publishing Ltd for permission to quote from: Rob Ritchie (ed. and introd.), *The Joint Stock Book: the Making of a Theatre Collective*, 1987; Andrea Dunbar, *Rita, Sue and Bob Too* with *The Arbor* and *Shirley*, Introduction by Rob Ritchie, 1988.

Yvonne Carroll of the National Library of Scotland was most helpful in dealing with enquiries about the Traverse Theatre Archive in its possession, as was Fiona Sturgess, Marketing Manager of the Traverse Theatre. Professor Richard Boon, University of Hull, was his usual incisive self; Lee Dalley, University of Leeds, was a great and tolerant help as regards computers.

For permission to consult company records, we thank: the Council of the Royal Court Theatre; the Traverse Theatre; Out of Joint Theatre Company.

Philip Roberts is obliged to the (then) AHRB for a Small Research Grant; to the University of Leeds for research leave; and to Margaret Flower for typing much of the initial draft. Max Stafford-Clark is obliged to Naomi Jones for monitoring the initial drafts of the case studies, and to Stella Feehily for reading them.

A Note on the Text

◀)) signifies a quotation from a taped interview.

✐ signifies an extract from Max Stafford-Clark's Diaries.

Introduction

This book falls naturally into four sections, which reflect the major stages of Stafford-Clark's career. The first section, the Prelude, chronicles his arrival at the Traverse Theatre, Edinburgh. Appointed as a Stage Manager in Spring 1966, he became Artistic Director in Spring 1968. In November 1969, he resigned as Artistic Director to be Director of the Traverse Workshop Company. The Workshop's final production was David Mowat's *Amalfi* in August 1972. Stafford-Clark then went on, together with William Gaskill and others, to form in 1974 the Joint Stock Theatre Group. Part One is occupied with this period, which for Stafford-Clark drew to a close at the end of the decade. Part Two shows the third phase of his career as Artistic Director of the English Stage Company at the Royal Court Theatre, London, from 1980. Part Three details how, in 1993, Stafford-Clark left the Court and founded, with Sonia Friedman, Out of Joint Theatre Company, which is still flourishing at the time of writing.

Each of Parts One, Two and Three contains a detailed account of three selected productions as described initially in Stafford-Clark's Diaries, to which has been added a new commentary by the director. These case studies reflect both the evolution of a directing style and also offer a view of the times which generated them. Prefacing each of these three parts is an introduction and an account of the period covered, which seeks to set the case studies in the relevant context.

Each of the sections tries to offer a different perspective on a directing life. The period at the Traverse shows the powerful influence of American avant-garde companies, particularly of La Mama, who performed at the Edinburgh Festival in 1967. The creation of the Traverse Workshop Company in large part stems from the innovative techniques of La Mama. It is ironic, given Stafford-Clark's reputation as a text-based director, that La Mama's work seldom left a text intact, preferring to use it merely as a platform. It was at Edinburgh that Stafford-Clark began the enquiry into the relationship between writer, director and, crucially, actor, which has hallmarked his work throughout. His later tendency to involve both himself and the actors in the creative process showed in such projects as *Dracula* (1969), which he described as a 'joint investigation between the team of writers and the resident company'. Equally, his suggestion, for example, in the late 80s that

Timberlake Wertenbaker make a play from the Thomas Keneally novel, *The Playmaker*, is anticipated during his time at the Traverse by his asking Stanley Eveling to fashion a piece around a book on Donald Crowhurst. The result, *Our Sunday Times*, transferred to the Royal Court's Theatre Upstairs in June 1971. The Traverse years saw in addition the proliferation of experimental companies, with the theatre hosting work from the Freehold to the People Show, from Portable Theatre to Pip Simmons, from Moving Being to Low Moan Spectacular. The range and diversity of the presentations created a climate of change, of risk-taking and of innovation.

The Workshop came to an end in 1972, followed by a brief period of free-lancing, which included raising some hackles at the Royal Court with his production of Howard Brenton's *Magnificence* in 1973. In 1974, Stafford-Clark and William Gaskill, who had left the Court in 1972, came together in an experiment which essentially involved two directors exploring each other's approach to rehearsing and directing. This led to the creation of the Joint Stock Theatre Group, the most important Fringe group of the seventies and beyond. The working pattern consisted of an initial workshop with actors and writer, followed by a gap in which, if all went well, a script was developed by the writer, which then formed the basis of subsequent rehearsals. During this time, Stafford-Clark was involved in the creation of work by David Hare, Caryl Churchill, Wallace Shawn, Barrie Keeffe, Howard Brenton, Snoo Wilson and Hanif Kureishi.

It was at the beginning of Joint Stock that Stafford-Clark began to keep a Diary. There is always one, frequently several volumes per year. He noted on 29 March 1977, 'Writing a diary is like civilising a jungle; it's making orderly and inevitable the chaos and mess of ordinary life. My passion for neatness finds an outlet.' From August 1974, the Diaries (which continue to this day) record in a minute, neat hand an exhaustive account of a director's public and private life. The entries were written sometimes in breaks between workshops/rehearsals, sometimes after a day's work, sometimes during and sometimes after a meeting. The characteristic pattern is to record factually, and then analyse the facts. The entries range from writing down the progress or otherwise of a rehearsal, to a view of an actor's development in a part, to observation of, for example, Bill Gaskill at work or in discussion at Joint Stock meetings, to consultations with the writer. The overwhelming sense is of a process, an emerging shape, a cumulative growth.

The Joint Stock section, of all the sections, shows how a text is made, modified, and brought to production. There is a careful analysis, for example, of precisely how Stafford-Clark's initial idea of a play about the Crusades modulated, via Caryl Churchill's reading, into *Light Shining in Buckinghamshire* (1976), and how there were two writers originally working on the project. Or the extent to which the *Fanshen* workshops in 1974 produced a way of looking at theatre which suffused all of Joint Stock's working life. The piece entitled *Yesterday's News* (1976) began life as a project with Jeremy Seabrook about a particular community. It failed to develop and was replaced by a piece about mercenary soldiers. Brenton's *Epsom Downs* (1977) involved a research day at the Derby, while his views about Emily Davison were upended by two feminist thinkers invited to a workshop. Perhaps most extraordinary is the use not simply of the performance abilities of actors but also of their sexual orientation as prime material for the workshopping series. The Diaries record in great detail how this led to the creation of *Cloud Nine* (1979) and the emergence of Caryl Churchill as a hugely important writer.

The next section is to do with Stafford-Clark at the Royal Court. Moving from a work process which involved the relative luxury of the production of one play at a time to the multiple obligations involved in running a theatre necessarily altered his preoccupations. Over the following thirteen years, the Diaries record the business of managing a theatre with its own jealously guarded history in the face of political hostility, economic threat, and the sustained efforts by some to bring him to heel or replace him. Here are found confrontations with the Arts Council and with, on occasions, the Chairman of the Royal Court's Council, as well as the endless manoeuvring and rejigging of schedules in order to build a season which could be financially sustained. The Court, like the arts generally, was fighting a rearguard action in the eighties, and survived. It also produced work of great quality by Andrea Dunbar, Caryl Churchill, Edward Bond, Howard Brenton, Ron Hutchinson, Wallace Shawn, Jim Cartwright and Timberlake Wertenbaker. The Diaries for this decade reflect these difficult times, including the crisis over Jim Allen's play *Perdition* (1987), but also its high spots, such as the processes that led to, *inter alia*, *Our Country's Good* (1988) and *Serious Money* (1987).

Stafford-Clark, at the time of writing still the longest serving Artistic Director of the Royal Court, left on 1 October 1993. However, a new venture was emerging. Stafford-Clark notes on 24 May 1993 that, 'As of last week I have a name: Out of Joint.' This company, founded with Sonia Friedman, was to tour outside London, and initially took as its model the combining of two related plays in 1988: *The Recruiting Officer* and *Our Country's Good*. Thus *The Man of Mode* was coupled with Stephen Jeffreys's *The Libertine* (1994) and *Three Sisters* with Wertenbaker's *The Break of Day* (1995). This policy was not systematic. Other pieces, such as *Shopping and Fucking* (1996), were stand-alone. Stafford-Clark and Friedman gambled that touring new work outside London would revive an audience for whom the opportunity to see new plays had diminished. The piggybacking of classic and new clearly represented a tactic to draw in good audiences.

Out of Joint is the fourth phase in Stafford-Clark's career to date. As in the first phase, the impulse is towards new work, with a classic included from time to time. The record of the work by Out of Joint to date has secured the company an international reputation. Plays by Sebastian Barry, Mark Raven-hill, April De Angelis, Caryl Churchill, Timberlake Wertenbaker, Simon Bennett, Judy Upton and David Hare reflect the lifelong preoccupation with new writing which began in the mid-sixties.

This book is about the making of theatre. It is, above all, about the making of theatre by one theatre director over a lengthy period which has not yet concluded. On 2 April 1978, Stafford-Clark noted in his Diary that 'Today's *Sunday Times* makes it clear that I am not to figure large in the 1980s'. In October 2004, some twenty-five years later, the Theatre Management Association's Award for the best touring company went to Out of Joint for Stafford-Clark's direction of David Hare's *The Permanent Way*. A year later, the Fringe Reports Awards named Stafford-Clark as the 'Theatre Person of the Year' in the Outstanding Achievement category.

Prelude

THE TRAVERSE THEATRE, 1966–72

Prelude

THE TRAVERSE THEATRE, 1966–72

Stafford-Clark, Maxwell Robert Guthrie Stewart (Max)

b. 17 March 1941. Educated: Felstead School; Riverdale Country Day
School, N.Y.; Trinity College, Dublin . . .

🔊 I did English with a subsidiary subject of Irish History. I don't think
I decided to be a director until I'd done it, but at some point when I was
at Trinity I stopped wanting to be an actor, and at some point when I'd
got to the Traverse I started wanting to be a director. At university I
acted in productions, but directing seemed more of a fulfilment and also
there weren't so many people who were good at it.

I was on a rugby tour to Edinburgh. I'd read about the Traverse. I loved
playing rugby [scrum-half] but everyone else would be out getting drunk
at night and I'd be reading, so I did sneak off and go to the Traverse, and
met Ricky Demarco. They were in the process of stuffing envelopes, so
I just got involved in it. Then I got talking through Ricky to Jim Haynes
and that's how the arrangement to bring over the revue, *Dublin Fare*,
came about. [Demarco and Haynes were two of the driving forces in the
creation of the Traverse.]

Letter to Philip Roberts
The Oxford and Cambridge revues that summer were particularly weak,
and *Dublin Fare* thrived in comparison. The critical coverage was generous,
and we transferred to the Arts Theatre [in the West End] full of confidence. However, in order to fill up an evening, new material had to be
incorporated, and the technical requirements proved utterly beyond my
limited capabilities. The drama critic of the *Evening Standard*, Milton
Shulman, wrote: 'The one good thing about this infantile undergraduate
revue is that none of these young people will ever be seen near the
professional stage again.' Triumph and Disaster were my first theatrical
acquaintances, and they have been firm friends ever since. *February 2004*

Stafford-Clark was appointed a Stage Manager at the Traverse in Spring 1966. Sacked by the then General Manager, he himself had become acting General Manager by July 1966, and General Manager, as well as Assistant Director to Gordon McDougall, the Artistic Director, by November 1966. By May 1967, he was Assistant to the Director. His first professional production was of James Saunders's Double, Double, *August 1966.*

◀) I'd never seen a stage arrangement like that at the Traverse [where the audience was seated either side of the stage]. The intimacy above all struck me. The theatre at Trinity was equally small, but the back row at the Traverse was never any distance. It did seem very particular and very exciting. The sixty seats meant that you could experiment. With a sixty-seater, as opposed to a three-hundred-seater, you could take many more risks. Edinburgh was a city which, because of its annual Festival, was accustomed to experiment and so it welcomed that.

He directed a triple-bill in February 1967, of pieces by the American playwright, Paul Foster. The umbrella title was Dead and Buried. *The pieces were* The Recluse, Balls, *and* Hurrah for the Bridge.

Programme note by Paul Foster, February 1967
I have attempted in this play [*Balls*] to reduce every aspect of the theatrical experience to an irreducible minimum. I have eliminated actors from the stage, eliminated lights as much as I could, limited words and their meaning by making a statement *and* then denying it so that algebraically, we wind up with zero. The players and their allegorical counterparts, the balls, one by one subtract away the sounds, the motion, the babble of surface logic, so the play simply is an attempt at finding a solution by stating the conditions. Perhaps it is, after all, merely a game.   *Traverse archive*

◀) I'd already got my foot in the door and had been doing some directing. The contact with Paul Foster gave us the contact with La Mama. I was very pleased with the production. *Balls* in particular was quite influenced by Beckett. That contact led to the La Mama coming as part of the official Edinburgh Festival, so it was the Traverse Theatre which produced La Mama.

In May 1967, the La Mama Troupe, founded by Ellen Stewart in 1961 at Café La Mama, New York and directed by Tom O'Horgan, set off on its third European tour. The Troupe performed Rochelle Owens's Futz!*, Paul Foster's* Tom Paine*, Leonard Melfi's* Times Square *and Sam Shepard's* Melodrama Play *in ten European cities, including their debut in Scotland at that year's Edinburgh Festival.*

Letter from Paul Foster to Gordon McDougall, 8 April 1967
I am greatly pleased with [*Tom Paine*] to date. I think it is some of my best work. At present I am testing certain scenes with the La Mama Workshop. This is the body of ten actors which you will meet during Festival. They are using scenes as exercises. They perform acrobatics, create scenes standing on their heads (yes, this is true!), use some scenes in rotational chance form. Chant speeches. Play medieval instruments such as the crumhorn and recorder. Interpolate parts back and forth. Improvise the concept of a character while disregarding the actual words to 'open' up the guts of a character. They are assigned 'homework' by reading at least two books on Paine's life . . . In short, the contributions they bring to the texture of the play is most stimulating to my imagination while writing the play itself. I assure you, a massive amount of work is being done to test and re-test in true laboratory fashion every word and comma of this play . . . Love? Of course, baby, love is what it's all about.   *Traverse archive*

Letter from Ellen Stewart to Stafford-Clark, June 1967
Paul Foster has returned in a blaze of glory, thanks to you and Gordon. I know just what a presentation of this sort must have meant, and particularly since you were pioneering the Off-Off-Broadway move- ment in Scotland. You were very courageous and I am sure your efforts were not received with open arms by your public but remember, you have begun and you will in time win. What is most important is that you were the first one of your country to embrace the movement. You will receive rightful recognition.   *Traverse archive*

◀) Certainly the impact they had was huge, an ensemble who all played instruments, the physical aspect of their work . . . I'd never seen anything like that before . . . There were a number of groups coming out of America at the time – the Open Theatre, the Living Theatre and the La Mama – but it was the La Mama who were the ones I was influenced by, through their coming to Edinburgh. The impact of their work made the work I'd been doing look a bit shallow. The dream of an ensemble is one you constantly pursue as a director. Sometimes you get close to it and sometimes it eludes you utterly. This was the first time I'd seen it. The depth of the ensemble they had was hugely impressive and did expose the work I'd been doing, and it wasn't until Joint Stock that I was able to get to that depth really. It certainly was a pivotal moment, but equally there was a pivotal moment with Joint Stock and Bill [Gaskill] later. The difference was that Tom O'Horgan would not have thought of himself as a great text man. What he did was take a scenario and embellish it, transform it with the work he did with the music and so on. It always went beyond the word. The text was less important. The workshop to *engender* the text was something that came out of Joint Stock. That wasn't anything that La Mama did.

Traverse minutes, 15 January 1968
Mr Stafford-Clark was granted six weeks' leave of absence from 26 January 1968. Three weeks' holiday pay was due to him, the remaining three weeks' leave would be unpaid. He planned to work with the La Mama Company in New York.   *Traverse archive*

◀) I stayed with Paul Foster. I operated a follow-spot and I went with Tom O'Horgan down to Philadelphia, where a show was opening. I had access to rehearsals, and I also went while I was there to Nancy Meckler's rehearsals before her arrival in this country. So I was a kind of hanger-on. I was minimally useful. But at that point, having done a bit of work myself, the opportunity to absorb from another director was very important. I think that a director's life is artistically a bit lonely. You don't see other directors working in the way that actors see other actors working. As a director, you are constantly thrown into a state of competition with other directors, and as a freelance director, as I learned when I left the Traverse, you're in a state of competition for jobs. You're offered a job and you think, 'Am I first on the list or am I third on the list?' You don't have that sense of comradeship or companionship or opportunity to learn off each other that actors get. So, the time with O'Horgan was hugely influential, as was, in the same way, the time with Bill Gaskill later.

In Spring 1968 Stafford-Clark was appointed Artistic Director of the Traverse, in succession to Gordon McDougall.

Traverse minutes, 25 March 1968
He hoped to engage, at little cost, a small cast who would form a permanent theatre workshop to experiment and improvise and, from time to time, present plays. Meanwhile, the main programme of plays would be put on by outside directors and actors chosen as occasion demanded. Such a group would come after the Festival, in the first instance, but with the hope that the period might be extended.

Some discussion ensued as to whether such a policy was (a) desirable and (b) within the financial resources of the Traverse. The Committee was divided on both these points and wished that the proposal should be put in detail in writing and circulated to the Committee.   *Traverse archive*

Traverse minutes, April 1968: memo from Max Stafford-Clark
At the meeting last Monday it did seem as though I was proposing a radical change in Traverse policy. On reflection I don't think this is quite the case. Over the last two years the Traverse's greatest strength has been that we have built up a stable of extremely strong playwrights whose work we have nurtured and cultivated . . . Encouraging and developing new playwrights is and must remain the most important single aspect of the Traverse's work if only because we are uniquely equipped to do this.

At the same time, I feel it's time the Traverse experimented in another direction as well. For some time different groups in Europe and America have been trying to find a new theatre language and new ways of presenting plays. Simply, there's a growing dissatisfaction with actors standing on a stage making speeches and people sitting in an audience listening. This 'movement' is groping towards additional methods of expressing emotion and feeling, through voices, through dance movement and through a much greater physical involvement. Jerzy Grotowski in Poland is the Arch Druid of this whole movement, and the La Mama and the Open Theatre have picked up many of their techniques and exercises from him . . . By having a company in Edinburgh, who won't necessarily be appearing in every Traverse production, we will have time to develop our own experiments, exercises and improvisations. There's no time to develop new plays if you go into rehearsals for one play as soon as the previous one is up. It's a long-term project. I don't know if three months will really tell us very much. If we find one good thing, it'll be worth continuing. I feel that artistically the Traverse has a really solid basis at the moment, but that now is the time to strike out, for, unless we undertake this work now, another year or two will see us left in the rearguard.

ON THE PROPOSED SUMMER PROGRAMME

Disadvantages:

'We're paying out more money for no increased box office returns.' True.

Between now and the Festival the company will cost us an extra £165–£200. I'm sure this is an investment worth making, although I don't know that it's right to expect any immediate and tangible artistic returns.

In the Autumn season the company will probably cost less as we will be able to build up a repertoire of three to four plays, which we can perform for an eight-week season.

A small amount of money may be recouped through two late-night shows which the company will be performing.

'All Paul Foster and *Balls.*' Not true! I know it's important to maintain a balance, and between now and the Festival only one out of four plays we're doing will be very different from those we have been doing for some time.

'Paying actors for doing nothing.' Certainly not true. They will all be working intensively for a minimum of five hours a day to a discipline which will probably be more physically and mentally exacting than anything they've done before. Since we will only be paying them £5 a week they may have to get temporary jobs outside this time, i.e., as waiters in the evening or something.

'Same actors for a year is too long.' True but not true. Certainly no actors can be contracted for a year – there must always be a get-out clause. Also getting a company is like marrying six wives – there's bound to be a settling down period – there will be actors who don't fit in or who don't like what we're doing. On the other hand a year is not enough. Grotowski has been working for ten years with the same actors, and the Open Theatre's work has developed over five years with the same nucleus of actors.

'We may get no return at all – artistically or financially – from this venture.' Absolutely true.   *Traverse archive*

Letter to the Arts Editor of The Times, *30 April 1968*
We are going to establish a company of permanent actors who will appear in about half of the Traverse's productions. The remainder of their time will be spent in a daily workshop where they will be working on some improvisations and exercises designed largely to increase spontaneity and also to explain and deformalise the relationship between actor and audience. We will be trying to bring more physical presence and excitement into our productions. At the moment it seems that soccer teams and pop groups alone express what is really happening in 1968.

◀) We did a show called *U2*. It was a one-person show, that is, the audience was one person. People who rang up were told that the show was absolutely booked out, there's no way, but if you leave your number and there are cancellations, we'll let you know. So then one person was rung up and told there was a single return. The person then arrived in the theatre and, as soon as they had gone into the auditorium, the door was shut and the lights went out. They weren't even sitting down. They were trapped in the theatre. Then this girl [Linda Goddard] descended a ladder – face lit – and she did a dance with this person and then led the person out of the theatre back to the old Traverse and they watched a scene through a keyhole, where a couple were getting undressed and going to bed. And finally made love. So that the experiment was with an audience and what power you had over them.

We have undertaken a number of projects, including the fermentation of a closer actor–audience relationship. The result of this was seen in a play called *Comings and Goings* by Megan Terry [performed June 1968]. The play progresses through a series of transformation scenes which trace the relationship of a young couple from smooth take-off to forced landing. But although only two characters ever appear on stage at one time, the play is designed for a flexible company as any actor can substitute for any other at any period of the action . . . The means of changing the actor was by giving the audience two batons (one for actors and one for actresses), which they could raise at any point in the course of the play. In later performances a second sophistication was added, and the audience were also able to change the scripted text to an improvisation on the same theme, and back again. Nobody would claim that this was an enormous breakthrough in audience participation, but by entrusting the audience with this simple responsibility a very close and easy atmosphere was established. It also made the audience directly responsible for a 'good' or 'bad' performance, but most important of all, it made each particular performance very special to the audience there that night.

Most ambitious of all is a project called *Dracula*, on which eight different writers are currently working. This will be the first play to have emerged from our workshop and is a joint investigation between the team of writers and the resident company on man's preoccupation with evil. Scenes are improvised, written, fed to the actors, regurgitated and rewritten. Whether it will be horrific I can't foretell . . .

Plays and Players, March 1969

◀) We began with a lot of physical work every day. We used to do at least two hours of yoga and physical workouts . . . and it did help the voice and it did give a sense of unity to the company. It did lead to images, and a more imagistic theatre. It wasn't an intellectual theatre. It was more sensory. No research. Then we'd get a writer. In the case of *Dracula* [February 1969], a number of writers. Because it was a group-authored project, it didn't have, in retrospect, a unity. But it did have intensity, and it did have a sense in which we used the Dracula story to make comments about self-exploration. There was also a Brechtian influence, since we used to announce each scene.

In November 1969, Stafford-Clark resigned as Artistic Director to be Director of the Traverse Workshop Company. The new Artistic Director was Michael Rudman.

Traverse minutes for 23 December 1969 and 11 January 1970
It was agreed that the Traverse must have a theatre workshop. Since Max Stafford-Clark already had plans in this direction, the Committee felt

that he should be given the opportunity . . . The responsibilities
included raising whatever funds are necessary to run the Company . . .
To be personally responsible for all the finances . . . To submit quarterly
reports. The arrangement could be terminated by three months' notice
on either side.   *Traverse archive*

◀) We did have to pay for ourselves and we did. I remember it was £6
because it was a huge drop in salary when I left to form the [Workshop]
company. I used, at the beginning of each week, to put £1 in six drawers.
At the end of each day, I'd put the change into a seventh drawer. Then I
opened the drawer on Sunday, and find 15/6d, or whatever, and you had
to live off that. One of the members of the company, Angie Rew, used to
do a stew which kind of kept going all week and things got added to it.

Stafford-Clark's 'Traverse Workshop Company Report' (1969) summed up:

The initial idea was that the Company would be able to do work
without rehearsal or performance deadlines, and the Committee agreed
to this policy as long as it stayed within certain budgetary limits. In
other words, there would be certain periods when the Company would
be paid for doing workshops only or, as a Committee member put it at
the time, 'for doing nothing'.

In fact the amount of time the Company has spent on doing workshops
exclusively has been strictly limited for financial reasons. We have spent
time on tours to such diverse places as Boston, Amsterdam, York,
Glasgow and London. This has had a certain value. It has earned money
and spread our name abroad, but it has meant less time in the workshop.

The time actually spent in the workshop divides into three parts:

LAST SUMMER: this was a fairly tentative period which was frankly
experimental. I was finding my own directorial feet, having returned
from America. It was an initial discovery period and some of the things we
found then were used in *Dracula*. Immediately out of this there emerged
our successful Festival Programme with a very tightly knit company.

AUTUMN AND WINTER: specifically work for *Dracula*, split either
side of rehearsals for *The Line of Least Resistance* [by Rosalyn Drexler,
December 1968]. *Dracula* epitomises why I believe in a Company

policy, and it is, so far, the most explicit manifestation of its work. It demonstrates 'unique' quality . . . because of its physical element and because it evolved from the actors themselves. They therefore had a direct relationship to the material in the same way as actors in *Oh What a Lovely War* did for Joan Littlewood.

THIS SUMMER is for helping writers to evolve plays, using actors as a creative/interpretive tool in helping writers to stage plays.

Traverse archive

WILLIAM WATSON: [This] . . . is where a creature like the Traverse Workshop Company comes in: to explore, as a group of trained actors under an experienced director, the language of theatrical techniques — that other vocabulary they draw on in the normal course to put into life the language of the dramatist. This is perilously close to the business of being creative, and can lay vexed expressions on the faces of dramatists when they hear about it; but it should not. Theatre writers, good ones too, have explored language as part of the act of winning their play out of themselves on to the stage. This other language or vocabulary of the actor's ways of using himself in his art is just as eligible a call on the sources of dramatic imagination.   *Scotsman, 8 August 1970*

The first production under the title of Traverse Workshop Company was a double-bill of David Brett's Ultramarine *and David McNiven's* Mother Earth. *The productions opened on 30 July 1970.*

CORDELIA OLIVER: Now that the firstborn has been delivered, so to speak, anyone can see that, in the two months of its existence, both Max Stafford-Clark's and the company's time has been marvellously well spent. As it happens, the firstborn is twins, but not identical, for *Ultramarine* by David Brett and *Mother Earth* by David McNiven are conceptually as different as complementary colours. *Ultramarine* is fascinating because of its form, conceived on constructivist principles in permutations of unit-scenes (36 in all, any six making up a bill), and a complete set of permutations . . . which assume different colours and moods depending on their relationship with other scenes. *Mother Earth* is a larger conception . . . The cycle of birth, maturity, death and rebirth is carried along on a river of movement and colour, words and music and sound . . .   *Guardian, 3 August 1970*

The follow-up to this was a double-bill of plays by Stanley Eveling, Oh Starlings *and* Sweet Alice, *rapidly succeeded by the same author's* Our Sunday Times (*12 January 1971*). *Stafford-Clark's association with Eveling had begun with his direction of* Come and Be Killed *for the 1967 Edinburgh Festival.* The Lunatic, The Secret Sportsman and the Woman Next Door *followed in July 1968 then, a year later, the two-handed* Dear Janet Rosenberg, Dear Mr Kooning. *The writer-director partnership extended to* Shivvers (*April 1974*).

STANLEY EVELING: [Max] has the technique of getting a performance out of his cast. He's good at manipulating people without it being too obvious . . . he has a nose for holes. When Max says, 'Look, do you think you could put a little bit in here, or there?', I tend to listen.

Guardian, 16 April 1974

Memo to Michael Rudman, n.d.
I have talked with Stanley at length about writing a play round Donald Crowhurst, and am convinced it will be a meisterwork if he can get it done in time for us to go into rehearsal. I think this could be a major coup for the Traverse if we can get it done, and it does give a kind of focus to the season.   *Traverse archive*

STANLEY EVELING: Max lent me a book on poor Donald Crowhurst and suggested I do something with it. I did and we went over it with the company who were encouraged to offer opinions. In rehearsals we all mulled over what went well and what didn't, and I would go away and fiddle.   *Letter to Philip Roberts, 27 September 1999*

Our Sunday Times was deliberately constructed as a verbal framework to which a company of actors and musicians could have their own contributions. It is an attempt to find yet another Total Theatre, but this time one which included a writer as part of that total as well as movement, music and sound, an attempt to make a physical and tactical synthesis. It was also the first time that our own relationship moved recognisably beyond the professional writer/director/actors triangle into some kind of stock fund of common and egalitarian contribution. At the moment, that's the kind of theatre I enjoy most as a director . . .

Plays and Players, June 1971

Our Sunday Times, *together with* Sweet Alice *and* Amaryllis (*both late-night shows*), *transferred to the Royal Court's Theatre Upstairs in June 1971. During the period of playing at the Court, Stafford-Clark's company met Keith Johnstone. Originally a script reader in the fifties at the Court, Johnstone was a member of the Court's original Writers' Group from 1958 and co-wrote and co-directed with William Gaskill a largely improvised, controversial documentary about the treatment of African detainees during the Mau Mau guerrilla campaign in Kenya. Called* Eleven Men Dead at Hola Camp, *it was performed as a 'Sunday Night' in July 1959. Johnstone also worked with Gaskill at the Royal Court Theatre Studio from 1963. The Studio formed a workshop for actors but also undertook research into improvisation. The fruits of this research can be found in Johnstone's book* Impro: Improvisation and the Theatre (*Methuen, 1981). John Arden called Johnstone 'the unpaid conscience of the Court'.*

◀) What was happening at the Court was something I'd read about but knew very little of. When we were in London, Keith Johnstone was still around the Court, and we did one or two workshops with him; he too was quite keen to meet our Company because we were a non-proscenium arch company, and we had a band. We had been invited to the Court's *Come Together* season of experimental work [Autumn 1970], but we didn't have a show at that point. And so Keith was keen to work with us, and we were very keen to learn from him. The status exercises and the theatre games were ones which I went on to develop further, which took me in different directions from him. But what I did later came in part very much from those workshops.

After Our Sunday Times, *the Workshop Company presented John Spurling's* In the Heart of the British Museum (*August 1971) and, in January 1972, Howard Brenton's* Hitler Dances. *The play was developed with help from the Mickery Theatre, Amsterdam, whose Artistic Director was Ritsaert ten Cate.*

HOWARD BRENTON: I first worked at the Mickery with the Portable Theatre who were doing a play of mine in 1970 . . . While we were in Eindhoven, I saw some children playing on a bombsite; above them there shone the neon sign of the giant Philips Corporation. I told Ritsaert of this. 'Grow it into a play,' he said. A year later I was back, trying to do just that, living and living it up in the lofts and outhouses with a company that Max Stafford-Clark ran.

Hot Irons (Nick Hern Books, 1995), p. 54

In 1971, Stafford-Clark and the Company went to a conference of experimental theatre companies.

Letter to Philip Roberts, 15 May 2002
The International Theatre Institute festival was outside Paris in an up-market holiday camp. Experimental and radical theatre companies came from several countries. We represented Scotland. Each company occupied a cluster of chalets. We began with an interminable discussion about why we were there, and, more pertinently, how we were going to work together over the week-long conference. The opening session dragged on all afternoon in the September heat but was kicked into life by the Swiss group who launched into an immediate and surreal improvisation in the middle of the conference. One of the group, Roderic Leigh, was later in Joint Stock's first production, *The Speakers*. Robert Wilson did a still life which featured a dead rabbit. The Polish group, led by Kantor, were sombre and impressive. The Italian group from Turin had a charismatic and autocratic director and his largely female company were students, shop assistants and waitresses who had run away from home telling their mothers they were at an academic conference. Their show wasn't up to much, but they gave the best parties and got drunk with vigour and determination. The Swedish group announced they would hold an open-air performance outside their chalet, which was at the top of a small incline. As I approached I could see a large and breathless crowd. In the centre of the clearing a young man with long blond hair was very slowly fucking the group's volatile leading lady. There was also a Marxist French group who declined to mix with the rest of us and who everybody resented. They staged a protest against our bourgeois inertia by arriving in the dining room swathed head to foot in bandages, where they sat in silent protest at each table while we ate. I was impressed. We played the role of court jesters and staged scenes from John Spurling's *In the Heart of the British Museum* in the garden. Part of the Traverse Workshop Company were an accomplished band, Bread, Love and Dreams, who had their own following in Scotland. In retrospect I can see that they gave the company much of the light and airy feeling that we had at our best. As for the serious political idea, it would have died of loneliness . . . we were interested in exploring ourselves.

From a memo to Michael Rudman, 28 September 1971
We will be rehearsing Howard's new play [*Hitler Dances*] in Amsterdam
as soon as we open *British Museum*, but it's certainly possible that the
project will never come to anything as his style is so different from our
own, but by about the middle of October I should be able to tell.

Traverse archive

From a letter to Michael Rudman, n.d.
We did a workshop today and astounded this incredibly bizarre
conference by playing children's games.

We have made enormous progress with Howard after three weeks'
work. We come back from Sweden on 21 Nov. and thereafter could
perform it at the Traverse any time from mid-December on. The play is
a spy story set in the Second World War. Very different from our usual
stuff. Ho, ho.

Traverse archive

The Company's final production was of David Mowat's Amalfi *in August 1972, after
which Stafford-Clark freelanced for a period:*

◀) . . . I did realise in the brief time there was between the end of the
Traverse Workshop Company and starting Joint Stock in 1974, i.e., my
time as freelance director, that you only get offered the plays that the
Artistic Directors of theatres don't want to do themselves.

Stafford-Clark became associated with the Royal Court in 1973:

◀) And I was for a time the Resident Director, and I lived in the hut at
the back. There was an idea to create a company – I think it was before
Bill Gaskill was involved – that would do shows both in Edinburgh and
in London, and it was to be called East Coast Joint Stock, which is the
name that was given to the pool of coaching stock that the Great
Northern, the North Eastern and the North British railway had on the
East Coast mainline going from London to Edinburgh . . . So the first
tilt at the name was East Coast Joint Stock.

Stafford-Clark directed during this period: Pinero's Trelawny of the 'Wells' *for the Long Wharf, New Haven, USA; Peter Shaffer's* The Royal Hunt of the Sun *for the Palace Theatre, Watford; David Hare's* Slag *for the Court, and Brenton's* Magnificence, *also for the Court in 1973.* Magnificence *caused some turbulence at the Court.*

◄)) The struggle to get *Magnificence* on was quite a bitter one, and, once it was on, it was by no means embraced by all the directors working in the theatre. Lindsay [Anderson] didn't like it. In fact he came up to me in the interval of the first preview and said, 'You seemed such an intelligent sort of chap. You don't really think this is a good play, do you?' He positively disliked the play. His attitude was extremely contagious . . . In a way the wheel's come full circle, because certainly I make younger directors fight for the work they want to do. You have to both listen to new voices, and at the same time challenge them. I just think Lindsay's challenge came from a particular dislike and resentment at plays which articulated a stronger political position.

But ultimately you had to be in a position to initiate work. Certainly if you wanted to experiment in any way you had to have your own company. That was the impetus that led to us starting Joint Stock.

Part One

THE JOINT STOCK THEATRE GROUP, 1974–81

Part One

THE JOINT STOCK THEATRE GROUP, 1974–81

As with many other theatre ventures, coincidence and serendipity played a part in the creation of, arguably, the finest experimental theatre group of its time.

BILL GASKILL: During my last year or so at the Court I became friendly with Max Stafford-Clark, [who] is about ten years younger than me, from a generation more interested in pop music and football than Shakespeare and classical ballet . . . We started talking about methods of work and what we felt like doing next. Out of this grew our collaboration in the Joint Stock Theatre Group, founded . . . for what purpose no one was quite sure but Max kept calling it 'an umbrella' organisation. It looked as if it might keep the rain off Max Stafford-Clark.

A Sense of Direction (Faber, 1988), pp. 134–5

BILL GASKILL: A dream we all had, this wonderful thing of a great permanent company, long rehearsal periods . . . If you want to rehearse a play three or four months, you ought to be able to, and not be under pressure to do one every six or seven weeks . . . To create new work you need a different nursery . . . *Plays and Players, April 1973*

BILL GASKILL: We decided we would have a workshop in which we demonstrated our exercises, improvisations and rehearsal methods with a group of actors invited by us. Nobody was to be paid and we were not necessarily planning a production after the workshop . . . I suggested Heathcote Williams's *The Speakers*, which was first given to me by Harold Pinter.

R. Ritchie, ed., The Joint Stock Book: the Making of a Theatre Collective
(Methuen, 1987), p. 101

TONY ROHR, *actor*: The idea was for us to investigate the lives and eccentricities of various fanatics, down and outs and other people who spoke at Hyde Park Corner, and this involved us in going out interviewing people and begging in the streets . . . At that time there was no long-term goal in mind; it was just a one-off experiment. Because everyone found it so valuable and such fun it carried on from there.

Plays and Players, February 1982

ROGER LLOYD PACK, *actor*: What? Speak directly to the audience and have them walk around us, wherever they wanted? Who had heard of such a thing? I was used to the audience sitting still, in one place . . . A new approach to acting was needed to suit the context, a certain kind of reality is demanded when you are talking to your audience only a few feet away . . . We were engaged in this new way of working which made us feel particularly vulnerable, uncertain how it would work.

Ritchie, pp. 103, 104

The Speakers *opened on 28 January 1974. Its success led inevitably to discussions about the next project. Between the Williams play and the choice of* Fanshen *came a series of productions of pre-existing scripts*: Eveling's Shivvers; X *by Barry Reckord;* Colin Bennett's Fourth Day Like Four Long Months of Absence. *All were directed by Stafford-Clark.*

🔊 *Fanshen* was Joint Stock's second production. And if *The Speakers* had been the honeymoon period, *Fanshen* was the marriage. Both Bill and I had been intrigued by the idea of collaboration. We had each come to the end of demanding periods of work . . . The next project was harder and not so straightforward. Bill had produced a copy of William Hinton's *Fanshen.* [*Fanshen: a Documentary of Revolution in a Chinese Village* (New York/London: Monthly Review Press), 1966]. It is a six-hundred - page account of the struggle to implement Communism in a backward village in rural China.

BILL GASKILL: I approached David Hare about adapting it and, rather to my surprise, he agreed. The night before we were due to start the workshop I rang up Max and proposed that all decisions made about the work should be made communally to reflect the character of the book. Rather grudgingly he agreed. Joint Stock was about to become politicised.

Ritchie, p. 105.

After Fanshen *(see Case Study, pp. 30–43) came* Yesterday's News, *which began on 21 January 1976, with Gaskill and Stafford-Clark co-directing. This show is a good example of an idea which in its initial stages took one form, but which subsequently became quite different. The project was to have been scripted by Jeremy Seabrook, dealing with the theme of community. Early on, Stafford-Clark wrote in his Diary that*

✍ . . . listening to Bill talk about it, I do believe that he has a personal ideal of what he wants the show to be about. I don't. I can see that we have to find a microcosm quickly, otherwise the work won't have depth . . . I hadn't much wanted to work with Bill again. I do find myself swamped by his personality but it's also true that the joint shows have a weight I don't get by doing shows by myself . . . Self-criticism: I don't think my attitude was good through the *Fanshen* workshop or even in the early days of rehearsal.

Gaskill subsequently wondered where the project was going:

◀) I tell you, for five weeks, we did everything. We bared our souls. We told our life stories, and then we went through a terrible discussion . . . And it went on, and it became impossible. Finally, you have to have a subject, you have to. You can't create from a vacuum, and you can't create from your own life unless you are a writer.

By 27 February the group had reached crisis point. The Diary records that things were:

✍ . . . at an all time low . . . We sat around discussing what we should do, and David Rintoul [actor] said there was this newspaper story about mercenaries. Bill said we could do a verbatim account, and that's what we resolved on. Paul Kember [actor], who had been a journalist, tracked down the paymasters who organised the mercenaries, and through Ken Cranham [actor], we got the addresses of two mercenaries. And they were terrifying.

After Stafford-Clark and Rintoul met two mercenaries in a pub, they appeared to de-cline an invitation to talk to the group, and it seemed that nothing would happen . . .

To Philip Roberts, 20 May 2002
. . . when the door was kicked open with a shattering bang. The two mercenaries strode in; one came straight towards us and stood in the middle of the group, while the other walked round the hall kicking open each exit door and checking outside. They had thought we might be IRA . . . The two of them talked for three hours. One had been a Para, and the other had been in the SAS . . . We learned about the compelling attraction of violence. When they left, we were agreed. We had a show.

Yesterday's News *opened on 6 April 1976.*

Stafford-Clark's next show was the first Joint Stock piece directed solely by him. It marked the beginning of his long collaboration with Caryl Churchill, and it was to become one of the most fruitful partnerships of modern theatre. The venture was the first experience of Joint Stock for Churchill, and a novelty for her as far as working methods were concerned. In October 1975 (before the work for Yesterday's News *began), Stafford-Clark had pondered in his Diary an idea for a play that*

> ✍ at times seems good and at others a fledgling fantasy. It's about the Crusades . . . Women, old men and boys left to look after land, the half starved life they were leaving behind to become soldiers, the skull left in the helmet, women's monologues about why men do it . . . all gloom, wood fires and misery.
>
> CARYL CHURCHILL: Max asked if I'd like to do a show about the Crusades. He had stayed at a house in the country where there was a crusader's tomb and had wondered what would make someone uproot himself and set off for Jerusalem. *Ritchie, p. 118*

The workshop began on 5 May 1976, and the Diaries record in some detail how the 'Crusader show' became Light Shining in Buckinghamshire. *Initially, both Churchill and Colin Bennett were engaged as writers, but Bennett subsequently withdrew. As part of the workshop:*

> 🔊 Caryl was reading Christopher Hill's *The World Turned Upside Down* [Penguin Books, 1975]. In Hill's book, there was a chapter about the Crusades, but there was also a chapter about ecstatic religions and the Civil War, and Caryl said that this looked even more interesting, so that's how we got to it.
>
> CARYL CHURCHILL: . . . and when I read Norman Cohn's *The Pursuit of the Millennium* [Secker and Warburg, 1957], with its appendix of Ranter writings I was seized with enthusiasm for changing it to the seventeenth century. *Ritchie, pp. 118–19*

Stafford-Clark's Diary records the progress of the workshop:

> ✍ *29 May*   Scene: magistrates examining poor. Church wardens examining poor. Two poor people standing by the poor box.
>
> *1 June*   Read information about immigrants and eccentricity. Going naked. Eating veg. only . . . Quaker meeting about beliefs. A day rather

like thin gruel . . . Did read stuff on vagabonds and tried improvising peasants before the magistrates. A lot of Mummerset coming in, my dear.

6 June   Caryl went to Quaker meeting. She reports: 'Seats are in a circle. Came in. Settling in silence. Anyone who wishes to speak stands up and does so.' Wants to do a Quaker meeting tomorrow.

8 June   The meeting . . . didn't quite work. Try meeting as ourselves and get that to Ranter level. I've been a bit lazy in pushing some work through to a conclusion. Have only worked mornings today and yesterday. I was feeling tentative about which way to go . . . Do more work on characters with those who haven't developed one yet. Push Ranter meeting through. Nothing is too silly for the Ranters.

9 June   I'm not putting myself into it properly and the weather's too hot. Meanwhile we've been doing a lot of music. Colin Sell has set two pieces of Isaiah to music and most days we've been singing and got pretty good at it, too . . .

Caryl Churchill's reaction to the workshop process showed a steep learning curve:

CARYL CHURCHILL: So there was reading and a wall chart; talking about ourselves; and all kinds of things mainly thought up by Max. I'd never seen an exercise or improvisation before and was as thrilled as a child at a pantomime. Each actor had to draw from a lucky dip of Bible texts and get up at once and preach . . . They drew cards, one of which meant you were eccentric to the power of that number, and then improvised a public place-a department store, a doctor's waiting room – till it gradually became clear who it was, how they were breaking conventions, how the others reacted.   *Ritchie, p. 119*

CARYL CHURCHILL: It attracted me as a method of working, but I'd no idea what it was going to be like, and I'd never worked in a co-operative way. I'd always been shy about showing anyone my work before it was finished, but I liked being more open, and learnt enormously from it.

Sunday Times Magazine, 2 March 1980

Rehearsals began in August 1976, and, as was often the case with Joint Stock, only three Workshop members — Linda Goddard, Will Knightley and Colin McCormack — went into the full rehearsal. They were joined by Jan Chappell, Bob Hamilton and Nigel Terry.

> CARYL CHURCHILL: . . . the first part was like another workshop, making the history real again . . . We went to Max's uncle's farm in Buckinghamshire and read the Putney Debates in the farmyard; the actors were sent in to explore the house without anyone in the house knowing they were coming, and Linda described being startled by seeing herself in a mirror: that led me to write the scene where one woman got another to look at herself in the piece of mirror she has looted from the great house . . .   *Ritchie, p. 120*

🖎 *Early Aug*   Should there be men and women in the Putney Debates scene? Should there be 'hat' acting or one cossie for everyone in each separate part?

9 Aug   Seems a bit arid, dried up and barren at the moment. Must keep it juicy and fertile. Open up the actors and the possibilities of new material . . . Talked with Caryl and decided to make the parts non-specific, i.e., not have a particular actor identified with a particular part all the way through.

11 Aug   Got stuck yesterday both in morning and afternoon. Actors blocked and me blocked too . . . For tomorrow, go back to the kind of work we were doing. Talk about sexual repression in each of our own lives and then talk as characters . . . Decided on read through. I've let it go too long. Should have rehearsed the scenes earlier. Three and a half weeks left and it seems one and a half, or maybe half a week wasted.

20 Aug   Run-through. We rehearsed the 'Putney Debates' — Colin and Will listening well. Baton points not always picked up. Bob, you're aiming at a cool character and I don't think that's right. Nigel, can't follow you. Emotion comes from the words and you *must* use them. In only one speech does [Rainborough] show any signs of incoherence. You must reason with the opposition. You must all begin to follow Putneys. It's no use looking down at the script.

Light Shining in Buckinghamshire *opened on 7 September 1976 at the Traverse Theatre, Edinburgh, before transferring to the Theatre Upstairs at the Royal Court.*

✍ Is this boring the arse off them? How much easier it would have been if there had been a star . . . There's not one laugh in the whole show except at the idea of Christ coming next year . . . A Traverse Festival audience is not the one for this show . . . Are they going to come back for Act 2?

9.21 p.m. I begin to feel relaxed. Got them going. Quiet.

25 Sept   It's certainly reached the stage where I've got nothing useful to contribute any more, but then shows should do. Why is the first half so difficult? Why isn't it the definitive show I had hoped for? Why and how and in what way do I know it hasn't worked out? It's not as good a show as it would have been had Bill done it with me.

26 Sept   Bill said I should have been there for the first two weeks of *Light Shining* and he's right. Otherwise, how would the show improve?

17 Nov   Light Shining has been extended again and will have nine weeks in all in the Theatre Upstairs. I enjoy it . . . it does have a clean, spare beauty and passion in it. I love watching it. The scrubbed table . . . the figures . . . the actors lit against the black . . . the skull, the hourglass . . . Soon it will be gone for ever, but it is beautiful. All that stuff about the Crusades a year ago hasn't surfaced in any direct way at all, but I sense that somehow it was relevant.

The early months of 1977 saw a critical moment for both Joint Stock and Stafford-Clark. After a Company meeting of 28 February he outlined his private definition of the Group's importance to him:

✍ What Joint Stock means to me is the opportunity to follow and develop my own taste. The moment that right has gone, I shall go. On Friday, Bill said the Court should be for people who need it. So should Joint Stock. And I need it because I don't have much of a career outside Joint Stock, and I have absolutely no opportunity to instigate work that I feel should be done. I am therefore absolutely opposed to the laying down of any rigid principles about what particular kinds of plays should be done because it will change as we change . . . The opportunity to do

Light Shining is absolutely unavailable to me elsewhere. Nothing about working with Joint Stock has changed my opinion that it is a director's job to instigate work.

By 5 March the Group's crisis was in full swing.

✍ 22 people at mammoth policy meeting. Pip [Donaghy] begins to talk. We all need to fanshen. He talks very emotionally and we are a little embarrassed. Joint Stock must fanshen. I stay looking down and don't want to meet people's eyes. Simon [Callow]: 'The personality of Joint Stock has come from the directors. We adapt to the theatrical precepts of the directors . . .' Gillian [Barge]: 'Other people can have the bright ideas which I can then support, and get my energy from that.' Hayden [Griffin] opens up the question of whether we should have a home or not. Will [Knightley]: 'What we tried to do with *Yesterday's News* was to arrive at a consensus without the guidance of a clear political point of view provided by a book like *Fanshen*.' Paul [Freeman]: 'If we were going to have a coherent political point of view, it would have emerged by now.' Max: I spoke and I think I said what I wanted to say, albeit somewhat incoherently. I remember using the metaphor of us being like a lightly armed and mobile attack force . . . Tom [Wilkinson]: 'Unless there's some kind of articulate credo, the work will founder. Who do you wish to address?' Bill [Gaskill]: Really feels that our standard of work has dropped off since *Fanshen*, 'and that is because we have lost what we are doing it for, what centre we are operating from.'

After Light Shining *came a jointly directed revival of* The Speakers (*October 1976*), *followed by Wallace Shawn's* A Thought in Three Parts (*February 1977*), *Barrie Keeffe's* A Mad World, My Masters (*May 1977, also jointly directed*) *and, in August, Howard Brenton's* Epsom Downs (*see Case Study, pp. 44–67*). *It was in 1977 that Stuart Burge became Artistic Director of the Royal Court. He appointed as his Associates Jonathan Miller and Stafford-Clark. The latter took up his appointment in May.*

◀) STUART BURGE: I knew about him and I'd seen one or two productions of his [but] the main thing was Joint Stock and that was really where I knew him. And I just thought he was a very likely Associate Director . . . I think the first thing you have to do when you become an Artistic Director is seek out your successor. I thought he would be a candidate. I tried to get him to come as co-director but the Board wouldn't have him . . .

As Associate, Stafford-Clark's first production was Snoo Wilson's The Glad Hand *in May 1978. From early that year his thoughts had been turning more to the Court:*

✍ To say truth, I feel a bit disenchanted with Joint Stock and I don't want to step straight back into that fight again. I'd rather help the Royal Court, but if I'm to do that I must have power. I must be able to take decisions. Otherwise, it's simply frustrating.

A day later: The Royal Court should be open house to the Fringe, but should also develop its own projects and its own writers. Unless there are projects, people, energy plugged into it as an organisation, and depending on it, we're fucked.

Two more productions completed Stafford-Clark's work with Joint Stock. Churchill's Cloud Nine *opened in February 1979 (see Case Study, pp. 68–95), and Kureishi's* Borderline *(October 1981) ended Stafford-Clark's directorial association with the Group. The other co-founder of the Group, Bill Gaskill, ended his association with his production of Nicholas Wright's adaptation of Balzac,* The Crimes of Vautrin, *in May 1983. The partnership was one of the most influential of the seventies and beyond.*

◀)) BILL GASKILL: After *Yesterday's News*, we did just sort of go our own way. The creation of the year-long Company (1977) made a great deal of difference, because I did *A Mad World, My Masters*, which Max was sort of around, and did occasionally take rehearsal, but it was really my show. And Max did *Epsom Downs*, which was entirely his show, and I had no part in that whatsoever.

I had to share things with Max, who was, after all, a good ten years younger than me, and I had to adapt to him, and sometimes bully him. And it must have been very tiresome for him to work with someone who expected to be not obeyed but acknowledged as having senior authority. But in the process good things came out of it.

Case Study

FANSHEN
David Hare

Workshop: from 20 August to 20 September 1974

Rehearsal: from 28 January 1975

First Performance: 10 March 1975, Crucible Studio Theatre, Sheffield.
Then at the ICA, London, and subsequently at Hampstead Theatre

Workshop Group: Oliver Cotton, Kenneth (Ken) Cranham, Marty Cruikshank, Paul Freeman, Bill Gaskill, David Hare, Carole Hayman, Cecily Hobbs, Roderic Leigh, Roger Lloyd Pack, Pauline Melville, Toby Salaman, Max Stafford-Clark

Cast: Philip (Pip) Donaghy, Paul Freeman, Cecily Hobbs, Roderic Leigh, Philip McGough, Tony Mathews, Pauline Melville, David Rintoul, Tony Rohr

Published: Plays 2 (Faber, 1997)

I'm aware how petulant my early Diary entries about Joint Stock sound. I wrote most frequently when I was miserable, while moments of pleasure and discovery tended to go unrecorded. Beginning with *The Speakers*, Bill Gaskill and I directed the first three Joint Stock shows together. That in itself is unusual: never before and never since have I experienced true partnership with another director. Bill was a charismatic magnifico of the old Royal Court school. He believed his only duty was to the truth. And this had to be taken pure and undiluted. This often led to the stark exposure of an actor's shortcomings: 'Is that really how you intend to play the scene?' he caustically challenged one actress during rehearsals of *A Mad World, My Masters*, and to Simon Callow, who was yet again resisting a note: 'Simon, you will remain forever in self-ignorance until you are able to take a note . . .' Generations of actors at the Royal Court, Joint Stock and RADA have been lashed by his merciless and unforgiving analysis. But at the same time, the precision, detail and focus that I observed in his work have lasted me a lifetime. Though my Diaries record my frustration at his dominance, in fact I was in a good position to learn. I had directed a number of plays at the Traverse and one or two with some success at the Royal Court. I was no longer an apprentice, but each production I undertook made me more aware of my own limitations. Bill Gaskill was my mentor (a word we didn't use in 1974), and I learned the world from him. So don't altogether credit the sulky tone of some of the Diaries; it was a thrilling time. I knew just enough to appreciate how much more there was to learn.

Later I came to understand that our partnership was fruitful because he was learning from me too. With the Traverse Workshop Company I came from an entirely different tradition to the studied precision of Royal Court practice. Largely ignorant of Brecht and European models, my big influences had been the wild American companies: the Open Theatre, the La Mama and the Living Theatre. I had seen plays in Poland staged on a table over the heads of the diners, so I was confident about the staging for *The Speakers*, which was to be the first promenade production in the country. The action was often simultaneous and the audience were forced to choose which character or encounter they intended to follow. Bill and I cut out chunks of Heathcote Williams's book, and laid them side by side on the floor of Bill's Fitzroy Road flat to discover which bits could overlap or be played simultaneously. Our practice would be for one director to take the morning rehearsal and the other the afternoon, with a period either side of lunch, when we would either work together or simply observe the other's direction.

We used the same method with *Fanshen*, but it was difficult to find a way to grasp a culture so alien to our own. *Fanshen* is a huge book by William Hinton which documents the implementation of Communism in Long Bow, a small village in China. It covers five years between 1945 and 1949. It begins with the triumphant overthrow of the landlords and ends with the village delegates returning after a conference to explain that too much has been taken, and that the villagers are going to have to return some of the appropriated land to the disgraced landlords. It was written by Hinton with clear polemical purpose, and although this was attractive, it wasn't an approach necessarily shared by David Hare, or indeed, by any of the rest of us. The book was over six hundred pages: the purpose of the workshop was to find some way of showing David how it could be dramatised.

THE WORKSHOP (*20 August–20 September 1974*)

PAULINE MELVILLE, *actor*: There we all were in St Gabriel's Church
Hall, a group of well-fed western actors, trying to come to grips with
what it was like to be a Chinese peasant, often close to starvation,
who had taken part in the most massive revolution of the twentieth
century. Although we had all read the book, we were still hugely
ignorant about Chinese life, politics and culture. Parts of the early days
of the workshop were taken up with each actor researching a certain
area and then giving the others a lecture on it so that we pooled a great
deal of information . . . One of the ideas that we adopted from the book
and gradually absorbed into our way of working was the notion of
discussing everything through until it was resolved to everyone's
satisfaction without taking votes. This idea remain[ed], to some extent,
in the structure of Joint Stock itself and the way meetings [were]
conducted.   *Ritchie, p. 117*

✍ *21 Aug*   Built up high status and then reversed it. Try and find
exercise to give status to a particular character, e.g. a landlord, and then
break it. Masks, costumes, shoes . . . Long, boring discussion about what
are lice and what are scabies. General and rambling. Then discussion
about drugs. But when will we stop talking and do something? Trouble
is nobody knows quite how to begin. Oliver advocated acting out the
whole story in about twenty minutes. Carole: 'Perhaps you could tell it
like a story.' Bill: 'I think it's a bit huge to tell as a story.' Bill begins to
talk over and stop criticism. Roderic begins to tell story. Go over details
of book. Extremely tedious. Rather like an awful school exam.

22 Aug   The next day we try and bring the story closer to ourselves.
The material is very remote and impersonal, so then we told stories
about the Second World War, which were closer to our own cultural
experience. Degenerated into talk again. Discussion about working
method. Oliver taking the class. Hot-seating: put somebody in middle
and quiz them as if they were peasants . . . Much disagreement about
working methods, and in the end little got done. Another frustrating day.

26 Aug   Tried improvisations but did not get beyond problems of how to portray an alien culture. Did improvisations in a cart. Medley of different country accents. All very different. Using any regional accent seems wrong.

28 Aug   More status improvisations. Transformations in and out of China. Work with Roderic. Two people (Cecily and me) acting out story with masks. Parable about enlarging Communist Party. Three widows with marriageable daughters using masks. Begins to look promising. Very clear and slow. Roderic trying to isolate actions during story. Carole resisting. Bill explaining that actions alone can advance the story. David told Dracula story. Ken and Carole acted it out. Certainly gave a clearer rendition . . . Obviously, there is a scene here in which we could use masks. A play within a play seems a good idea . . . A bit of directorial conflict. 'It's not finished,' said Roderic. 'It is,' said Bill. 'It isn't.' Very hard. We can't all direct at once.

But we did! The actors and David, Bill and I all acted in the workshop. Bill had introduced an exercise which separated the action from the dialogue. The actor had to speak his actions aloud. But 'I pick up the glass' became 'I move my hand to the glass . . . I grasp the glass' if the movements were slower. The exercise gave a choreographed and aesthetic feel to perfectly ordinary domestic actions, and I began to understand how Bill had directed the final moments of *Saved* where, after all the violence, Len mends the chair in silence: a moment which the author, Edward Bond, had described as 'irresponsibly optimistic'.

1 Sept   Main difficulty is still finding some way of getting into a subject that we don't have much instinctive sympathy for and understanding of. Or much knowledge. The most productive work so far has been Carole's transformation exercise, going between being the village delegates criticising their own hard-line approach to the disgraced landlords, to self-criticism about ourselves and the workshop process. Some status improvisations that I set up were good, and Bill's action-by-action exercise was very interesting. Part of the problem is that we have no collective purpose in undertaking the show and not even a cohesive and united idea about what theatre should be like. [We had a loose, left-wing idealism which was never transformed into a concrete political position.]

2 Sept   Physical work is very difficult to get into, too. What exercises would be useful? We've tried corridors [This was a physical exercise in which three people stood behind each other and worked together to make a strong and often surreal visual image. I had picked this up from observing Nancy Meckler's work with the La Mama Company in New York] and that kind of worked once, but something else is needed to depict the extremes of violence . . . Realistic improvisations haven't worked.

Things got easier when David Hare began to write some scenes, and when we began to improvise the working day of the peasants of Long Bow. Fairly early on Ken Cranham giggled and said, 'We're not going to start this play by all pretending to be Chinese peasants hoeing, are we?' Bill and I hastily reassured him, but in fact that's exactly how the play did begin. One morning I observed Bill working on the opening scene, which presented the village at work.

✍ *2 Sept*   Bill directing David's scene of the peasants working and talking. Beginning to come alive with Bill instinctively, carefully orchestrating the moments. David often writes in terms of effects. The whole scene is a visual confusion. Carole: 'Is it naturalistic?' Bill: 'We'll find the answers as we go along.' Later. David made the point that he would like to continue writing scenes and facing the actors with them, and then taking them away and re-writing them. He said the basic problems of the show were contained in the scene we did this morning and that the problems of technique of presentation could equally well be solved by rehearsing a scene as by rehearsing techniques. But we all felt the workshop should stay alive, and we should not move into a rehearsal situation.

Clearly we were enjoying the unstructured chaos of the workshop and reluctant to submit to the authority of the writer so soon. But of course David was right. All technique comes from content and endeavouring to rehearse without the play will always be an arid enterprise.

We only began to come to terms with the material when we applied the process the peasants put themselves through to our own lives. Ken Cranham had been offered Hal in a production of *Henry IV* at Nottingham. It was clear that he would not be available for the rehearsals of *Fanshen,* and the collective put him 'on trial', to debate the responsibility of his decision. It sounds frivolous, and indeed it was fun. But it gave us some understanding of the exposure that the revolution brought to people's lives. We decided that his decision was careerist and politically irresponsible. He himself had doubts about the tavern scenes in *Henry IV*, and admitted that there was no great financial gain and it would mean leaving home for five weeks. His decision was roundly condemned. Ken groaned at the prospect of the tavern scenes as we discussed how unfunny they would be.

We also 'classified' each member of the group, asking questions about income and outgoings. David was classified as a rich peasant whereas Bill himself was a middle peasant. The rest of us were poor peasants. *Fanshen* literally means 'to turn over'. But it meant much more than this. It meant to enter a new world. Our next step would have been to confiscate Bill's flat, sell it, and redistribute the proceeds among the rest of the group.

Of course we didn't, but David had been beadily observing our efforts to find a way into the intransigent material, and, in a way, his play dramatised our frustration and drew a parallel between that and the struggle of the village leaders to make Communism work.

2 Sept   A very good day. The discussion revealed a common area of concern and interest in attitudes to the book.

10 Sept   Bill sets up an exercise where we have to advocate anti-foreign propaganda. Toby on Indians, Pauline on American psychology, Oliver and Cecily on American TV series, me on foreign cooking, Marty on religion, 'a pernicious foreign influence which has corrupted our whole lives'. We devised a slogan for each speech. Mine was 'Back to British Food'.

11 Sept   Telling morality tales round in circle. Improvisations about women and roles and Chineseness. Discussion about Chineseness, and how we could get those qualities. I want to work from selves in, i.e. anything must be approached from the standpoint of ourselves. Whereas Bill thinks authenticity or as near as possible is desirable.

12 Sept   Simultaneous improvisations of family life in separate parts of the room. The well in the centre is where they meet and talk.

17 Sept   Life in Long Bow improvisation. All have different characters, jobs, roles. Begin the day. Ken, landlord, asleep. Bill talking to Cec-ee-lee [Cec-ee-lee was Cecily Hobbs and we were rehearsing appropriately enough in Pim-lee-co]. Marty characterising fiendishly as old lady. Question of placing energy correctly. Cecily getting a bit bossy. Paul tentatively approaching Ken to borrow some money from the landlord. Cecily dressing up as Roger's wife to fuck the landlord. Use a different device of talking directly to audience. Should be more public, extrovert. Improvisation was forty minutes. David will probably use five.

David advocated winnowing down material. Placing the monologues the actors had worked on at any point. Placing specific incidents. Bill said Pauline's life story was best because she wasn't feeling sorry for herself or even aware things could be better. Second time around. More energy and purpose. Begins to look good for opening section, which will depict life before the revolution.

20 Sept   Ideas for structure of eventual piece. Toby: Flashbacks from meeting at village gate. Starting from ourselves, and being seen first as actors. Oliver: Narrator indicates feeling (affection, warmth) towards the subject. Max: Houses could be made out of village hall props like we did the other day. David: Purity of ideas contrasted with particularity of people's lives. Bill: Problems can be solved by thought, application and practice. Pauline: Difference between presenting something and endeavouring to transform the audience so they accept it. Oliver: Nobody knows anything about China. We would be educating them.

Discussion. Max: Have we worked in the most efficient way? Could it have been better? Has it been much help to David? Tolerance for discussion on an equal level has emerged. Will to work beginning to come.

◀⁾ At the end of the workshop, you say to the writer: 'Here's all this material we've researched. Now you can write a play about North Sea Oil exploration if you want, but that's the work we've done.' And certainly early on with *Fanshen*, we explored a lot of stuff about women with bound feet, but it was of no interest to David Hare at all. It was, however, fascinating for *us* to become acquainted with that world.

The workshop had been frustrating because we were unclear where we were heading, but I recall the rehearsal period as being Joint Stock at its best. The group had become politicised by the material and infused with purpose. David Hare's pellucid and uncluttered script passed several scrupulous inspections by William Hinton and was deemed sufficiently optimistic about the process of Communism. It provided us with both story and style. It demanded both clarity and simplicity, and Bill and I began to attack the text with a sense of direction.

THE REHEARSAL PERIOD

PAULINE MELVILLE: The rehearsal period was a rare fusion of the political and the aesthetic. Bill Gaskill and Max Stafford-Clark worked with us on different scenes at different ends of the hall and sometimes with all of us working together . . . One crucial development . . . was the decision to look at each scene in order to discover what the political point of that scene was and how best to make it clear. This, in fact, was an extremely unusual if not revolutionary step for an English theatre company to take. It affected the style of acting that was to develop. Questions about whether we were going to paint our faces yellow or whether the women should have bound feet . . . gradually ceased to be asked as we grappled with ways of making the political ideas clear . . . There is no doubt that the ideas in the book were affecting and being deeply integrated into our method of work. We began to have self-criticism sessions. At the end of each week we would gather together and criticise the week's work and criticise ourselves too.

Ritchie, pp. 117–18

✍ *29 Jan*   Argument about form of staging. Me trying it as a kind of Grotowski-like walkway, over the audience's head, which Bill objects to and thought too complex. It would also restrict the numbers.

30 Jan   Argument about staging continued in rather better temper than yesterday when [there was a] rather sharp disagreement between Bill and me about the need for a discussion at all. Part of the problem is that

some people (Pauline) would like to do the show somewhere as large as
Wembley stadium and some (Toby) in the Old Traverse (that seated
sixty-six). Debate re size of venue and, hence, the function of the piece.
Are we doing an epic about a national movement or an intimate play
about life in a particular village? 'Akenfield Chinoise' or 'sweet and sour
Akenfield'? David [Hare] feels the former. I suppose he's right.

This was a crucial debate, to be repeated when we did *Epsom Downs*. Pauline
Melville's objective was to win hearts and minds . . . so the bigger the
audience the better. Toby Salaman, on the other hand, relished the detail that
would be intrinsic in a more intimate space.

✍ *3 Feb*   Bill: Further questions about background and daily life of
individual peasants. What time do you get up? What do you get paid?
Long discussion about agricultural matters. Would they hoe backwards
or forwards?

4 Feb   Bill: 'Don't drop your ceiling of ignorance too low on emotional
temperature – unless there was a boiling point, how could there have
been a revolution at all? . . . You all feel you have to explain things. Just
be there and feel it.'

6 Feb   Did 'divisions of spoils' scene. Decision to absorb sections of book
at the point when the peasants arrive in the hall and see the fruits they
have confiscated from the landlords laid out before them. The narrative
then becomes directly spoken. Toby was upset yesterday because Bill
kept stopping the rehearsal before the actors could get into it. Later:
weaknesses still there, but the passion and commitment very good.

11 Feb   Opening should be simpler. Whether or not they are actors,
they're not writers.

Each actor had developed a monlogue about his or her particular peasant.

🔊) BILL GASKILL: Working with two directors wasn't easy, but we
were both committed to making it work, and the actors relished the
curious set-up. They never took advantage of any disagreements between
us and never hesitated to scold us if either of us was feeling negative.

✍ *12 Feb*   Finding things pretty difficult too. How can you rehearse when [Bill] changes everything we found yesterday? Get over it a bit. A few basic questions have got to be sorted out though.

22 Feb   10.45: Roderic hoeing too much. Do as little as you need. Seems much clearer. Placing not right. Peasants should be further away. Sense of development now there's silence to start with. Feeling of passion aroused. What do the others do while Pauline is talking? I think she needs to be by herself. Hardship of people must be set up clearer at very start. Why it's important is because it makes revolution possible.

Sc. 2. Testimony not played with much conviction or purpose. Why are you re-examining your lives? With what purpose are you doing it? Should be much more naivety . . . Scene got lost because it needs more rehearsal, balls and passion . . .

5 Mar   Run-through.

10 Mar   Dress rehearsal. Sheffield.

Letter to Philip Roberts, May 2002
One morning during the middle of a *Fanshen* rehearsal Bill came in and watched me working. He had made us analyse scenes from a Brechtian perspective. What was the author's intention? What was the political purpose of the scene? Most of the actors were happier operating from the point of view of the characters, sort of sub-Stanislavsky, and Roderic Leigh was claiming that his character was too intimidated by years of oppression to play any part in bullying the dispossessed landlords. I was clear that the whole political point of the scene was to show the creation of a new underclass, and the task was to discover and invent the manner in which each character *would* participate in the bullying. At lunchtime Bill took me aside. He said the work was very good and very clear; I should keep going for the afternoon and he would go to an art gallery. This imprimatur from someone of Bill's stature was exciting and heartening.

🔊 BILL GASKILL: I suppose I first wanted to work with him [Max] because he seemed to be working in a different kind of theatre. I thought it was something outside my own experience really, and it was wonderful to be part of that, to be actually part of a joint effort, and so, I think, it turned out. There was this very significant day when we were rehearsing a scene in *Fanshen*, a rather straightforward comedy scene where someone comes on, and there's a person who doesn't want to go to the meeting, and he's kicked up the arse and has to go to the meeting. And we said that there was something wrong with this scene, and I said, 'Well, I think we haven't looked at its political purpose.' We did it again, and it suddenly became transformed just by that very decision. Now Max, at that point, absolutely seized on this as the basis of the work, and that everything thereafter was to be looked at from this political point of view, what political statement was being made. Now, I had never done that in my life. Max took hold of it, however, to a much greater extent than I had really envisaged. And I remember being very shaken by it because I thought that he had taken my way of working, and taken it further. When Max finds the schema, he will then become quite fixed in it. Max followed it through, and I think it's that which gave *Fanshen* its austere and severe qualities.

◀) NIGEL TERRY, *actor in other Stafford-Clark productions, speaking about 'actioning'*:   You break the whole thing into sections, and you use transitive verbs on every single act and action. Max might have done that himself, or partly done it before rehearsal. Then he'd go through it with the actors. So you've got a structure, like a framework that you can always refer back to. And this would go on for quite a while. Max doesn't get you on your feet until you've gone through that process, reading it, saying the action, changing them. He might change them, you might change them. It's a flexible thing, but it gives you the framework, the structure which is malleable. You can change it if it isn't working for some reason. It doesn't stop instinct. It means you can refer back to it all the time. Often, in the later stages of rehearsal, if something isn't working, you go back to the actions, and see if it was right. It just makes you think about what you are doing, how you affect somebody else. Which is what you do in life anyway.

◀) I learned about 'actioning' from Bill and began doing it with him. He would 'unit' certain scenes, and I think I took it further. It was on *Fanshen* that I began to use actions.

The one thing Bill and I had been clear about during the prolonged rehearsal period was that we were engaged in work with a limited popular appeal. Chinese peasants weren't box office. To our surprise this wasn't the case. *Fanshen* was seriously received and houses at the ICA [Institute of Contemporary Arts] in London were full. Later we revived it at Hampstead. The first night coincided with freak storms in the Swiss Cottage area, and water poured down the hill and into the theatre itself. Bill directed the willing audience and cast in a mopping-up operation which increased spectator solidarity and seemed at that intoxicating moment to be a significant political act that had its own momentum.

Success always transforms a production – not always for the better – but my Diary catches the heady desire to continue working together.

30 April 1975   Actors' meeting both about *Fanshen* and the next project. Bill: 'There is one area we cannot get into and that is rough theatre. I feel absolutely temperamentally unsuited to rough theatre.' Pip: 'I would like to be a star.' Everybody: 'Then go anywhere else.' Pauline: 'I think Joint Stock should do things relevant to people's lives.' Tony M: 'Has anybody read a book called *The Sheep Are Still Grazing*?' Tony R: 'I'd like to do a show with Snoo Wilson. My agent said [*Fanshen*] was too political.' Pip: 'My agent said some of her best friends are quite left-wing. I would like to do a show with music and dancing and having a good time.' Me: 'Well, it's called pantomime and it happens every year . . .'

10 May   Actors' meeting about the future of *Fanshen,* and of Joint Stock. Pip doesn't want to do *Fanshen* again at all. Paul would like to do it for six weeks as a maximum. Roderic would like to play in youth clubs and community centres if it were revived: 'I have a certain amount of energy and a great deal of idealism, but I don't find Joint Stock absorbs all my energy. I find it very difficult to be an actor. What I've found good about working with Joint Stock is the core of people together and the attention to detail and working with fellow actors. I enjoy other actors giving me notes.' Tony R: 'Rubbish!' Roderic: 'If *Fanshen* has taught me anything it's that television and repertory companies won't take me as I am, and Joint Stock will . . .'

Pauline: 'I came to *Fanshen* back to front, not because I wanted a job but because I wanted to do things I see around me. Always in a factory or in a theatre I want to change things as they are. And I didn't know where best to put myself to carry that out.' Bill: 'Pauline's contribution was very important to the work, but I would not like to do the play entirely with people like her.' Tony R: 'I wouldn't like to go on doing *Fanshen*. I'm bored with it . . . I don't feel the commitment to it I did to *The Speakers*. The reason I like working with the Company is you get such a long time to rehearse. I want to do new work. I don't want to go off and do Shakespeare. *The Speakers* ruined me for anything else.' Paul: 'Yes, it has ruined me for other work in the theatre.' Tony R: 'I've become much more critical about other work I do. I feel a certain loss when I go outside this company.' Paul: 'Have we got the courage to commit ourselves? Joint Stock annoys me a lot. Why were there so many weeks off in the middle?'

There had been sixteen weeks between the end of the first phase of rehearsals or the workshop, and the beginning of the second phase. During that gap the actors had been unpaid, but David had written the play.

✍ Bill: 'I feel that the attempt towards democracy has been worthwhile.' Roderic: 'Could we push it further?' Max and Bill: 'Only if we were going to form a unified group.' Pip: '*Fanshen* forced me to be more disciplined as an actor. I don't mind if the next play is not political.' Roderic: 'Success has turned it into a cultural event.' Bill: 'Our attitude is what has made it a success, together with the way Max and I have staged it.' Bill: 'Can I make a confession? At the moment I feel very close and very warm towards you all. When I am away from you, I don't feel that.'

14 Sept   What should we do? Follow *The Speakers* and *Fanshen* with another adaptation from existing source material? Find an old classic that we can use as a quarry and become *auteurs*? . . . Or do a classic anyway? Why not? A production of, say, *The Beggar's Opera* by Joint Stock would be very different . . . Why do we expect so much from theatre? Why do we expect fulfilling work to land in our laps? Until we work out our own particular philosophy, what kind of work we want to do, with whom, for whom, what we're aiming at, it won't happen. Why should it?

Fanshen was seminal both for Joint Stock and for me. I absorbed the first lesson of hard-line Royal Court doctrine: that the play comes first. I started to develop a methodology that I still employ, and I learnt that the best theatre is both inquisitive and determined to learn about other worlds. And I acquired a political sensibility that in a diluted form is with me still. When, at the height of their involvement with the Workers' Revolutionary Party, Corin Redgrave or his sister Vanessa came to talk to the company and told us that the demise of capitalism was imminent, I knew they were deluded. But looking back I realise how much we were also in the grip of a dream. Did we really believe that by doing *Fanshen* at the Hampstead Theatre whole areas of St John's Wood, Swiss Cottage and Kentish Town would turn Communist? Perhaps we did. But even if the political philosophy was a fantasy, the criteria that it imposed on the work was of enduring value.

It was the material in *Fanshen* that had politicised the company. Joint Stock never became a proper collective but, even if the two directors dominated the selection of the material, all decisions were monitored and scrutinised by meetings of the whole company. The actors were a majority and some decisions reflected that. 'Should the actors travel by the company van?' 'No, they should get train fares.' But the most difficult discussion was always about the scale of work we were attempting, and the debate, for instance, about whether *Epsom Downs* should go to the Roundhouse, a large, former engine shed in Camden Town, north London, was a long and bitter one. It was an argument I lost.

Joint Stock's third venture, which I also directed with Bill, was a verbatim play about mercenaries in Angola (*Yesterday's News*, 1976). This was followed by my first play with Caryl Churchill, which began as a workshop about the Crusades but ended up being about ecstatic religion in the English Civil War: *Light Shining in Buckinghamshire,* 1976. Then came *A Mad World, My Masters* by Barrie Keeffe at the Young Vic. Then *Epsom Downs*.

Case Study

EPSOM DOWNS
Howard Brenton

Workshop: from 12 May 1977

First Performance: 4 August 1977

Workshop Group and Cast: Gillian (Gillie) Barge, Simon Callow, Paul Freeman, Bob Hamilton, Cecily Hobbs, Will Knightley, David Rintoul, Tony Rohr, Max Stafford-Clark, Jane Wood. Designer: Hayden Griffin, later replaced by Peter Hartwell. Bill Gaskill also attended some earlier meetings.

Published: Plays 1 (Methuen, 1996)

I had worked with Howard Brenton on two occasions before Joint Stock undertook *Epsom Downs*: on *Hitler Dances* for the Traverse Workshop Company and on *Magnificence* for the Royal Court. Howard's writing moves always towards the big political gesture (which became so unfashionable in the nineties). But the plays were both subverted and supported by the generosity of his spirit. He was an ideal writer for *Epsom Downs*, a big genre piece that celebrated the boozy camaraderie of Derby Day. It was the first large-scale play Joint Stock attempted without the steadying influence of Bill, and the fretful and fractious nature of our discussions reads now like the shrill voices of so many anxious children left to play in the nursery without the discipline of nanny.

Howard's father was a policeman who left the police force to become a Methodist minister, and the guardians of temporal and spiritual order feature heavily in Howard's writing. They are opposed by the rebellious spirit of the young. In the opening scene two senior policemen on horseback are planning the day. The horses were played by naked actors with the riders mounted on their shoulders. Paul Freeman and David Rintoul were to be the horses and both displayed a manliness that did the company proud. David in particular revealed assets which had the rest of the company stunned with admiration. At the last minute an extra scene was added at the start of the play which meant that David had to be replaced by Simon Callow. Simon wasn't coy about taking off his clothes, so I was surprised when he looked downcast. Simon confided that half his acquaintance had already booked for the show in response to his enthusiastic description of David Rintoul's manly charms.

Epsom Downs, like *Our Country's Good* years later, was a semi-workshopped play. That's to say Howard had written an initial draft that was chewed over and tested in rehearsal before the official rehearsal period began. Derby Day itself occurred during the workshop and became a crucial piece of research. Howard's early draft had police beating up gypsies beneath the stand, but our trip to Epsom failed to reveal the class war we had been so eagerly anticipating. It is to the credit of both writer and company that observation triumphed over theory, and we set ourselves to depict what we saw.

My stubborn and wilful resistance to the idea of performing in the Roundhouse was fuelled by a deep-seated suspicion of the different theatricality that a larger space demands. I don't recall that the houses for *Epsom Downs* at the Roundhouse were any greater than those for *A Mad World, My Masters* at the Young Vic so, in that respect, my opposition to the bigger space was justified. You don't become populist simply by moving to a larger space, and neither Howard's play nor Joint Stock's approach contained the necessary elements of populism. We didn't have stars or music. The arguments were heated, particularly about design, and, to my relief, Hayden Griffin, the original designer, resigned. He was replaced by Peter Hartwell, with whom I was to have a long association. And it was Peter who was to show me I was wrong about the Roundhouse. His set was a large, grassy, green hill. Rather than making a conventional entrance, the actors appeared head and shoulders first as they toiled up the far side of the rise and came into view. The good humour of Howard's play and the breezy open-natured embrace of Peter's set would have been diminished in a smaller space.

Epsom Downs tested the resources of the company. Nine actors doubled and trebled roles through the course of the evening to create the epic world the play demanded. I learned that it was possible for an actor to play three roles in the course of the evening, but that four was too many. Howard's play is often described as a genre piece, and William Frith's famous genre painting of *Derby Day* (1858) was often referred to. Certainly the ambition was to present a cross-section of society in the year of the Queen's Jubilee, and we

were eager to apply our bright new political analysis to the boozy spectacle that we found. But before we even started rehearsal there was much
manoeuvring about the Roundhouse. We had embraced discussion as a way
of decision making during *Fanshen*, and my Diaries record our attempts to
embrace this new methodology. Sometimes I refer to myself in the third
person. Although the Roundhouse had been home to Arnold Wesker's
Centre 42, it had never been successfully used as a theatre.

BEFORE THE WORKSHOP

✍ *9 March 1977*   Simon: 'Well, here we are again, staring baffled and
bemused into a circle.' The subsequent discussion covers: 'Does the
work we've been doing lead towards the Roundhouse or towards a
smaller auditorium?' 'Would Howard still write *Epsom Downs* for us if
we were doing it at the ICA?' Howard: 'If I can't get four hundred
people a night then I'd rather blow up and end up in the debtors' jail.'
Gillie: 'I feel incredibly enthusiastic about going to the Roundhouse.
More and more enthusiastic.' Howard: 'You've always needed enormous
overkill to fill the Court. Two stars, middle-class jokes and rock music.'

23 April   Of Howard's play, Will: 'It needs a large space, and a focused
space. But we do seem to be a bit buggered with the Roundhouse if . . .'
He leaves the sentence unfinished.

4 May   Howard: 'I feel I've made something for the Roundhouse. Max
feels I haven't. I'd like to know what you feel.' Bill: 'I think you get an
Elizabethan atmosphere by moving the action into the audience.' Gillie:
Wants to do what Howard wants. Hayden: 'I don't see us creating the
space Howard demands anywhere else.' The feeling of the meeting is
that we should go ahead with the Roundhouse. Bill: 'I'm not at all
convinced you could hear the text in the Roundhouse, and I'm not
convinced that we could fill it.' Likes the play, but doesn't feel it 'would
get notices twice as good as Barrie's play [*A Mad World, My Masters*] and
play to houses twice as big'. Howard: 'So what do you suggest?' Bill: 'I
don't know really.' Then goes on to suggest several things, including that
he would hate to see it in pros. arch, and that the Young Vic would be
perfectly possible. Bill is certainly the dominant male baboon. A
different quality of listening when he speaks.

Alison [Ritchie, Stage Manager]: 'Every time I go into the Roundhouse, it gives me the willies.' Feels that Howard's ambition will bounce back on us and could become an albatross round our necks. Cecily stirs it up by asking emotive and unrelated questions with great energy and determination. Tony: Favours the Roundhouse. 'We'll be cutting Howard's balls off if we don't do it. Howard: 'It's kind of Tony, but my balls are all right.' Will: 'I'm not at all convinced that it's a play for the Roundhouse, but I speak out of ignorance and faint-heartedness.' Howard: 'I'm not that wise about theatres. I just know I want to write for that one.' Hayden: 'I don't want to work with a director who is only helping the actors out.' Howard: 'I see a rather lazy show, sometimes with nothing happening on stage at all. I'm not really a horse-dung man.' Simon: 'It is just that that I find most hard to imagine.' Paul: 'I think the Young Vic is too small for it, and so is the Royal Court. What are we going to do with the rest of our lives if we don't go to the Roundhouse? Go round with our tails between our legs saying that we did not think we would get an audience so we didn't go?' Hayden: 'I would withdraw from the collective if it wasn't done at the Roundhouse.' Howard: 'Not the Young Vic, because it's a spiritual cul-de-sac, and not the Royal Court because it's the epitome of an aesthetic, bourgeois ethic. One does feel panic too about the Roundhouse, because it's the graveyard of Arnold Wesker.'

Discussion about the Roundhouse took up a lot of time, but Simon Callow wanted to talk about the whole structure of Joint Stock. His presence in the company was odd. His belief in a particular kind of charismatic performance aesthetic was at total odds with the Royal Court credo that both director and actor should submit their egos to the service of the play. The conflict that resulted was tiresome, but his work was excellent.

✍ *4 May* Simon wants to talk about internal policy. Had thought that a permanent collective would harness and release both energy and commitment . . . But the only criteria, it appears, has been the director's judgement, and that was the most autocratic he'd ever worked under. Any attempt at discussion was brutally cracked down on. 'I was very unhappy and I have given the best work of which I'm capable.'

My opposition to the Roundhouse was splitting the company and, as a result, there was discussion about finding another director.

✍ Bill: 'I think that's absolute nonsense . . . to let Max go . . . You run the risk of losing the whole project. I don't think it makes sense. You'll end up with second-rate material and a second-rate director. There are very few good directors.' Paul: 'But there are not only two good directors.' Bill: 'There are hundreds and hundreds of good actors, and only two directors who have created Joint Stock.' Howard: 'I have been waiting for a clear sound like a gong from this meeting, which I have not had, so I will not come to the meeting tomorrow.'

There was a final meeting when matters came to a head: my notes dip in and out of the first person.

✍ 5 May   Amazing – Bill starts talking of doing Howard's play at the Young Vic, and suddenly support for the Roundhouse begins to slide. Hayden: 'We're a very nervous company, aren't we?' What a stupid bullyboy Hayden is. Bill: 'The impulse for the Roundhouse comes from Howard and Hayden.' Will: 'I've become more and more turned off by the Roundhouse . . . There is a huge crisis in the company, and I cannot be a sleeper.' Paul: Accuses me of deliberately getting bad dates for the tour, incompatible with the Roundhouse, and says that my opposition has single-handedly brought [people] round. 'I propose that we ask Max to direct the play at the Roundhouse . . . that the post of Artistic Director be abolished . . . that we explore other directors . . . that we get a tours director . . . that if he [Max] will not direct it, then he should leave the collective.' [The discussion continued, but Paul's proposal was never put to a vote.]

Hayden: 'We should have the will to lead. If we take the decision to go to the Roundhouse, then the energy will follow . . . We have to take a decision today.' Simon: 'I would be amazed if we did not know the directors and texts we wanted to do between us . . . I think it would be extremely harmful to Joint Stock if Max were to leave. The Roundhouse is not the only place you can expand to.' Tony: 'I want to go to the Roundhouse, but I'm scared about what Max said about whether it was the right space.'

The group finally comes round to agreeing that we should go to the Roundhouse. Feeling of tension ebbs a little. They are all keen that I should give in, and do it there, except Hayden, who doesn't think he could work with a director who doesn't believe it can happen. Why am I always so negative? Because I'm timid? Because I know what I like? Could we do *Fanshen* in the round? Anyway I give in, and all of us, including me, feel a sense of relief.

The discussions about the Roundhouse weren't remarkable. In fact they're the kind of half-baked conversations familiar to anyone who has worked in a group. But it is remarkable that they took place at all, and that we expected them to lead us to a decision. And they did. David Hare's comment on *Fanshen* in the published text expresses astonishment at the interminable discussions that the acceptance of Communism involved: '*They talked for six hours.*' During the rehearsals of *Epsom Downs* we were to experience this for ourselves.

✍ *11 May*   Read through. Howard kneels on the ground to talk to the actors. Howard: 'It sounds a bit pretentious but my intention was to base Emily Davison on *Hamlet.*'

The ghost of Emily Davison, the suffragette killed at Tattenham Corner, was played by Jane Wood and appeared intermittently throughout the play. Ghosts are another characteristic of Howard's writing.

We tried to cast the play by group consensus too. This was a doomed decision. Bill had attempted something similar with his production of *A Mad World, My Masters*, but had been so disappointed with the actors' bland and predictable choices that he had overruled them and confined them to their second choices. This had worked out surprisingly well, but the taste for democratic decision-taking is alluring, and recklessly we plunged into casting *Epsom Downs* democratically.

✍   Simon: 'I do not think we should cast it lightly.' Max: 'Or perversely.'

An enormous discussion followed, which occupies several pages of my Diary. Tony Rohr was reluctant to play Doc, one of the buskers at the beginning of the play. He thought the part was silly and too small.

✍   Tony: 'I don't want to come and do that little bit. I'm an egomaniac. I don't want to ponce about. I don't care, Paul. You're creaming your rocks off. You've got something to say.' David: 'I think you're behaving like a child of two.' Tony: 'Yes, I am.' Jane: 'I'm leaving,

too, if we go on working mornings. I've got an eight-year-old child.'
Everybody getting ratty. Tempers lost quickly and flaring up. Everybody
speedy to say what they won't do, particularly when their own holidays,
time off, and peace of mind are threatened.

Group passion won the day and Tony Rohr played the busker, but in retrospect it seems a perverse ambition to determine an issue as delicate as
casting by group decision.

THE WORKSHOP

Unlike *Fanshen*, the workshop for *Epsom Downs* presented us with the opportunity to meet people from the world we were investigating. We scrutinised
Howard's script in the light of our freshly acquired expertise. The first
person we talked to was Robin Soans. Robin is a wonderfully supple actor
whom I have worked with many times at the Royal Court and with Out of
Joint, but on this occasion it was his familiarity with the racing world and his
expertise as a punter that we were drawing on.

✑ *12 May*   First workshop session for Howard's play. Robin talking
about racing. Peculiarities of the Derby course. A most peculiar course
on which to have the world's most famous race. Not allowed to have
practices. You have to have a horse with a good temperament because of
all the picnickers. The last mile is a funnel of shouting people. One
hundred and fifty thousand people, more than at any other meeting.
Every horse in the Derby is trying to win, unlike smaller races. Horses
are extremely competitive, but they either end up in a tin of Kit-E-Kat
or in a field of lush grass and buttercups with the equine equivalent of
Raquel Welch arriving every five minutes. Simon: 'Why do they race
better when emasculated?' Robin: 'It affects them more psychologically
than physically.' If you want to live off gambling, you have to have capital
and patience. A thoroughbred racehorse in full flight 'is the most
aesthetic sight in the world'. The lad. The head lad. The travelling head
lad. Some horses have to have sheep or goats or a special lad in with
them to keep them calm. Racing is socialist in that the rich pay for the
entertainment of the poor. Riddled with hierarchy. Old Etonians.
Snobbery. Not taking Jewish money.

13 May   Howard talked clearly about his play. Emily Davison was an important character for him: 'She is a more humane figure than Jed, but I cannot find a political line for her.' Jed was the protagonist in Howard's earlier play, *Magnificence*, and he too aspired towards a grand political gesture. He was a left-wing activist who had kidnapped a politician. 'In the next few years, a kind of dullness is going to settle on us, a spiritual logjam.' Howard went on: 'The brains of people with political vision will boil.'

Simon was still fretting about his role in the collective, as we romantically called ourselves.

✍ *14 May*   'I have reservations about the end product, and about the relationship with directors. How do you direct plays in a collective? There's an unconsciously held feeling among directors that you have to slap a straitjacket on actors. Otherwise, they overact grossly. Actors should have a personal relationship with the shape of a scene, and the play in general. Am I a lone wolf in this, or do others feel the same?'

The answer is that Simon was a lone wolf, and his yearning to have a controlling voice in the direction of the play, like an actor-manager, went unheeded. The other actors may have wanted a voice in the choice of director, but they were in no doubt that a director was needed.

Our research continued; on 17 May we met Dr Kendrick of the Gypsy Council:

✍ *17 May*   Gypsies are descended from Indians. Mixed with Irish travellers. Half live in caravans; half in houses. Various tours provide stopping places. They are suspicious of outsiders. Don't bother with the Welfare State. Don't like others calling them gypsies. Boys and girls get married very young. Once a girl is fourteen, then she's not allowed out. Families tend to marry off their children at fairs: Cambridge, Appleby, Derby Day. They make arrangements with families of similar status. Hardly any gypsies can read or write. Nor are they numerate . . . Dr Kendrick sees himself as a civil rights worker, not as teacher. He's learned in his own life not to worry where money comes from. Doesn't tend to accept long-term contracts. Only works as much as he needs to get the money to get by on. And then does what he wants. Howard enthuses: 'An old pre-capitalist life, completely outside society.'

Rehearsals went hand in hand with research. One story-line dealt with the feckless Sandy (Simon Callow), his wife (Cecily Hobbs), their little boy (David Rintoul) and an infant (Gillian Barge). There was generalised child acting to begin with, but there's something perennially satisfying about playing children: 'Cecily being very good as long-suffering mother,' I wrote.

✍ *19 May*   Status exercises. Improvisation – Sandy's young wife, Margaret, meets Bud, an itinerant busker. Tony as Bud: 'I spend half me life outdoors, and the other half in bed.' Howard: 'Good: Tony thinks as an anarchist.' Howard reveals [that, as a child,] he spent an hour praying in a church in Truro for Christ to appear. When He didn't, the young Brenton gave up religion immediately. Howard finds status games and animals interesting. Improvisations always state the obvious, but Howard says it's good to have that in mind for rewrites, because then he's not too subtle. The play is written already, so it can now be checked out against the facts.

20 May   Paul Freeman produces somebody from Gamblers Anonymous. A compulsive gambler. Took him twenty years to give up. Ran up debts of £40,000. Lied to his wife: 'A compulsive gambler has to become a compulsive liar.' The first thing women think is that he's having an affair with another woman. Dragged by his wife to a meeting of GA. 'Thought everybody there was living a ridiculous life, but I was the one leading a ridiculous life. I was very lucky I didn't end up in prison . . . When I gave it up, there were two hundred and sixty-four packs of cards at home . . .' Talks of grandfather and how he won £48,000 at Haringey. Ran out of the stadium with two bags and his short trousers stuffed with white £5 notes. 'I've seen a hundred people working for an owner on a track putting money on for the owner,' so no big bets are clocked by the bookies. A team of international pickpockets comes in for the Derby.

21 May   Two members of the British Feminist Socialist Movement – Mandy Merck and Angela Phillips. They are suspicious of us. Mandy said Emily Davison did buy a return ticket to Epsom. They seem reluctant to see her as a martyr: 'What's the point in getting arrested? You've only got to pay fines and that's expensive.' Our level of attention is very high. Will listening very hard. Angela: 'You don't have to throw yourself under a horse to get on camera.' The BFSM is a synthesis of different views. It's almost impossible for someone within the Women's

Movement to be a star. If anybody puts their heads above the rest it would be slapped down. 'Germaine [Greer] got into a position where she could not produce any more.' Unless plays are done by feminists, then distortion will inevitably take place. 'Gay Sweatshop has got better because feminists are in plays instead of out-of work-actresses.'

They ask why Emily Davison is in the play. Howard says: 'To use one of the few facts people will know about the Derby to provide a kind of critical searchlight,' and he believes that 'creating a spectacle' is a protest that will 'loosen the pinions of society' Angela: 'People who are prepared to do that must have their own reasons too.' Angela and Mandy are very opposed to a 'star' action. 'The reality would be that she doesn't have time to do the gesture because she's got to go and relieve the baby-minder.' They ask about Joint Stock. Will: 'Joint Stock is a quasi-socialist group. The hell we live in is that we each have a different attitude to any problems that arise.' Howard: 'Joint Stock spends a lot of time trying to get the windows right, the perspective right, and it involves chewing down a lot of nails . . . a lot of old aesthetics. Constantly in the scenes we're trying to get the social relationship desperately clear.' Later: as we were finishing, Angela Phillips said she did not think that we had come to terms with the group's own feminist inclinations, and that any push in that direction should come from the group.

23 May   Simon: Buskers are 'a theatrical reality, not a real reality'. Hmmm. Paul: Not interested in Emily if she turns out to be some individual neurotic. Max: What will the *Daily Telegraph* say? 'Joint Stock takes a warm look at a cross-section of English society.' Howard: 'I do think romantically. My people do behave in a heightened way. We are involved in a global system which is not helping us. And one way of exposing that is by having someone who is trying to disrupt it. The class system is a swindle.' He goes into situationist theory. Then following Howard's talk we essay an exercise where you begin with a slogan, e.g., 'Work is the curse of the drinking classes', and then devise an improvisation which exemplifies that, using the characters from the play.

We divide into three groups. The Marxists (Paul, David, Jane); the self-described Thickies (Cecily, Bob, Tony); and the St John of the Cross group (Simon, Gillie, Will). I work with the St John of the Cross group and our slogans are very clear, even if we don't fulfil them. 'Gambling can never fulfil expectations.' Thickies fight over drink. Their slogan was something about self- and mutual destruction. Marxists do an improvisation and have one slogan for the lot, 'Socialist peer is a contradiction in terms.'

25 May   Howard suggests we try working the other way round, i.e., start with the characters and then find the slogan to suit them. Start with two characters, Pearce and Blue, a Horse Trainer and a Police Superintendent, which seemed difficult. Something about them knowing their position. Who depends upon whom for a living? Jockey on trainer; trainer on owner; owner on horse. They're celebrating their status. We should define them a bit first. It seems to me that you can make the points best if they are lower middle-class, grammar-school boys who have arrived. What slogan do you choose to illustrate that? 'The lower middle-class uses upper-class skills and morality to consolidate their own position in the class hierarchy.' The unseen element in the Blue/Pearce scene is approval/disapproval by class superiors, i.e. the owners. [Socialist peer was a reference to Lord Rack, who was being played by Paul Freeman. He was a peer with a love of horseracing and a murky past. The character was speculatively based on Lord Wigg, who came to talk to the group on 28 May.]

28 May   Lord Wigg: 'If you understand racing, you understand England. Racing is highway robbery without the glamour of the highwayman. The rich robbing the poor.' The relationship between owner and trainer and jockey is the 'last surviving relic of the feudal system'. Obviously a great, passionate hatred of the class system informs him. 'I'm basically uneducated . . . What disciplines I've got I found for myself.' He's spent his life fighting 'the Tory bastards'. Tells how he advised Harold Wilson that betting could be taxed. Board set up. Tax imposed is a huge success. £30 million raised in 1966; 200 million in 1976. 'How sterile our society must be to go and spent time in a betting shop. The great mass of people in this country never take a decision except in a betting shop. Not everyone who goes racing are rogues and vagabonds, but all rogues and vagabonds seem to go racing.' Jockey Club holds official enquiries – 'an organisation that really believes it has a divine right to rule'. Until recently, a jockey at an enquiry was not even represented. [Lord Wigg is a charismatic figure; Paul Freeman got a clear idea of the weight and status his character, Lord Rack, should have.]

30 May 'I'd like to talk about wit,' says Tony Rohr. Everybody agrees this is a vitally important subject too long neglected. 'I think we should have the Whit Monday off,' says Tony.

We did the Parade Ring scene. Horses straining. Overbred. Owners. Crumpet. Trainers. The different class strata at Epsom are something we must observe beadily.

1 June We all go to the Derby.

We had done some excellent research and worthy rehearsal, but we always knew that Howard's play, set of course on Derby Day, would have to be measured against the real event. 1 June, the First Tuesday in June, Derby Day. On the train down to Tattenham Corner Howard revealed his plan to have an actor play 'the Race' and another play 'the Course'. This moved us firmly into the area of surrealism, and I felt a strong challenge to my inventiveness and powers of staging. And there were still a number of questions unresolved at this mid-stage of rehearsal. Clearly the actors were going to play kids, but were they going to play horses too? Could we learn the tick-tack language? Were the actors playing jockeys to act on their knees to show how small they were? Were the actors playing horses really going to be naked? Could everybody be the Race? Nine tick-tack men; nine jockeys; nine horses, and then nine characters hanging about after the race has finished?

2 June Talking about yesterday at the Derby. General jollity. Works outing. Gillie: A prodigious amount of alcohol being consumed. Beer bottles everywhere. Components for vacuum cleaners being sold. Not many middle-class people at all. Chefs hired by works outings. Absolutely working-class celebration. David: Like a medieval encampment early in the morning. Talks of regional differences between bookies. Villains sitting in their yellow Rolls-Royce Corniches. Howard: The care people had taken. Like a fifties British film for Ealing Studios. Screwing legs into their tables. Vast picnics brought. Slowness of the build-up. The violence and ecstasy of a football match not there. A different kind of celebration. Gypsies were wonderfully dignified. Paul: No idea England had so many bookmakers. Found the arrival of the Queen and the whole aristo thing absolutely obnoxious. 'At the end, those people had removed themselves by money and class.'

Small sense of frustration because there was no natural consummation. People taking their clothes off, trying to make a climax that wasn't there.

Jane: British eccentricity. The Queen one moment . . . next: 'Have you
had a letter from Jesus?' Cecily: So vulgar. Not seventies at all. A sort of
timeless feel about it. Diversity of bookies. An anticlimax, because the
race is over so quickly. Tony: Backing the winner lost my head. Gypsies
were so well off. Beauty of gypsy girls, 'hair all beautifully done in
ringlets'. Sense of it building up. Once the Derby is over, everything
seems to be petering out. Timeless. Hallucinogenic feeling. Great tables
groaning with food. As the day went on, people got more and more
drunk. Just two minutes . . .

Loonies were walking the course to tread the divots between races!
Guardsmen. Willie Carson [the jockey] must have had the shits when
he couldn't throw Lester [Piggott] off. Milliondollarman nearly won.
'I would have been eating at the Ritz.' Bob: 'Buy a charm off an old
gypsy.' She was twelve. Bob took photos of villains, but did not dare
do it directly, so Tony and Dave stood in front of them. Max: Smell of
hamburgers and onions. Cheap, cheap, cheap. Bookies had come from
all over the country. How hard the jockeys work and divide the day
between them, reappearing in race after race. Like a colourful swarm
of bees when you see the jockies in the distance, but the sense of effort
when they are in front of you. Swearing, sweating and huge clogs of
earth kicked up. No class clash at all. Kept away from each other and
both parties preferred it that way. Simon: The racing enclosure . . .
trapped up there in their morning suits unable to move. To show how
great the power of the crowd has become, and swing on that tide.
Would be a misrepresentation to show they were being manipulated and
unhappy, because they were having a good time.

Will: Play should culminate in short, sharp scenes rather like the
vignettes we've been doing. Jane: Worried about the blending of
documentary and fantasy. Max: Why is Emily going to kill herself?
Because of personal oppression, or oppression of women in general?
Tony: 'I would like to see the characters in the first half fleshed out and
followed through. The character of Emily does worry me, because she
has no muscle. What is it that Howard wants to show?' David: 'What is
it we want to show, and how? About the Derby . . . about class today?'
Howard: 'It's a play about the class struggle. That's what it's about.
Derby Day itself is half-time in that struggle. Emily is important because
she connects the past with the present. Fact or fiction? It's got to be

fact. You are picking tea leaves out of the ocean, but each scene has got to make a point.' Simon: 'So how can it be a swindle? I'd like to push you on that.' Howard: 'I would like the people to own the horses.'

Conversation comes down to Simon and Gillie versus us again. Gillie doesn't really want to show how horrid the bosses and upper classes are. 'I get tired, I suppose, of always being on the right side, us against them.' Howard: 'Scrap the play so far and use it as lumber with which to reconstruct. The play has been smashed against the reality of the event.' Will suggests we should do lots of quick scenes. We're enthused . . . then crisis. Hayden comes in and says he doesn't want to work with me, and says he needs somebody with Bill's experience to do it. 'Needs a strong director. Max is not a director I feel a particular sympathy with. Play needs a director who has experience of working on a large scale.' Company rally round, and confidence is expressed by all. Paul [to Howard]: 'Nobody is indispensable, except possibly you.' Howard: 'Only indispensable people are the actors . . . I'm getting Parkinson's disease, I'm so furious.' Howard [of Peter Hartwell, as a replacement for Hayden Griffin]: 'He would be better than one of the burnt-out heavies.'

The long simmering crisis with Hayden came to the boil, but unlike the discussions on the Roundhouse we were able to resolve the situation swiftly and without rancour.

✍ 3 June   There is a general nastiness in Howard's play which we certainly did not see the other day. No policemen beating up tramps or mothers talking of abandoning their babies. Nor did we notice anybody with their pocket picked. But it's difficult to write a vibrant play about people having a good time. We begin to pool our observations and use them to assess the accuracy of the play.

A list of the groups of people at the Derby who we haven't got in the play. These include: hamburger-sellers; works outings; religious fanatics; heavy drinkers; hawkers; vendors; mental deficients; tipsters.

6 June   Gypsies: Unlike the play, they had a variety of accents. Coaxing, but not ingratiating. Insistent. Cecily surprised by their wealth. Unlike the play, they did not go round picking pockets. Like the play, it was the women who worked the crowd. David saw gypsy men playing pitch and toss. Unlike the play, a sense of nation. Presentation of selves very upfront. Day-glo colour. Unlike the play, they do not have a

guerrilla sense of being besieged. Like the play, it felt that they had a different set of values. Hairstyles early fifties.

Bookies: unexpected that they come from all over; that they were so varied in dress – smart *and* scruffy; that there were so many of them. Wildly different odds on outsiders. And that they could deal with such small-time bets. Unexpected: the wit and bonhomie, and the difference and variety of cards they handed out. Howard 'learned that bookies are softer round the edges than we thought'.

Policemen: like the bookies, the police were on a sort of working holiday. It felt they were not present in the crowd, but ready to protect the Rolls in the stand. Paul: Like the play, found the police presence ominous, but they did not mingle with us. Police are there to protect property, and the most important piece of property is the Queen. Howard: 'They underscore the structure of the day. There is no aggro because everybody adheres to that structure.' It's clear that we do not want to show the police as jolly and avuncular bobbies. Howard wants a rank-and-file police scene. Idea that it's their day out and proud they're making a good show of it. Howard enthusiastically reassessing his ideas. What an oral man he is: cigarettes, chocolate, cigarettes all stuffed in.

7 June   Howard: 'Gypsies are geared into being predators by our society.' Paul: 'Gypsies have chosen to live outside society.' Howard relishes a scene of gypsies burying the caravan of a dead man. Do not pass possessions on, which is the foundation of the class system. Everyone to think of a slogan. Max: 'The middle class admire and fear gypsies for their apparent lack of middle-class values.' Howard: 'Gypsy life is an impossibility that persists.' David: 'Meeting one set of social mores makes you question your own.' Will: 'The gypsies are as trapped in their culture as we are in ours.' As always Will Knightley's grounded sense cuts through our eager analysis.

We move back to bookies. They are a product of gambling. What is gambling? Slogan about gambling – 'Gambling provides a necessary element of chance in our over-rigid and stratified society.' Simon: 'Gambling is a form of acceptable madness.' Cecily: 'Gambling is the marriage of science and superstition.' Paul: 'Gambling is the logical sport for a society devoted to the accumulation of private wealth.' Tony: '. . . about the ability to predict events, not about winning money.'

Howard: 'Gambling is an illogical suspension of belief logically exploited by an industry.' Oh very good.

We discuss works outings: Very formal. There's a *placement* for the seating. Trestle table with beer and trestle table with wine laid down. Works outings must be big business for some people. High spirits – shaking the bus to dislodge someone on top, who then jumped onto the roof of another bus. A fat pearly queen with union jack dress. Singing songs. Accordion player hired to provide continuous music. Organisation enormous. Home-made jubilee regalia. People stripping off on top of buses. Mooning. Pale, tight bums on display. Little ropes out round areas. Geography of the area worked out. Buses became full of people who had passed out.

8 June   Should do naked horses p.m. A.m.: the set. Everybody taking turns with blocking scenes. Action easy. Howard comes to block a scene: 'Oh, my God . . . where's a child? They're all being played by so-called grown-up actors.' A jolly time is had by all and blocking scenes seems terribly easy. We do the race. One person commentating/acting it out. Howard: 'The solution is that we do everything ourselves.' This was unexpected after our discussion this morning about real tanks in Howard's *Weapons of Happiness* [National Theatre, 1976]. It works well and everyone is happy and energetic. Basic costume for the actor is the principal part they are playing, and otherwise they assume a hat to become an aristo or a horse or whatever – and it's cheap. Howard: 'God, it's exciting.' He kneels, then sits, then kneels.

A long discussion then follows in my Diary about the class system, the Queen's Jubilee and how Derby Day could be better.

🖎 Bob: 'Coming from the working classes, I felt that was not a good place to be. I'm still trying to make some sort of shift.' Still feels very conscious of origins. 'I always wanted my dad to go out and buy a car when I was a lad.' Max talks of accuracy and representing the truth of what we've seen, and its credibility. Paul says that's not good enough. Howard must not go off and write what he wants. He must represent what we've seen from the point of view of the left wing.

Paul Freeman's idea – that the writer should be beholden to the will of the group and that his function was to articulate the group position – was always provocative. The strength of Joint Stock's work, which stemmed from Bill's time at the Royal Court, was that in the end we handed the material back to the writer. *Epsom Downs* showed the company at its most boldly interventionist.

✍ Slogan for the whole race: 'A cat can look at the sport of kings', but we cannot find a real point of view. Simon: 'How could Derby Day be better?' Paul: 'You could get rid of the Queen.' Gillie: 'How would that improve things? She would be replaced at the top of the pyramid by somebody else.' Simon: 'Derby Day is a myth . . . and an extremely successful publicity job, and if it's unquestionably an enjoyable day the conclusions you draw from it about English society are not true.' Gillie: 'Envy is at the root of the class system.' She cites me as wanting to have the view and have the horses, and therefore it's my own spiritual problem. We must fight our own individual greed and woolly ideas we sort of hold between us. Howard: 'I'm going to rework, sharpen and articulate' the events seen, but agrees with me that it must be based on our experiences.

Two and a half weeks after we had been to the Derby, Howard delivered a new and revised draft. The read through was always tricky with Joint Stock. The actors' enthusiasm, commitment and expectations came up against the reality of the parts they were to play. They could no longer fantasise about what Howard might write. Of course, a long discussion followed. In retrospect Howard's patience and good temper seem little less than astounding. No wonder Caryl Churchill is the only writer to have worked with Joint Stock more than once.

✍ *27 June*   Max: Lord Rack has now got pain in him. Simon: 'It's a rich tapestry but some of the threads don't seem to lead anywhere.' Will: First half very strong, but it slides away after the Derby. Doesn't see where it goes after that. Needs a scene there to sum it up. Max: 'Disagree. I like the dying fall.' Tony thinks it's a bit simplistic. Not enough meat. Thinks there was more of Howard's personal bile in the earlier draft and says, 'I still don't know about naked actors.' [I don't know why Tony was so reticent about getting his kit off . . . It made him a star and he's dined out on it ever since.]

Gillie likes it. 'A paean of praise to the working man.' Paul: Doesn't see the class swindle that Howard has talked of. Has to be some attitude. Howard thinks the Derby is a con, but unless a character says so, the point will not be made. Howard thinks adding is better than cutting, 'which is a mindless affair'. Agrees that some political element is missing. 'I think of myself as a political writer. It must be nailed down.'

[The question of how many parts each actor could play was raised.] Howard: 'What would doubling do?' Max: 'Increase the costume budget.'

[Now that the parts in the second half were clear the roles were finally allocated.] David very concerned and keen to play Epsom Derby Stakes. Gillie pretty clear about what she wants, but, otherwise, actors surprisingly easy about what part they would play.

Howard embraced everybody's reservations with astonishing good grace and proposed undertaking another draft immediately. Howard: 'I just find my brain might burst if I don't finish the second draft first.'

Of course Howard's writing wasn't all journalism. The charming but harassed young family who finally determine to gamble their savings to buy a house had an element of autobiography. Howard talked about what he wished to achieve: 'A sense of loss. Beginning of middle age. Freedom's been lost. Somehow they never grasped what it was about. A lot of wear and tear. How can Sandy and Margaret possibly find out what's happening to their marriage under an onslaught of children?'

Now that we were spending more time rehearsing rather than discussing, Simon's talent became clearer. The trouble was that his own philosophy about acting led him in an increasingly contrary direction. My notes record this with some exasperation.

✎ *2 July*   Simon acts every part as if he were Superman. So his Sandy becomes a romantic lead, wonderfully charismatic, full of energy, and brimming with affection towards his children. Not a failed and emotionally immature builder who can't hold down a job.

Another story-line concerned a disaffected stable lad, Jocks (David Rintoul), and his attachment to Primrose, a young gypsy girl (Jane Wood). Their mutual attraction provided an element of romance against the background of the race.

✎ Jane: 'It seems a bit easy, their relationship at the moment.' Max: 'Parade Ring scene is where doubt and the impossibility of the relationship occur to them both.'

4 July   Assumptions of gypsies are that outsiders are punters to be sold stuff, and that's how Primrose must regard Jocks until there's a reason to change. Howard talks of Romeo and Juliet: forbidden love. I point out that the hatred of the Montagues and Capulets has been set up in the play, and here it hasn't. Howard says Primrose's behaviour is outrageous when she is picked up by Jocks, because she's by herself and not with her gypsy family. But how are the audience to perceive that? We talk again. Tension. Finally, we agree. Energy flowing. Primrose should agree to Jocks's invitation to go to the fair only at the very end. Resistance to going should be expressed. Jane suggests they should meet Pearce the trainer, who has fired Jocks at the beginning of the play. Howard says it's a bit *Crossroads*.

Howard's draft had the two young ones split up at the Parade Ring scene before the race. The offensive spectacle of the rich should alienate them both, but Primrose should see that Jocks is still part of that world.

✎ *5 July*   David tells story of the play from Jocks's point of view. Not in control of his own destiny. This to trace his politicisation throughout the play. In the final scene, he feels he should be angry and energised. Also positive that that's it as far as racing is concerned. He will leave that world. Jocks must have an awareness of his own life, but there is a danger of overwriting. We spend the day working through the material for each set of characters. Hard work but it began to pay off. I could see what Howard's purposes and intentions were. And began to see too where it did not work. Chipped away at Parade Ring scene for four hours, and at last the mammoth edifice that is Brenton's determination began to shift and slide, and Primrose's freak-out, motivated by a look, begins to shift over to Jocks.

Two of the more unexpected characters in *Epsom Downs* were a pair of Evangelists who were campaigning against the twin evils of drink and gambling: Howard was succinct and clear about their characters.

✎ *8 July*   Howard: 'They are weak. Their sea wall has been breached and will always be weak. Jesus is a surrogate and a replacement for the drink.' Character based on a butcher called Tillery who had huge arguments, spitting and shouting, with his father during prayer meetings. Cecily: 'The scenes have a burlesque, music-hall feel to them.' Howard: 'That's good. Miss Motrom . . . brittle . . . flakey . . . tight.'

The detail is emerging. Tony giving good value by reminding us of the stage directions. Jane: 'I did not throw myself under a horse for you to sit on the grass making sandwiches for your men.' Howard mutters, 'Sunday School tracts. I'm against bold statements because they diminish the reverberations.' Max: 'Don't worry about characterisation. Get the philosophy right.' Finally a run-through after a not very good day.

10 July   Run-through solid. Seemed a little long. After the run, we had old talk about the point of the scene versus richness of character argument. Paul versus Simon. Simon arguing that scenes cannot exist without characters. Paul arguing that characters must serve the overall political ambitions and purpose of the play.

13 July   Discussion with Howard about the ghost. Howard: 'In the old days one would have had a violent lighting change to indicate the ghost's presence, but we don't really have a ready-made convention.'

The race itself was over eight and a half minutes long and, because it came midway through the second half, and led to a long anti-climatic ending. This was a true enough reflection of the day itself, but not good news theatrically.

✎ *15 July*   Phone to Howard. We agree the build-up is OK. The race itself is what doesn't deliver; it's strange coming midway through the second half. Howard: 'You're looking at the top of a mineshaft, and there are great geological strata underneath. The racing industry should be displayed in the way we stage the race.'

17 July   Work through second half, and then run it to show Howard after lunch. Howard starts giving me notes about the Derby and the Parade Ring scenes. Howard: 'There's no objective correlative to the Derby scene itself.' And of course there was much discussion. Will: 'The race is staged pedestrianly. The naturalistic acting during crowd scenes doesn't seem right.' Gillie: 'Detailed work is necessary for the crowd. It's currently not placed enough.' Tony: Second half certainly seems lightweight. 'Early Traverse Workshop,' he says dismissively, knowing it will hurt. David: 'Style of second half different and at the moment too refined in its dealings with a rough theatre event.'

The cast were critical of my tentative moves towards a bolder and more surreal form of staging. They were quite right. Encouraged by them it became more forceful and theatrical, and Tony Rohr brought his own quixotic approach to playing a racehorse. When asked for a monologue on the thoughts of his horse in the Parade Ring scene he said:

✍ *19 July*   'I'm quixotic and overbred, and not thinking about the race at all. I am a Derby outside chance, and my function in the scene is to show that I have my own horse thoughts.' I'm flagging today and punishing Howard's perfectly valid and correct suggestions to try it slower and give it room to breathe. Also worked on Lord Rack (Paul Freeman), eliminating accent, and making him more direct, pugnacious and charismatic.

20 July   Pissed off with Howard because I finally feel we are functionaries to his ambition and drive, and it all costs so fucking much. How miserable and shrunken of me. Discussion about taking money from the Racing Information Board. Gillie thinks it's absolutely immoral if we are saying that racing is a swindle. I provokingly suggest that we should send back the Arts Council cheque. Howard says, yes, we should. 'We only take money from them with fear and loathing.' We all say, 'Rubbish.' Perhaps I am just jealous because Howard has two interviews set up, with the *Observer* and the *Guardian*.

23 July   First complete run-through.

24 July   Trying to cut first half. Howard feels big speeches are not paying off. We must make more direct contact with the audience.

General feeling of euphoria and confidence from actors, but that's not necessarily good. It's certainly not in the bag, and we all know how the critics can fetch you one.

25 July   I had a dull day. Because of the pressure I put on last week, things are settling into patterns, and it's necessary to jolt people out of them. The difficulty that emerged today was of different ways of working. I asked Gillie to think of an objective for her scene with Will. She laughed and said, 'Oh, I don't work that way.' I'm also aware that I'm not helping Simon: he has to have a broad overall image of the character, but at the moment his bookmaker is too genial. I think Howard had conceived a predator/pirate king with more envy and greed under the jovial exterior. David as Jocks is trying to turn him into a moody Hamlet with no coarseness and no wit. David and Cecily are taking it all v. seriously. The characters they play are not tragic figures, and they agonise too much.

28 July   Howard talks of the necessity 'to infect the Roundhouse staff' with our presence. We all talk about whether or not we should have a party with them or talk to them. Howard wants to talk with them about 'popular radical theatre'. He will give a lecture . . . 'Anonymity of big theatres . . . What we're trying to do.'

30 July   Roundhouse. Run. David Hare on the phone. 'Love the play's good-heartedness and that it doesn't proclaim its self-importance . . . Bit where the race is over I found very disappointing . . . didn't understand that Sandy had won.' The bet Sandy places on the race secures the family's future because they are able to purchase their first home with their winnings.

3 Aug   Famous sayings. Max: 'We're within puking distance of the finish.' Tony says after last night's run-through I looked like a pale and anxious schoolmaster. Come on now – sharpen your reflexes . . . and now get the laughs as well as the images and the point. Acting good – it's got body . . . gravy . . . Bovril.

4 Aug   First Performance: THIS SHOW HAS EVERYTHING . . . IT'S CRUDE THEATRE. Take it further. I've held it back. Because I don't do 'rude' easily.

Epsom Downs was successful. It didn't pack the Roundhouse, but it attracted approval. I look back on it with great affection, but I'm in awe at how difficult we made it for ourselves. Each decision, from casting to the set and the purpose of the show, was subject to endless discussion and inevitable disagreement. Nor was it over with the opening of the play; we plunged straight into yet more discussions about the future of Joint Stock. It is no wonder that few of us wished to commit to a further year's work.

✍ *11 Aug* Roundhouse discussion: Gillie: 'I have lots of ideas now . . . of what I don't want. I had thought the lack of a unified idea would be good. Now I'm not so sure. We need a stronger unifying idea . . . particularly politically.' Simon: 'The composition of the company and choice of writers are crucial. The managerial aspect of the collective has worked extremely well.' Will: 'It's become clear that we are asking the impossible from the writers. We want the writer to represent us, but his own creative juices must be involved. It's not till halfway through rehearsal that you know what you are involved in.' Tony: 'Danger we're becoming a very precious, tight-arsed group of people.' But on the other hand, 'You leave Joint Stock and then where do you go? The more foreign touring, the better. I can't stand this fucking country. I hear we're very big in New York, so why the fuck don't we go there? I'd like to see other directors coming. I'd also like to solve the Irish question.'

Paul: 'What makes this company unique is its relationship with writers.' Will: 'Most texts fall so short of any kind of ideological political direction that we seem to be letting ourselves in for permanent frustration.' Max: 'Because theatre is a collaborative medium you are always and continually involved in compromise.' It does demand an enormous amount of sustained energy to run a group. Will: 'The work together is brain-burstingly difficult to sustain, and you have to step back from it from time to time.' Gillie: 'What the fucking hell are we giving in now for? . . . I don't feel as if I've progressed at all, apart from being able to take my clothes off.' [Gillian Barge had performed a striptease in the character of Angela Rippon at the start of the second half of *A Mad World, My Masters*. It contributed a great deal to the box-office success of the play.]

Will: 'I can't see any way round the alternative of giving power back to the directors and the people who are prepared to stay on and do the work'. Simon: 'If people aren't prepared to stay together for longer than six months, then the experiment can hardly be called a resounding success.' Tony: 'What about this pension scheme?' David: 'There's a place for an artistic director because it focuses the decisions of the collective. So what do we talk about now?'

Well, the next thing to talk about was whether the group had a future together. Could we contemplate a year's work together? Would people stay or go?

✍ David: 'We've tapped a vein that has not been around for forty years, and it makes me excited.' Jane: Could not contemplate a whole year's work like this. Would like it if there were a pool of actors instead of a permanent company. Paul: 'I would not want to do a whole year's work, but would like to do a show.' Cecily: 'Don't know.' Simon: 'I'll leave definitely. I don't think I'm doing very good work, and I'm not in sympathy with the aims.'

So the idea of a collective, a permanent company, was approached, inspected and declined. But there can be no doubt of the commitment and vigour that it brought to the work. It must have been particularly punishing for Howard.

✍ Howard: 'I think the dialectic and the discussion is a gain, and is a lesson that will stay with me. One of the reasons I came to you was that I felt my work becoming diagrammatic. By talking to people and seeing them I enriched myself.'

And his note in the front of the script of *Epsom Downs* shows characteristic generosity:

HOWARD BRENTON: Joint Stock has a distinctive way of working with a playwright. The final text is the writer's alone, but it is written in full view of the company's constant, questioning gaze. I am indebted to them for their painstaking research, their encouragement and stamina, their endless but always creative criticism, their flair and invention in workshops and rehearsal, and for the many happy hours we spent together on racecourses during the flat racing season of 1977.

Author's note to Epsom Downs (Methuen, 1977)

Case Study

CLOUD NINE
Caryl Churchill

Workshop: 14 September–6 October 1978

Rehearsal: from January 1979

First Performance: 14 February 1979

Workshop Group: Julie Covington, Carole Hayman, Dave Hill, Jim Hooper, William Hoyland, Miriam Margolyes, Tony Rohr (Tony R.), Antony Sher (Tony S.), Max Stafford-Clark, Jane Wood

Cast: as the Workshop, minus Dave Hill and Jane Wood

Published: Cloud Nine (Nick Hern Books, 1989)

Epsom Downs marked the end of Joint Stock's agonising effort to define itself as a collective. My focus began to shift towards the Royal Court, where I had directed three plays in 1978. I had become close to Caryl Churchill when we worked on *Light Shining in Buckinghamshire* in 1976. The idea for a workshop on sexual politics was hers.

The Diaries show Joint Stock abandoning Marx and making a passionate leap towards Freud. *Yesterday's News* (also 1976) was the last of the three shows that I co-directed with Bill Gaskill. We had begun that workshop with each of the participants giving a detailed account of their own lives. In the end that particular play headed in another direction altogether, but that line of work provided a useful starting point for *Cloud Nine*. As my Diaries record, the workshop involved a great deal of talk about our parents and our own sexuality. We began collecting material before the workshop even began: an actor who auditioned for the workshop, but did not in the end take part in it, gave Caryl and me a vivid account of the expertise required for speedy oral sex on the train from Waterloo to Clapham Junction. It furnished the material for Gerry's monologue in the second half of the play, which was performed by Tony Rohr. As Tony Sher recounts, the group were chosen as much for their sexual proclivities as for their acting ability: The group featured two couples (one same sex, one not) an ex-couple and a healthy mix of heterosexual and homosexual men and women. The rich diversity of our sexual partnerships made for a varied diet of testimony and improvisation.

We may have been obsessed with the opportunity to discuss our own sexuality in the workshop, but the diverse sexual experience of the other people we interviewed had an equal influence. One actor talked of an up-bringing in rural Ireland that could have come from Maria Edgeworth's *Castle Rackrent*, published in 1800, while our caretaker's horrifying story about her brutal husband had Dickensian overtones. In the London of 1978 our own transgressive and confused sexuality was contrasted with lives that could have come from a century earlier. Perhaps it was this that influenced the structure of the play and led Caryl to set the first half of *Cloud Nine* in Victorian Africa.

The confidence of the rehearsal room demands to be respected in the same way and for the same reasons as the confidence of the confessional. Secrecy creates the maximum conditions for emotional commitment and truth. In order to secure this emotional commitment from the company a vow of confidentiality was made from the outset. Nothing said in the process of the workshop was to be revealed beyond the four walls of the Canonbury theatre where the detailed discussions of our personal lives had taken place. In attempting this book twenty-five years later I realised that the material that went to form *Cloud Nine* began to resemble one of those Second World War German bombs which has lain harmless in the mulch of a churchyard for sixty years but if tampered with would still be capable of causing a nasty explosion. For this reason I have made every attempt to obscure the identities of those involved. Everything in quotes was said in the rehearsal room although the source of the material will not be acknowledged. I have taken this decision not only to preserve that confidentiality agreement but also to maintain professional relationships which have become precious to me over the years.

THE WORKSHOP (*14 September–6 October 1974*)

. . . we would be using ourselves as research material. The group was
being chosen for their versatility not just of talent, but of lifestyle.
Thus the collection assembled for the workshop ... included a straight
married couple, a straight divorced couple, a gay male couple, a lesbian,
a lesbian-to-be, at least two bisexual men and . . . the usual large
number of heterosexuals.   *Ritchie, p. 139*

✍ *14 Sept*   Obviously the people involved in the project are drawn
from particular sections of the community and therefore it seems
important to do some *Yesterday's News* type work and to look at other
relationships in Great Britain today. 'I'm a heterosexual, feminist
socialist,' said Caryl as we were casting.

We began the workshop with some simple improvisations about our own
childhoods and, throughout the workshop, depended a lot on role-reversal
improvisations.

✍ *17 Sept*   Work as children hearing about sex for the first time.
Choosing an important object from childhood, e.g. a teddy bear, a
tartan blanket, and presenting it to the group. Improvisations about
parents and how they coped with things. Post-coital improvisation with
roles reversed. Man tender, woman reaching for cig and turning on
telly. Hilarious.

18 Sept   I asked what expectations people had of the workshop. The
responses were multifarious:

Obliqueness about sexuality. Suppression. 'Don't know whether I want
to opt into or out of nuclear family unit. The emotional support from
hetero relationships I have had has not been enough and should I
therefore turn towards gayness? Would that give her more emotional
support? 'I haven't worn a skirt for eight years. I have pushed that
femaleness aside completely.'

The way in which women are censored. How can they be considered a
minority? There was anger and aggression about being a woman felt by
at least two of the women in the group. 'I would like to examine
repressions put on me because I'm a woman.' Terrified of losing
independence.

One self-confessedly gay actor was interested in exploring how his lifestyle relates to everybody else. He has a permanent relationship, with as much casual sex as he wants. Realises how different his needs are. 'Almost like perfect at the moment.' He thinks it's necessary for the show to support that view. Should not be a shock to people.

Another actor wanted to find out how his relationship compares with other relationships in the group. Would like to find something in common and for play to be accessible and optimistic. Would like to find out what women are like and how they relate to gay men. Vast subject.

The conversation veered onto the subject of marriage. One actor commented:

'I look at my parents and I'm not sure I have the bottle to go through all that myself.'

Someone else (female) chipped in:

'Have always thought of men as the enemy. I never thought about a comparison because I did not think I would win. Hope we don't end up doing cute little improvisations. Need to show audience the brutality that exists in relationships.' Feels pessimistic about England. Gulfs between people. 'Minded terribly for a long time that I wasn't beautiful.' Childhood and adolescence very painful. Very moved hearing people speak.

Another:

'I've been married for thirteen years and I've got a kid. I have nothing in common with the girl I was when I was eighteen. I'm suspicious of feminist hard-line because all the problems of living with somebody are not just the man's fault.' Hard graft: negotiations over all that cleaning and washing.

Everybody had spoken rather tentatively at first, then inhibitions were broken, and we were all bursting with opinions. The conversation moved on apace, jumping from subject to subject, all of us eager to have our say . . .

'It's a relief talking to gay men because the sexual pressure isn't there.'

'Best friends should be lovers too. Emotional dependence and sex have become separated. Is that it?'

'The only way I could handle jealousy is if I don't know.'

'I insisted on a double bed when I went to stay with my boyfriend at his parents' house.'

Energised by the discussion and by our own curiosity, we began with a number of improvisations that explored sexuality. All of the group were encouraged to come up with situations, which were promptly improvised. Caryl set up one where women were competing for the same man with their attraction to him determined by playing cards they had selected at random. She then initiated some work on dependency. How dependent is one partner on the other in a relationship? Again both the amount of 'approval' required, and the amount the other partner was prepared to give were determined by cards. Julie Covington set up a passionate scene of sexual experimentation between two young kids which was discovered by a horrified uncle. Carole set up a hilarious improvisation with a casting director, an actor or actress and a director. Once again both the actor's talent and the amount the director was attracted to them were determined by the random selection of playing cards. The gap between the two led to some politically incorrect decision-making on the part of the director.

✍ *19 Sept*   I suggested we talk to Mrs Chapman, a widowed farm worker on my uncle's farm in Aston Clinton, who had never been more than seven miles from home in her life. Her experience of sex would contrast with our own.

We never did get to talk to Mrs Chapman, but the caretaker of the Tower Theatre, Canonbury, where we were rehearsing, was later to fill that role for us.

Tony Sher set up an improvisation with a paedophile counsellor and a lonely old man confessing how he ached to touch his grandson. It was strangely moving.

✍ *19 Sept*   Situation with men alone – boardroom meeting. Situation with women alone – changing room before dance class. We endeavour to isolate male and female characteristics.

And then we set up a number of situations where each sex 'intruded' on the other's world. We placed male doctors in a women's ward; then some female advertising executives discussed a campaign for the launch of a new ale.

✍ Still knots in the stomach. Nervous. The medical improvisation has an atmosphere of holy piety and the patients have the air of dopey lethargy. Carole as staff nurse giving hushed and reverential air while Tony S. as the consultant has a casualness that's absolutely right. We reverse the roles with a man as the staff nurse and a woman as the consultant. It immediately heads straight for agit-prop.

There's something there, but somehow the work is not yet hitting at it. Remember from *Yesterday's News* how much easier it is to get people talking than it is to show it in the work. Early improvisations make you realise how you have to go back and do more research and have yet more discussions. What is it we want to explore? – feelings of women being unfairly exploited? A gay couple's feeling that they have arrived at a happy sexual *modus vivendi*? Feelings of anger? Feelings that a heterosexual relationship doesn't provide enough emotional support? Perhaps we should go right back and talk about our lives from the start. Or perhaps I'm flannelling about too much and I should set up improvisations which get at what is interesting more explicitly.

So in the afternoon we reverted to discussion: We interviewed people about their own relationships.

✍ What attracts you to your partner?

Answer: 'Her intelligence.'

What about affairs?

Answer: 'Could not have casual sex. Moving towards affairs, as exciting as the sex act itself.'

About men:

'I cannot imagine a man having the tenderness . . . I just don't see men as being whole people . . . It annoys me that people think that feminism leads to lesbianism.'

The discussion moved toward childhood remembrances:

'I was totally rejected at school dances. An excrescence perching on this radiator. You sat there until you were picked by somebody. Until you decided to go home early. I cannot tell you what school dances were like for me. I felt ashamed.'

20 Sept   A day about children. Again we drew cards and the number meant you had to act a child of that particular age. We put Jim and then Carole through an afternoon of kids screaming with the partners demanding to meet in the evening. The women set the men an improvisation in which they all have to play women. We then change and the women improvise a City board meeting. Miriam is delightful as a pipe-smoking Harold Wilson.

Caryl then set up a series of improvisations where various characteristics were 'imposed' on a particular person. In the first one Julie was sent out of the room and an office situation was set up. Everybody was told that Julie was stupid and not up to her job. Within seven or eight minutes these expectations had been fulfilled and she was becoming an office catastrophe. Tony S. was then excluded and we were all told he had a vicious temper. An improvisation was then set up where he was a newspaper editor. Again, even though Tony had no knowledge of the 'characteristic' we were imposing, he became more and more short-tempered in the course of the improvisation. We developed this into a game where we tried to identify sexual characteristics. Each actor drew a card to determine how masculine (black cards) or feminine (red cards) they were to be. They were then questioned by the rest of the group. We became surprisingly accurate.

✍ *21 Sept*   Carole sets up an all-male Property Developers Party, with one woman coming in. The focus went to her immediately, and all the men started flirting with her. Miriam: 'I don't often get up North.' Dave: 'How do you fancy a team job?' Tony S: 'Christ, I haven't done that for years.' Miriam plays property developer lady wonderfully. Men disputing with each other over Room Service, and getting Miriam up to their room. Carole: 'Nobody listened to what Miriam had to say at all.' Dave: 'No wonder because the men were told their objective was to pull her.'

However the women were equally sexist when Dave set up an improvisation where a lone man got on the top of a bus with a party of women. I then developed a game where the actors selected cards at random to determine how eccentric they were. A card of two was mildly eccentric while nine would be an out-and-out madser. Only one person in the group was 'eccentric'; their identity was unknown to everyone else. It was revealed in the course of the improvisation. Were we more tolerant of male eccentricity?

First Julie was a mad tickler at a tube station, and then Miriam was an eccentric barmaid. Tony Rohr then did one, but he's so eccentric anyway it was impossible to tell any difference.

✍ *21 Sept*   I set up Royal Court tavern scene as an equivalent to a topless bar, but with men serving with their trousers round their ankles and the women staring at their balls. It's hilarious. Gay afternoon: A red card indicated you were gay and had to contact other gays (other red cards) in the group. Then we added a joker card which indicated policeman and which led to several arrests. Worried that Carole seemed bored and publicly disinterested in the gay world, and that Tony S. didn't seem so interested in women's problems. Perhaps we should expand the workshop . . . Perhaps the numbers are too small. Having said that, some of the work is very good.

The next day we had a morning of improvising particularly charged sexual situations.

✍ *22 Sept*   Tony S. and Julie: Lawyer and lesbian friend arrive at a conference. Tony S. and Jim: Two guys in a pub talking about pooftahs. Jim and Dave: Policeman arresting a bloke in a cottage. Brilliant. Dave and Miriam: Wife and gay husband who have not kept an appointment with a psychiatrist. 'Have you lost your manhood?' Miriam and Carole: Girlfriend meeting an old school friend who has now become a lesbian and needs to be reassured. Miriam: 'Is this just an experiment?' Carole and Jane: Anxious mother with child who has been playing with other girls behind the bike shed. Dave questions what we're doing. 'We should talk more about our own lives. We are of a generation whose parents were repressed sexually, and we are bound to start from that.'

In retrospect perhaps this was another moment that prompted Caryl to set the first act of *Cloud Nine* in Victorian Africa and enabled her to explore repression to hilarious effect.

✍ More discussion about what we have discovered about ourselves and about each other:

'Our imagination has uncovered ways of approaching situations we would not otherwise have thought of.'

'Homosexuality is the ultimate rejection of femininity.'

'Lesbianism and homosexuality are both rejections of masculinity.'

'We've discovered this week how prejudiced we all are . . . '

'Having a child is the point when somebody has to surrender liberty. It's no accident that most people split up in the first year of their child's life.'

Generalisations about sexual relations became specific observations about our group:

'I'd say that in this company the women are a bit paranoid. It's no good women becoming as aggressive as men.'

'The group is rather unbalanced. We have four dominating women.'

'You are diminishing us into stereotypes.'

'We are all dominating women.'

'I get very upset at being called dominating because I've been brought up to think that's unattractive'

'I do not care if people don't find me attractive. It changed four or five years ago. I don't care if I don't pull anybody anymore.'

We set up various improvisations that attempted to show the difficulty of coming out:

✍ *23 Sept*   Miriam is a lesbian MP, and the constituency party discusses whether or not she should be re-nominated. 'I have nothing personal against Miriam, but I have to decide whether or not she would help the party in the forthcoming election,' says Julie. Miriam: 'I have every right to a private life. I don't mind them investigating my private life if they do that responsibly.' Julie brings great energy to the improvisation: 'You are talking naïve claptrap. You have let all of us down. Your selection would not help the party.' Very well sustained.

In a second improvisation Miriam and a partner (Jane) go to buy a double bed. Dave is the salesman. Humiliating, but very touching. 'The lesbian experience seems to be a gloomy one,' says one of the actresses.

'If we appear grey and dowdy maybe it's because life has conditioned us to be like that. Women who are lesbians sometimes opt out of being sexually appealing.'

25 Sept   We decided to move from gays to parents today. We should all talk for fifteen minutes each about our own parents . . . and then decide on areas to improvise.

Through the remaining two weeks of the workshop we each had to tell our own life story, focusing in particular on our parents. There were some life stories which Caryl drew on more heavily than others. But the portrait which *Cloud Nine* offers has elements of all our testimonies within it.

✍   'Dad left school at twelve. Did education courses in the evening. Liked opera. Rose to be export manager. Did not marry until he was forty. Mum was thirty . . . Mum was always the dominating partner in the relationship. I hated walking to school in uniform because the other kids at the bus stop were horrid. Mum obsessed with the way we spoke. We did not own our house. We competed for Mum's affection. Mum had elocution lessons and encouraged me to better myself. Now Mum teaches Asian bus drivers in adult education class.'

After, we talk about the work in general. We try to sum up. Jim feels it's incredibly useful. Caryl comments on the danger of women being driven along a track of achievement. Besotted by it to the exclusion of everything else. Julie says how women don't have an inner sense of themselves, while boys are brought up to have one.

I was very tired today and couldn't get things going very well. Not satisfied with the improvisations. Don't feel we are getting into them in any depth. If Caryl was clearer about what she wanted to write we could be more focused. But I know that's not the point.

26 Sept   Dave said *Gloo Joo,* a play by Michael Hastings at the Royal Court, in which Dave was appearing, is transferring and therefore he won't be able to do this show. We discuss a replacement. Julie and Carole will draw up a list of approved actors over lunch, and we will consider it. Dave: Rich vein in this source of material. Julie: Awareness of mothers was that they were never able to relax and were always on the go. Dave: And that the relationship with fathers was . . . Carole: The subject is so emotionally loaded.

Back to parents and upbringings:

TONY S.:   'All four grandparents were Russian and settled in South
Africa. Dad found himself running a skins export business at the age of
twenty-six. The first fifteen years were bad. Dad drank heavily and went
out with the boys. Parents almost separated when the firm expanded.
More servants. Four children. Mum social and glamorous, while Dad
defined through work. Related strongly to his Mum. Mum never
worked after she was married. It was only in the last two or three years
that she hasn't been bringing up children. Remember hearing his Dad
say that they only stayed together for the children. Dad's drinking is still
a source of unhappiness. Between ages of nought to eleven he was
brought up by servants. Suddenly discovering at the age of eleven the
power of being white. The cook for the family of thirty-five years still
calls him Master. At drama school he had a relationship with an American
girl and cottaged with men on the side. Could not get it up with women
after that. Told his Mum first he was gay. Her reaction was calm and
unexpected – it didn't matter. 'As long as you can be happy, it's all right.'
Mum told Dad later in Italy. He was very, very shocked because he had
had no experience of it, no knowledge of that condition. Outwardly, he
did not show any change. When his Dad had got engaged to a non-
Jewish girl, Grandma had a heart attack. What would she do if she knew
he was gay? Mum is very talented, but she has never been able to express
that except through her ambition for him. In South Africa before drama
school, he picked up a coloured man, and had it off with him. Rushed
home afterwards, showered, and put all his clothes in the laundry,
delighted that he had not enjoyed it. Oppressive being Jewish because
the family network is very tight. Dad very rich, and it is like a magic
wand. He does give money and is very upset if people try to pay. It's
to compensate for the emotional support that he had not given.

We discuss a replacement for Dave Hill, and I broach the subject of the
actors' commitment to the, as yet, unwritten play.

Miriam: 'I feel quite passionately about this, and I'm quite prepared to
commit myself totally. I would do it if I have three lines.' Jim: 'I felt our
commitment was never in question at all. I'm shocked that we are even
talking about it.' Jane: 'I feel quite open about doing the play.' Julie:
'I'm absolutely committed to the process of work. I reserve the right,
as I would yours, to veer off in some way.'

I get Miriam to ask for two days off. She does it by playing cool and low status. Nobody opposes her, and then I say I have to have two days off next week. I play firm and everything with high status. Both of us get our own way. Is the conclusion that men instinctively get their way by playing high status? Jim sets up an improvisation with a film director: Jim is asking for a job. Low status. We work on how to get your way, and we do some master/servant improvisations to find out about dominance and manipulation.

William Hoyland was brought in to replaced Dave Hill, and we began with a briefing about the workshop and what we felt we had achieved. Later Caryl commented on how the group had adjusted to absorb a new dominant single male.

✍ *28 Sept* 'Career competition between gays is more disruptive. Traditionally, the woman accepts that the man is more successful, and gets more status from him.'

'You have to lessen the man's pain if he is earning less than you.'

'If there were more tender men, I don't think I'd be gay. I feel I'm open . . . but men are not open to me.'

'We keep forgetting that the country as a whole is not liberated at all.'

'When we had a kid, and I was looking after her for the first couple of years, I nearly went crazy. I put pressure on my husband to make him feel bad because he was going out every day and I was sitting at home. It's easier to be liberated if you've got a lot of money. His earning power was more, and I had to defer to that. I felt my career potential was sliding. Then I went to Liverpool for four months and left him to look after our daughter. It nearly finished the relationship but in fact was the point from which we could re-start.'

Discussion about titles: One woman in the group comments. 'I automatically accept being called "Mrs".'

Another adds:

'I like being "Mrs". If I'm "Miss", I feel less than if I am "Mrs". If I'm "Miss", it means no man has every loved me.'

The nature of the group certainly changed with William Hoyland's arrival.
He had been a member of a men's group and had a specific viewpoint on the
territory of sexual politics. He was a perfect replacement for Dave Hill, and
the focus switched to men and how they might be oppressed too. William
led the way in exploring a character who became Martin in the second half
of the play, a man who was bringing up children by himself:

WILLIAM HOYLAND writes: 'I was trying, as we all were at that time, to
deal with feminism. My point was that men were trying to change, trying
to embrace this new phenomenon and yet there was this stereotype,
perpetuated by the feminists of what men were . . . I counted myself as
one of those men who were trying to take on the criticisms men faced.
To give one example: I was taught by feminists not to say, "Women do x",
but to say, "Some women do x," so why do feminists say, "Men are . . . "
or "Men do . . . " and not "Some men do x . . . "? Why is that not
equally offensive?'

✎ *29 Sept*   Fathers are not allowed to look after children: 'When they
were small my kids were taken away from me on the bus.' Men are
constantly being told they are incapable. It's the other side of the coin to
women not appearing in boardrooms. Men have a fear at women's
prerogative.

The sensuality of cooking and how men are denied that side because
they are busy doing and getting job satisfaction and how men expect it.

Before the Industrial Revolution, 'I would have been a craftsman.'

How deep the breadwinning role is ingrained in men. Men often
collapse and die after two years of retirement. The same sexual
stereotype is held out by advertising.

The discussion moved on to sex and the protocols of the gay world:

'Penetration is negotiable. Overtures will be made to one's anus and
one either rejects or accepts them.'

'Men initiate sex' (said by a man in the company).

'I would feel I had to be fucked if asked' (said by a woman).

The decision about bringing in somebody from outside was pre-empted by
Miriam and Julie, who had befriended the caretaker of the Tower Theatre.
She had seemed a forbidding and rather frightening figure: laying down the

law about washing up the coffee cups and emptying the ashtrays and closing
the rehearsal room on the dot of 6 p.m. But Julie and Miriam made it their
task to charm her into submission. Her story revealed the complexity and
damage caused by a violent marriage. As soon as she started talking she
became much more open and engaged.

✍ *3 Oct* One of thirteen children. Nine lived. Mother was a herring
curer from Omagh. Boys and girls forbidden to look at each other while
having a bath in front of the fire. Brought up in rural Lincolnshire: 'You
can say I was brought up in complete austerity.' In the holidays, used to
pick spuds from 7.30 a.m. to 4.30 in the afternoon. Mother managed
the whole family. Dad gave her money. Mum was a devout Catholic. All
the kids have forsaken Catholicism. 'Mum taught us not to let men
touch us.' Went to a good school. Interested in cooking, so came to stay
with an aunt in the East End . . . Went on a catering course. Learned
from teachers and books. But did not see food. 'Realised that I had to
work. If I was to turn from a country mouse and get a boy friend, I
would have to think about making the most of myself.' Learned about
make-up. Nick was a French polisher. Earned £4 a week. Married him.
'He was a bastard. When we were courting he would have reached up
and given me the moon. Within an hour of getting married, he hit me
across the face. He beat me repeatedly. He put me in hospital seven
times. In those days, dear, you put up with it. No way would I put up
with it today. For thirty years he forced his attentions on me. Men got
married so they could own a woman and fuck.' But she wouldn't let
husband see her undress.

They moved back to the country because he had asthma. Saturday
shopping in Wisbech. He drove her in to do some shopping and said, 'Be
back in an hour or I'm off'. She hurried. Bag split. Shopping all over the
pavement. Put it back in the bag, but on way home, butter got on the
back seat. She put shopping away. Nick, cleaning the car, discovered the
butter on the seat. Came in. Kicked her into the fridge as she was
putting stuff away. Knocked her out. When she came round, she told
him to clear out. On the Sunday they didn't speak, and on the Monday
morning, he cleared out the fridge, took the car, and 'I haven't seen or
spoken to him from that day to this'.

Then she got work in the canteen of a pea-canning factory. Went on
a coach outing to Yarmouth. Sat next to Jim. He was a driver for the

factory. He'd been nursing an invalid wife for ten years until she died. On the way back, she asked him home and cooked him supper. They courted for a year and did not have sex in that time. He couldn't get an erection. Finally one night, he said, 'Tonight's the night'. He had been over a few bumps with the lorry 'and things had got stirred up'. 'So we had it that night and we both had an organism (sic) – that's terrific. I was fifty-nine and it was the first one I'd ever had in my life. Now we have sex sometimes as much as twice a week and I'm on cloud nine.'

This story gave Caryl the title, and also provided a prototype for Betty's final monologue. The caretaker's husband, Nick, had had a rough childhood himself. Threatened with the workhouse if he did not conform. He was illegitimate.

✍ 'He was brought up in a wicked sort of way . . . There are lots of things that turn men into beasts.' Maybe one thing is that they cannot satisfy their women. 'I have got a mind as big as this room, and I must open and close it as I want.'

Her candour, and the detail at the heart of her story shocked us all, but it set a benchmark for the rest of the workshop. Above all she felt great pleasure that her life had finally worked out: not great rage at the wasted years. She never asked us to empty an ashtray again, and sometimes she didn't lock up until 6.15 p.m.

As well as talking about our own upbringings we also met some some of the actors' parents and, in particular, grandparents. We met one rather formidable woman of much the same generation as the Tower Theatre caretaker. She was suspicious of our methods and the luxury of working on people's lives. She thought, 'It's a waste of time to waste time'.

✍ Sits very primly and straight. Protects herself. Gives very little away. 'I think it's all time you woke up anyway. I think politics is a man's job. I vote Conservative, but I would rather see a man there than Mrs Thatcher.' She thinks women get bogged down in their twenties by romance with one man.

Some of these beliefs were to surface in the character of Betty.

One of the recurring themes of the workshop was the strain that children place on relationships. Particular interests were: the difficulty of having children when you are young; the question of who instils discipline in the children, mother or father; and how should that discipline be enforced, should you smack a child? In the end these were to be important elements of *Cloud Nine*.

One woman, a mother, was eloquent on the demands that children make:

✍ Saw very few people. 'When I had the second one, I did find that I was getting terribly tired. I don't think I had ever touched a baby till I had one.' A day with a toddler and a baby: Shopping . . . constantly vigilant. Big highlight would be visiting a friend for tea in the afternoon. Difficult to convey how awful and yet how wonderful it was. One day at work, her husband messed up a job because he was so tired and couldn't cope with night feeds, so she always did night feeds after that, and therefore could not work effectively herself. 'I think I was fairly permissive with the children, but had rigid rules about television.' What astonishes some of us is that she had no idea about having children until it happened.

5 Oct   We set up improvisations involving kids and discovering the pressures they put on a relationship: Improvisations. William and Jim: Jim as Dad, William as a two-year-old. Jim cannot get William's shoes on. Finally he does, and William takes them off again. 'I don't want to go. I want to wee-wee.' Takes him for a walk. Jumps in puddles. Walks on top of a wall, but can't jump off. Keeps on asking why. Who's that lady? The Queen. Why is she the Queen? William forces Jim to assess his belief and say why he didn't like the Queen. Small, but as much force of personality as an adult.

Carole, Julie and Jane: Jane as a child, Julie mother and Carole friend. Jane admires Carole's diamond ring. 'I'd have diamonds on my toothbrush. I'd have diamonds on my dressing gown.' Julie: 'Jane, you are really being a pain in the arse.' Jane demonstrates ballet to Carole. Julie said, 'I've had that every day for two or three years'. We talk about the fear of using authority.

Tony S., Dave, Jim and Miriam: Miriam is a very possessive Jewish ma, while Tony is laissez-faire Dad. Jim and Dave are the kids. They both rush out of the loo with their trousers down. Miriam makes all the decisions for Jim and begins to dominate. Life styles are impossible because the attitude of parents is so different. Should they play on the

pavement? Nerve-wracking sending kids out for the first time. Jim
wanted to play with dolls but wasn't allowed to, because he was a boy.
Disapproved of. Dressing up as a girl would not have done any harm.

Some of these details surfaced in the first half of the play.

In both halves of *Cloud Nine* there are gay characters; it was always clear that
the information fed to Caryl would be influential.

✍   One actor spoke of his childhood: Trying to decide whether he
was happy or not as a child. Grandad worked in a steel works, 'which
helped kill him'. Mum trained as a window dresser for Marks and
Spencer, a comparatively high-status job. Dad was from Warwickshire
and came from genteel poverty. Left the RAF and came to the Black
Country to find work. Mother suffocatingly over-protective. His brother
was academically brighter and more popular at school. 'From ten
onwards, he was always in front of me.' In the conflict between parents,
the two brothers had to take sides. At first parents were always cuddling
each other, but they argued over money, and the fact that Dad did not
earn enough . . . Mum was manically clean, obsessive, always cleaning
and scrubbing, and eating at the same time. She was offered a window-
dressing scholarship but could not go. When told that her son was gay,
Mum said they knew all the time, and Dad said, 'There's a lot of it in
the army'. First affair was with a married man. He had also never been
with a man before. 'I have not slept with any girl for two years.' Could
not cope with girls emotionally. 'I think that because of the way I've
been brought up, I feel the need to be protected.' Feels he and his
brother have not fulfilled their roles as sons, so there's still pressure to
prove themselves. 'Parents are disappointed that we don't have
children.' Very debilitating being with parents now. Lets her be mother
because that's all she knows how. She feels frustration at what she could
have done. Reads a lot. 'I am all the time full of the sense of my
mother.'

We gave ourselves five minutes each to discuss how we relate to the person
we are with. Different people spoke.

✍ 4:32 p.m.   One said she would quite like to have affairs but
doesn't because it would hurt her partner. 'I used to run around and

I quite miss it in a way.' 'I think it's time we had a naughty', about two or three times a weekend. 'If relationship ended now, there would not be much of a mess.'

4:37 p.m.   Another: Lived with partner for nearly four years. Not monogamous. Could be improved if they were financially equal because then he would have his own car. 'I don't feel threatened.' Sex is called 'a bout'. 'We gradually worked out his sex drive was higher than mine.' Other encounters are simply sexual.

5:14 p.m.   Another: Had been very romantically in love. 'However first few days boyfriend was away, I felt relieved. A pattern is emerging in my own relationships in which I am getting involved with somebody else's man.' Both very emotional and very wary of romantic love.

5:20 p.m.   Another: Lived with partner for thirteen, fourteen years, pretty well a monogamous relationship. Come back at weekends and can go Monday to Friday without 'getting itchy'. 'It just works for us.' Cannot understand people not telling each other. 'Inconceivable to me. I could not countenance a relationship where I did not tell people what was going on, and I don't understand how people can sit in this chair and tell folk things they won't tell the person they're living with. We went through incredible difficulties, but they fade into the past.'

One of the actors shared his life story. It sounded like it was an upbringing from another century:

✍   Granny, Margaret Casey, was in service. She married William Walsh. Had five children. He died at age thirty-three of double pneumonia. She remarried and had three more children. Early life shrouded in mystery. His Dad, Harry Nicols, a sailor, was supposedly lost at sea. When born in London, Mum took him to Carrick-on-Suir, Tipperary where he was brought up by his grandparents with three uncles. Gran was 'proud, resourceful, domineering'. Granddad was slight, fond of drink and a Gaelic speaker. He managed a farm three or four miles away and returned at weekends. No electricity. No gas. Paraffin lamps. Grew own vegetables. Had own pigs, poultry, goats a pony and trap, and a donkey and cart. The three uncles and he shared a bed. He would sleep across the bottom and the Uncles would come to bed later and warm their feet on him. Mum was in England but she visited every summer and Christmas. Known as Peggy, she was attractive, vivacious, and beautiful, 'and I remember her surrounded by lots of men'. They would go to the pub, and he would be put on the table and would entertain by reciting and singing. She used to send home *The News of the World, Picture Post, The Eagle* comic and money. All the family keen 'to get out of the mud' and not to do manual work. A lot of cruelty around. Uncle beating Granny. He recalls coming in with an airgun to protect her. Granny herself had rheumatoid arthritis and would poke under the bed with her stick and beat him if he went to Irish dances in his new suit. Very little affection. He walked or biked six miles into Carrick to go to the Christian Brothers School, known as the monastery. The Brothers beat him with such ferocity he dreaded going the six miles and longed for the ride home. Grandfather said he would either be an archbishop or an arch-gangster! Early sexual experiences doomed. It all went on all around him but he wasn't getting any!

At the end of the workshop each company member endeavoured to sum up what they had experienced:

✍ 'Got through barrier of fear about improvising. Becoming political.'

'See a broader perspective about women. Can see more of the whole picture.'

'Thoughts confirmed. It is actually as bad as I suspect.' The work has pushed her further. Belittled by men, she sometimes has been tearful and nervous. 'The material has an explosive nature – sexual politics within the group.' Reached an understanding of the gay world, and now begins to have sympathy with the position of men. 'As to what you do about it, I don't know.'

'Surprised by the amount of trauma that belonging to this group entailed. Still finds it easier to associate with women and quieter men. Intensity of group experience.' Wishes she was more political. 'Don't feel I was able to give enough analysis to being a woman.' Was very conscious that other, commercial work that she does 'met with real hostility from the group'. The group had a rigid attitude to certain things. The experience tremendously rewarding and totally terrifying.

'Did not realise that sexual politics was politics. I'm now very interested in politics; it's all the same thing.' A revelation has been the life stories. 'We have not dealt with the relationship between women,' but now she can talk in the kitchen at least.

Confirmed her belief. At the start, had to justify the selection of the workshop members by their sexual experience. 'Awful feeling of pain being handed down in different forms. Earth the pain in your own generation so it is not passed on yet again.' Mothers and the huge influence they have.

'Encouraging to have beliefs confirmed.'

'Did not want to do workshops because frightened of the women in the group. Felt I had to hang on to my identity, which is in any case tenuous. Everybody had a terrible childhood and fought to get out. 'I've gone home and begun to sort out my life as a result of these workshops.'

'I have found the workshops very, very traumatic in many ways. I have been terrified and fascinated by the women in the group. I have been made to think, and to put my thoughts into speech. I'm proud that feeling that problems were common has been borne out. I had the fanciful idea that I might have children, and I don't want children now. I found working in the group very stimulating. I had thought about giving up acting altogether. Very satisfying work.'

'Early on I was freaked. Intense aggression . . . Max gave me a reassuring cuddle, which is what I needed.' Talked about nothing else since we have started. Did not know how strongly women and gays feel they've been oppressed. 'Can't advance until we remove sense of blame.'

During the workshop we had created a close bond between a pretty disparate group of people and, understandably, felt some ownership of the material. None of us had any reticence about telling Caryl what kind of play she should write.

✍ Dave goes for popular, accessible. 'You ought to try and find out where you can play it.' Carole: 'I certainly think it's an insult to the actors to say you couldn't play in small places.' Tony S.: 'I think it would be interesting to show the development historically. I think we should shock people and it should be explosive.' Caryl: 'You come to an analysis through individuals. You see it anecdotally, but you also begin to get a whole picture.' Tony R.: 'There is a danger if you get into the area

of hat jobs.' He means he doesn't want to play as many parts as he did in
Epsom Downs.

He went on to talk about the importance of including the character of a man
living alone, without depending on a general relationship. This also led Caryl
towards the character of Gerry, who Tony R. was to play in the second half
of *Cloud Nine*.

It would be quite wrong to imply that the experience of the workshop was
the only influence on Caryl's writing. She had been reading Genet's *The
Blacks*, for instance, and the idea of women being 'colonised' came from
there, as did the idea of the 'colonised' Joshua endeavouring to be as white
as or whiter than his master. Caryl is notoriously reluctant to write or talk
about her own writing, and I'm hesitant to say that this or that passage came
from this or that source. But I hope this chapter gives some idea of the
multifarious sources that inspired her. Journalism and autobiography are the
twin shire horses that pull every writer's plough. And in that respect Caryl
is no exception.

After the workshop there was a ten-week break in which Caryl wrote the
play. During this time we had to report on our progress to the wider Joint
Stock 'collective', which by this point was heavily dominated by the actors.

✍ *18 Oct*   Joint Stock meeting. Miriam: 'Extremely alarming and
invigorating to be involved in the workshop. I was continually astonished
that we were getting paid for doing something incredibly interesting.'

1 Nov   Joint Stock meeting. Bill Gaskill to Caryl Churchill: 'How
intimate will *Cloud Nine* be? Are there two-handed scenes?' Caryl:
'There will be eight main characters.' Bill: 'Sex and politics with Julie
Covington. You'll be packed.'

10 Dec   Joint Stock meeting. Tony Sher puzzled about his periodic
involvement with Joint Stock. Who is the company? Feels actors are put
under intolerable strain because of the alternative work he has now been
offered. He wants to wriggle out, but Miriam nails him. Miriam: 'I think
you are having the best of both worlds.' Tony R.: 'I know at least six people
who would love to take over Joint Stock, but they're no fucking good.'

THE REHEARSAL PERIOD

✍ *14 Dec*   Delivery of script.

Caryl's decision to place the first act in Victorian East Africa was a response
to the diversity of experience we had found. It rooted the play in an account
of Victorian patriarchy. This setting was a complete surprise when Caryl
delivered the script. The moment when each play was delivered always
showed Joint Stock at its most neurotic and carping. For actors, the customary process of selection is to assess the money, the length of the commitment
and the size of the part. With Joint Stock only the first two factors were
available for early inspection. The money wasn't much and the length of
commitment demanded was considerable, with an unpaid gap between the
workshop and the commencement of rehearsal. So job satisfaction depended
very much on the part. Each actor was to play one part in the Victorian first
half and a different role in the second half. The second half of *Cloud Nine* was
set in our own time (London 1979), but the characters had only aged twenty-
five years. Their post-feminist confusion about their sexuality, and the absence of repression certainly hadn't led to greater happiness or security.

Clearly the actors had exposed their own lives and their degree of ownership
put great pressure on Caryl. All of us were able to give approval to the high
comedy of the first act but found it more difficult to digest and give credence
to the reflection of our own experiences which Caryl had written for the
second half, set in contemporary London. Perhaps we wanted the play to
deliver the rounded conclusions to our own lives which we were so signally
unable to provide ourselves.

✍ *17 Dec*   The actors respond so that Caryl can consider rewrites
before we start rehearsal on 2 January.

Jim: Difficulty in making the leap from the Victorian period in the first
half to the modern second half. William: Also confused by the time leap.
Men seem to disappear in second half. Tony R.: First half not a broad
enough view of what we had unearthed. 'There isn't enough muscle in it
somehow.' Miriam: 'Very encouraged by it.' Peter [Hartwell, Set Designer]:
'Visually, the second act is more interesting than the first act.' Jane:
Could not follow why Betty was a man. Why not have all the women
played by men, and vice versa? Caryl: Point is that Clive has created his
servant and his wife in his own image.

The first half contained wonderful casting opportunities. There was a central patriarch, Clive. Both his wife, Betty, and his black servant, Joshua, were to be played by white males. Caryl writes, 'Betty . . . is played by a man because she wants to be what men want her to be; and in the same way Joshua is played by a white man because he wants to be what whites want him to be.' In addition Edward, Clive's nine-year-old son, was played by a woman and Victoria (aged two) was represented by a doll.

> ✍ Tony S.: 'One of the most brilliant pieces of political theatre I've ever read . . . one is constantly surprised in the first half . . . a shame that we have to leave the jungle at all.' Technical brilliance of the first half very difficult to follow. Caryl: Wanted to show white male dominance in first half, and the increased role for women in the second half. Max: 'The material of the monologues is terrific. The shorter scenes in the second half make it seem more fragmented, while the first half progresses with longer scenes. In the first half people avoid talking about relationships at all, and in the second half they talk about them all the time.' Caryl: 'I haven't caught a real momentum in the second half. It's hard to devise an action that will drive it along. But I will go back and start again. I have to get everybody talking about an interesting variety of problems . . . '

Caryl was not only writing against the deadline of an approaching first performance (14 February) but was also trying to satisfy those members of the company who hadn't yet committed to the production.

> ✍ *31 Dec*   Jane, Tony S. and Tony R. are the three who won't commit themselves.

Tony S. pressed for a lengthened first half and for dropping the second half altogether: 'The first act shows almost all the points we want to make.'

William Hoyland outlined a whole alternative plot for the second half and wanted to introduce a lady lawyer who Martin had on the side. Miriam was unhappy to have been cast so obviously as Maud and pressed for a lesbian love scene in the second half.

> ✍ *5 Jan*   We try reading it with cuts in from Act 2: in effect Act 1 becomes the play with flash forwards into the present. It works triumphantly to begin with. But strong reaction from Tony S. and Caryl is that the intercutting fragments the first half too much, and that it

won't work. What pressure for Caryl. She says gloomily: 'I can see a perfectly horrible play.'

Through January Caryl took part of each day off to rewrite the second half, while we got on with rehearsing the first half. The question of casting the second half was temporarily put aside, but there was still plenty left to disagree about.

✐ 13 Jan Argument about publicity. Will we do the *South Bank Show* (the television arts programme) or won't we? Julie is obviously keen to escape publicity. We ought to do it, and I do not think people should say, 'Yes, I'll do Act 2 for the *South Bank Show* but I won't do Act 1.' There's only one decision we can possibly take if we are being financially responsible. If you don't care how many people see it, then what's the point?

In retrospect my argument seems particularly dishonest and was probably written to persuade myself of my own rectitude. It was clear to all of us that Julie Covington was in a fair way to being a star. Her recording of 'Don't Cry For Me Argentina' and her appearances in *Rock Follies* on television had made an enormous public impact. It was also clear that her ambivalence about fame was one of the reasons she particularly wanted to work with Joint Stock. My own ambivalence was outed later when we arrived on tour at the Liverpool Everyman. The poster outside the theatre read 'Julie Covington in Joint Stock's *Cloud Nine*'. If I had really been *'financially responsible'* it would have been a decision I would have heartily approved; instead, I had the poster replaced.

Caryl delivered the remainder of the rewritten Second Act on 15 January. Once again we submitted casting to a consensus. And once again we let ourselves in for a whole lot of difficulty. Because she was playing the relatively undemanding part of Maud, the grandmother in the first half, we led Miriam to believe that the balance would be rectified when the second half was cast. But once the play was in front of us other criteria came into play.

✐ 15 Jan Oh dear, Miriam wants to play Lin. Carole also wants to play Lin. Send Miriam and Carole out of the room so we can discuss it. Are the criteria: 1. to serve the play? 2. to give Miriam first choice because she's under-parted in the first half? Tony R. also a problem. Is he going to leave too? 'I'm sick of dressing in boy's clothes.'

In the end Carole played Lin, the working-class mother of Cathy, and Miriam made an excellent Vicky, the rather middle-class daughter of Betty, who has an affair with Lin.

✍ *16 Jan*   Miriam: 'This method should be improved. The casting process is not a good one. It is in the changing of the method that the pain lies. I welcome Carole to Lin, and I will play Victoria, but I must say I feel hurt.' William: Where we went wrong was that we should not have cast the first act without having the second. Tony S.: The process of democracy cannot work in the end – 'as good a director as Max' will always get his way. Miriam: 'Equality of parts is an impossible brief. My expectations were incorrect.'

Our desire to possess the material even extended to a debate about the poster.

✍ *16 Jan*   Tony S.: 'We are doing a serious play about sexual politics and we have a large image of a man's face with a woman's make-up. Is that right?'

The rewrite and the debate about casting had eaten into our precious rehearsal time. We began to rehearse in the evenings in order to catch up.

✍ *4 Feb*   Disaster round the corner. Can it be pulled together? Do we have a second half? I've never done a show where we've had less time to pull it together. Everybody becoming bad tempered last week because of panic and because we are being rushed.

5 Feb   Did Scene 1 in some detail and it looked OK. Scene 2 done in evening, but everyone was very tired. Clive is a character we must keep exploring

Although Harry Bagley (played by William Hoyland) has had a romantic encounter with Betty (Jim Hooper), he is a homosexual, who in a disastrously mistaken moment reveals his predilection to Clive (Tony Sher), who immediately insists that he get married: 'You must save yourself from depravity.' This was to be one of the play's most hilarious moments. Harry is also being pursued by the nine-year-old Edward (Julie Covington), who urges Harry to have sex with him again.

EDWARD: Don't you want to anymore?
HARRY: I do, but it's a sin and a crime and it's also wrong.

EDWARD: But we'll do it anyway won't we?

HARRY: Yes of course.   [*Cloud Nine, Act 1, Sc. 2*]

One of the more remarkable, and unremarked, achievements of *Cloud Nine* is that it gives such a sympathetic picture of a paedophile.

✍ *8 Feb*   The actors all take the opportunity to air their fears. 'All those bonds we had are going out of the window.' 'Jim is frightened to death. He really must listen to the other actor.' 'I really do find Caryl's presence a bit oppressive. We must be given space.' William: 'I criticise myself for always putting myself in the right, which is clearly wrong'. Tony S.: 'Time could still be made to do the proper research, and I haven't done that.'

10 Feb   First run-through.

13 Feb   Dress-rehearsal.

First Performance 14 February 1979.

✍ *14 Feb*   Dartington . . . world premiere.

15 Feb   A hard week. The best performance was on Saturday, when the first half was really controlled and tightly played. The jump into the second half is a hard one, but I don't think it's going to get any easier.

22 Feb   Sparky row between Miriam and Carole about whether Carole should mop the floor in the dressing room. A big puddle has been left by Carole's umbrella, and Miriam's bag has been made wet. Miriam accuses Carole of being very selfish. Carole says she's going to the meeting and will do it after. A compromise is needed.

Miriam: 'It's not a subject you can tame.' Tony S.: 'It's much easier dealing with a reactionary society than it is a liberated one. A lack of an overview because we've never had time.' Jim: 'I've never felt so close to a play I've done, and I do feel defensive about it.' Tony R.: 'I'm not getting enough laughs. It's a struggle to go on every night.' Julie: 'Having said I'm thrilled, I'm nowhere near enjoying it.' William: 'I come off depressed partly because of the characters I play.' Jim: 'They tire themselves out laughing in the first half.'

The response to the play was warm. The first half veered from high comedy to farce, and there wasn't the difficulty I had anticipated in getting the audience to refocus on the second half.

After two weeks of performances Caryl and I went back and made further cuts which reduced the running time by twelve minutes. It made both halves much tighter, and particularly drew the second half together. Before we arrived at the Royal Court, the reputation of the play had preceded us. The producer, Ian Albery came to see the show on tour and offered us a West End transfer after the Royal Court run subject to certain conditions and cuts. The West End always places a certain pressure on a show, and we were in no mood to listen to somebody else's opinion.

✍ *5 March*   I don't want to transfer to the West End at all costs . . . cautious. Didn't like Ian Albery much, who said Joshua's character did not work at all, and ten minutes would have to go from the first half and a further five minutes from the second half.

After all we'd been through, we weren't prepared to tailor our work to perceived West End demands.

✍ *6 March*   Julie says it would kill the show to go to the West End because it infects and diminishes everything, or it will in the end. Others press for a limited season: three months only. Julie suggests television. We all say how impossible it is to get our work on the telly because of censorship, and because I wouldn't direct it. Julie keen to go to Belfast because that's where she's always wanted to go. That leads to a debate about who we want to play to.

We were snobbish about the audience who might come to see us in the West End.

✍ William: 'Tourists from Japan, and bankers from Haywards Heath deserve good theatre as much as anybody else.' Julie: 'I don't wish us to work for a West End Manager. I can't articulate why, but I know they are subversive in some kind of way.' Miriam talks compassionately of Julie's special position and how we can see by her unusual emotion it's very upsetting.

If we were to transfer then her name would certainly feature large and particular pressure would be put on her to undertake publicity. But there's no doubt that the others led by William and Carole would love the focus it would give their careers.

27 March   Royal Court preview. House full. People queuing for returns. Michael Codron here. Suddenly nervous. Julie's punk supporters with green hair. Subdued and very respectful audience, who give enthusiastic support at the end. Invigorated again.

28 March   Row with Miriam, who was ill and who thought I was taking insufficient notice of her illness. Row between William, who thought a scene was not being played properly, and Carole, who wanted it cut. Now I feel depressed. Why rehearse any more? We're been rehearsing endlessly. I long for the day when I can walk out in a tantrum too. I'm not really concentrating. Not much exuberance either.

There is no entry in my Diary to mark the success of the first night, or the warm response accorded to *Cloud Nine* in its brief run at the Royal Court. The reviews were broadly favourable, although by no means ecstatic. Michael Billington in the *Guardian* called it 'Cloud three and a half', though, to be fair, he rated Caryl Churchill pretty highly. Among women writers. He wrote:

MICHAEL BILLINGTON: It is a curiously hollow evening. It's so busy covering the waterfront and trying to provide an anthology of sexual attitudes that it ends up illuminating almost nothing.

Guardian, 3 April, 1979

Billington's disapproval and our own exhaustion were perhaps two of the reasons it took so long to realise that we were involved in a popular hit that would become a modern classic.

  24 April   Royal Court run at an end. Feeling tired, skin stretched over face. Awful get out. We wanted to save the set in case we revive the play, but it wouldn't fit through doors. Everybody older, tireder, whiter, paler.

Success doesn't always lead to contentment, but the play was revived with a slightly different cast in September 1980 and was the first new play to be a hit in my regime at the Royal Court. But it was in New York that the full appeal of Caryl's wonderful play was to be exploited. A production off-

Broadway ran for over a year. None of the team who helped create the play was involved.

It was clear at the time how the material of *Fanshen* had politicised Joint Stock. The prolonged and agonising meetings about whether *Epsom Downs* should go to the Roundhouse were a direct attempt to democratise the management of the company and to put into practice the organisational structures that we had read about in William Hinton's book. It was less clear how the workshop for *Cloud Nine* affected us, but what was immediately evident was how willing and enthusiastic people were to reveal the most intimate details of their sexuality. Since *Cloud Nine* I have always been confident that people would be keen to tell their stories if I said I was doing research for a play. From *Falkland Sound* to *Talking to Terrorists* I have taken advantage of this. Society gives us so few opportunities to talk about our own lives. The territory of the workshop overlapped with group therapy and revealed the wildly differing partnerships available to people in 1978. Hippie expectations of permissive relationships co-existed with the gruelling account given to us by the caretaker of the Tower Theatre of vicious beatings by her husband. No wonder we couldn't agree on a transfer. We were emotionally drained.

In 1999 I saw a revival of *Cloud Nine* at the Old Vic. At the interval I was able to indulge in the patronising approval that one aspires to when seeing revivals of plays with which one has been closely involved. The production was good but not so brilliant that it threatened my treasured memories of the original. But at the end of the second half I was winded and tearful. Of course, twenty years on, Caryl's brilliant capturing of our own hippy-go-lucky self-involvement had become as quaint and distant as the sexual mores of the repressed Victorians. The first half had always been a history play, but our endeavour to articulate our own sexual confusion had become history too in the intervening twenty years.

Part Two

THE ROYAL COURT THEATRE, 1979–93

Part Two

THE ROYAL COURT THEATRE, 1979–93

Stafford-Clark's initial assumption was that his tenure at the Court would be brief. He noted on 31 July 1979, that, given the paucity of scripts, he would have to compromise over his choices and 'that may be the only big decision I have to take in the ten months that I'm at the Court'. Gaskill is recorded as arguing at a Court Committee that 'it's an unreal position for Max to decide policy for nine months alone'. The issue had arisen because Stuart Burge, then the Artistic Director, had indicated late in 1979 that it was unlikely, given his television commitments, that he would return in the spring of 1980. Stafford-Clark was therefore asked by the Council to continue until the end of 1980. He was, however, aware that Gaskill himself, after leaving the Court in 1972, had struggled to find a base. The Court's Literary Manager at the time, Rob Ritchie, observed both Gaskill and Stafford-Clark closely:

◀) ROB RITCHIE: He learned from Bill. He watched Bill become homeless. Max is the last of that generation of directors who showed no interest in simultaneously developing a movie and television career. And Bill was the same. Bill just wanted to be with theatre. I can remember several occasions watching Max watching Bill getting depressed, and you could see that Max knew that, unless he got his act together, that was one possible future. As Bill went freelance, he was still working, but he wasn't able to sustain a career without a base.

Meanwhile, applications were invited for the post of Artistic Director. Amongst those interested was John Dexter, whose association with the Court went back to Devine's days. As he was to do several times later while at the Court, Stafford-Clark applied, and lobbied Court staff. For Gaskill, the choice was clear:

◀) BILL GASKILL: We had to choose between Max and Dexter . . . there was no question but that Max was a much better idea than John. Jocelyn [Herbert], of course, was very strongly for Dexter [she had designed several of his shows], but because David [Hare] and I were so positive, it went to Max.

Stafford-Clark was appointed for two years from April 1981.

Dexter and Stafford-Clark invited a comparison between the ancien régime *of the Court and a new generation. Stafford-Clark was the first Artistic Director who had not met George Devine. There was, predictably, hostility on both sides. John Osborne weighed in with an attack in the* Sunday Telegraph *of 10 February 1980. Stafford-Clark replied a week later, and reflected that 'Once Osborne's letter had appeared, it was as though war had been declared'. A later Artistic Director, Stephen Daldry, knew that some of the Court's luminaries (Jocelyn Herbert, Lindsay Anderson) felt cheated of their say in the succession. As late as February 1998, Herbert wrote to Stafford-Clark about 'the feeling that you engendered of animosity towards all that had gone before in George's time', while Stafford-Clark replied to point out that he was subject to 'the perceived hostility of the great figures from the past, including at times yourself'.*

The initial task was to programme the incoming season. It looked very difficult:

🔊 ROB RITCHIE: When I arrived in 1978, it felt as if the place had lost its bearings, and the cupboard was bare . . . Max brought with him the possibility of repairing those relationships between the Court and the Brentons, Hares and Churchills, who had been alienated by the previous regime. But it would take time to do it . . . Max brought in a Joint Stock approach to organisation and management. He was a great believer in the idea that you get the best from people if you can get their commitment. At the same time he had a strong personality and a clear vision. He was also immensely skilful at surrounding himself with younger talent . . .

While engaged in repairing relationships with writers, the Court settled on Hamlet, *directed by Richard Eyre.*

🔊 ROB RITCHIE: Well, we didn't have a play, so we sat down and thought, if we don't have a good play by a living writer, let's do a play by a dead writer. So then we thought, let's do the best play ever written by a dead writer. Why don't we do *Hamlet*? Richard Eyre's interest in doing it must have been part of the reason. It was a necessary decision, because there wasn't anything else to do. We didn't know when *Hamlet* was scheduled that *The Arbor* was going to succeed Upstairs . . .

In July 1980, Stafford-Clark had his first encounter with one of the Court's great figures. It was an association which was to end in hostile silence. To begin with, the proposal was to revive Edward Bond's first performed play, The Pope's Wedding, *along with a new piece,* Restoration. *By early 1981, it appeared to Stafford-Clark that two new Bond plays were on offer,* Restoration *and* Summer. *Eventually,* Summer *went to the National, and* Restoration *went to the Court, and ended wildly over-budget. The animosity was reprised in 1984, when the Court revived* The Pope's Wedding *and* Saved, *to Bond's vehement dissatisfaction. His work has not subsequently appeared at the Court. In the Diary, Stafford-Clark listed his influences:*

✍ *3 July 1981*   Through *Fanshen* I became politicised and learned about the practice of collective decisions. Through *Light Shining in Buckinghamshire* I learned about the richness and diversity of a period of English history which had become suppressed. Through *Epsom Downs* I learned how to read the racing page of the *Mirror.* And through working with actors for fifteen years I learned that you have to keep on learning. Filter experience, distil it and tuck away. Influences; Hilton Edwards [who co-founded the Gate Theatre, Dublin, with Micheál Mac Liammóir], Tom O'Horgan and Bill Gaskill.

Part of the Court's problem was that other spaces were encroaching on the Court's original monopoly of new writing. The other theatres could frequently pay more, or provide better facilities:

✍ [*Draft letter to David Hare*] I read *A Map of the World* twice yesterday and I think it's magnificent. Any reservations I have concern its resolution and the last twenty pages. I would love it to be done at the Court and this colours everything I write, BUT I believe it would be good for the play: the central theme is a personal debate, which would be best heeded in a public space which does not tend to the epic or the rhetorical. Also I believe new work is treated more seriously at the Court. We are still perceived as the centre of public debate while the National is not. There are also, of course, personal reasons, like the Court needs it more. Like, what is the point in running a theatre committed to new work if the new plays you are most passionate about don't get put on there . . .

The play opened at the National Theatre in January 1983.

🔊   When I went to the Court, the two writers I most wanted to bring in were Kureishi and Hare. When I left, I hadn't done a single play by Hare, and Hanif [Kureishi] had departed to film. So whatever the jewels in the crown of my administration were, they certainly weren't those two. I did see David as the outstanding writer of my generation who was writing public plays, who ought to have been on at the Court. It was just unfortunate that it coincided with Richard Eyre's regime at the National, which offered him a sympathetic home and gave him a bigger stage and a much more substantial income.

In 1982, Stafford-Clark's association with Caryl Churchill was renewed with the arrival of her Top Girls *on 1 March. He began rehearsals on 19 July and noted on 23 August:*

✎ First preview. Best play I've ever directed. How quickly the audience accepts a surreal convention.

1 Sept   First night. Peer-group approval. Critical disapproval.

In October came Andrea Dunbar's second play, Rita, Sue and Bob Too, *also on the Court's main stage (see Case Study, pp. 109–23).*

On 6 September 1982, Stafford-Clark's contract as Artistic Director at the Court was renewed for three years with a review date in March 1985. However, the pressures of economic retrenchment were beginning to become apparent, as was the dilemma of forging an artistic policy in the face of increasing competition.

✎ *18 Dec*   The disenfranchisement of the Royal Court from performing its duty. We cannot: rehearse as long; keep a company because we can't pay actors a living wage; cast plays of more than ten roles; costume and set budgets are cut below minimum acceptable standards. We have to think like paupers. No understudies, and long runs to disguise the fact that we can no longer afford to put on plays.

30 Dec   Went to the Pit [the studio theatre in the Barbican Centre, then run by the RSC] and it was full. May go to the Bush tonight and it will be full . . . I think we have to broaden our taste, and embrace work on a wider scale, as well as retaining the loyalty of writers we are committed to. Too much work ahead is duty, and not enough is flair.

Nevertheless, some valuable scripts arrived:

✎ *15 Nov 1983*   Sarah Daniels's *The Devil's Gateway* . . . a real original. Very funny and very particular. Lethal on families.

12 March 1984   Robert Holman's *The Overgrown Path* . . . fine writing and serious work . . .

4 Aug 1984   Ron Hutchinson's *Rat in the Skull* . . . Our ignorance of the background information makes it hard to gain access to the passion that fuels the play . . .

At the end of 1984, a new Chairman, Matthew Evans, arrived to take up his post. The almost instant hostility between the two men coloured the Court's work for the next few years. David Hare's undated letter of advice to Evans was precise. Evans should

> . . . drag the Royal Court back into the mainstream and replace the siege mentality . . . As long as Max is working there, then you see on the stage the best work with actors that is done anywhere in London. But the representational and promotional side is absolutely dire. It is worse sold and worse marketed than any theatre in London.

1986 saw Stafford-Clark directing Karim Alrawi's A Colder Climate *with some uncertainty; dealing with Louise Page's new* Hawks and Doves; *considering bringing Jim Cartwright's* Road *from Upstairs to the main stage; and developing a conversation with Caryl Churchill about the idea which would produce* Serious Money (*see Case Study, pp. 124–46*). *Pushed into the background from 1985 was a piece by Jim Allen called* Perdition. *On 28 July, he returned to the Alrawi play:*

> ✍ My state of mind is sharpened by humiliation. *A Colder Climate* is a particular kind of defeat. I do not think I've put on a play before which I've lost faith in halfway through rehearsal. Or one which got bad houses and deserved them. Or one where I have no defence against the critics, who have been largely very kind. The play is overexposed on the main stage, and would have been better off Upstairs.

> *30 July*   My life is too small. I see it at last. Endlessly directing new plays is an evasion more than it is evidence of integrity. My work tends towards the detailed and the small . . .

By October, the matter of Perdition *was beginning to surface. It was to accelerate, intensively, into 1987, as the piece attracted a huge lobby to prevent it ever reaching the stage. On the evening of a Council meeting called on 20 January 1987 to debate the play, Stafford-Clark withdrew it. His account of this is recorded later in this book (pp. 131–7).*

In the wake of the affair, Council of 8 February saw its Chairman asking it to accept that Stafford-Clark's contract would finally end in April 1989. Privately, Stafford-

Clark recorded in his Diary that evening that the issue was 'not so much about Perdition, *ghastly though the mistakes have been over it. It's really that they think I pursue too independent a line, and don't appreciate them enough. The suspicion is that I despise them. The truth is that I do despise a lot of them.'*

A casualty of the affair was the friendship between Stafford-Clark and Gaskill. The latter resigned from the Council over the withdrawal of the play, and Stafford-Clark's letter of 23 April 1987 to him concludes: 'I can think of no colleague or friend whose approval I value more and whose disapproval causes me more dismay.' The friendship only resumed some fifteen years later.

By July, Stafford-Clark was considering leaving when his contract was up:

> ✍ I think I've decided that I will leave the Court in eighteen months' time, and not fight it. The prospect of having my own company and being able to work in more detail on one or two plays gives me some relief, and the work of nurturing the up and coming writers (who?) can be equally well done by somebody else . . .
>
> [*But by 2 August . . .*] As of this second I'm of a mood to stay and fight the war of Sloane Succession. I can see why it would be good for me, but it is a question of whether it would be good for the Royal Court to have a change . . .

On 17 May 1988 Council resolved that Max Stafford-Clark be reappointed Artistic Director of the English Stage company for a period of 3 years from April 1989. Carried nem. con.

As well as rehearsing Timberlake Wertenbaker's Our Country's Good, *which opened on 10 September 1988 (see Case Study, pp. 147–68), Stafford-Clark was necessarily preoccupied with the economic state of his theatre. The Diary lays out the problem:*

> ✍ 11 January 1989   My concern is that we are being marginalised. That we no longer have the facilities to compete with the Manchester Exchange, or the National Theatre Studio, or even, as far as Upstairs is concerned, with an imaginatively run pub theatre. We are being pushed closer and closer to a cliff edge of viability. Writers we discover – Jim Cartwright, Timberlake – move towards the NT Studio or the RSC because there they can be promised a living. The NT Studio gave Jim Cartwright six actors for six weeks to complete his new play. We haggle over whether his delivery payment was £250 or £300.

In March 1989, Stafford-Clark began work on two new plays by Caryl Churchill, Hot Fudge *and* Icecream*:*

✍ *6 March*   Hot Fudge sounds great but it needs more work. Cast very good. Too many people at the read through. We should start charging. Began to read *Icecream* again in the afternoon. Hard to locate exactly what links both plays. They're terrific, but because they're small it would be easy for them to be dismissed as slight.

9 March   Ran a scene which slipped by in a flash. Problem is that if the play is about weighty matters, the structure of so many short scenes means it may seem slight. Should there be one or two longer scenes which arrest the momentum?

13 March   Sleepless night about *Hot Fudge*. Is it OK, or is it brill? If we just keep going, would its best be 7/10 as good as *Icecream*? Is *Icecream* pellucid, brilliant and economical, or just plain underwritten? Could we do *Hot Fudge* as foreplay in advance of the main event or as a kind of platform show? If we do them as a double-bill, will it simply take the focus away from the main event? Caryl is now so clearly at the top of her profession that she can write the rulebook. If she wants to do a fifty-minute play, that's fine.

15 March   Decided not to do *Hot Fudge* . . . as it would distract and defocus the statement from *Icecream*. [Hot Fudge *was given a 'performance reading' Upstairs in May 1989.*]

18 March   Once again feel we're scratching the surface and not grappling with *Icecream* in any depth.

29 March   I could not do the 'Party' scene until Caryl made us make it a much tighter, denser group, and then the sense of confidences being made were much more easily achieved. It's beginning to yield, but with such a short play we still seem surprisingly far behind. What have we been doing all these weeks? I have little idea of how it will all go together. When we began, the main problem seemed to be whether we could tune into those short scenes with sufficient grip to make them make their point before they had gone. The problem remains.

Icecream *opened on 6 April 1989.*

For the rest of 1989, Stafford-Clark was preoccupied with life after the Court as the expiry date of his contract approached. Despite a warm endorsement of the Court by an Arts Council Appraisal team, the issue was to do with losing a base. The Diary laid out the dilemma:

> ✍ *21 August*   When (if?) I leave the Court, I must start my own company, no matter how unpromising the economic circumstances promise to be. Without it, I will be doomed to a life of exile, where it will be impossible to achieve or instigate work.

On 15 September he drafted a letter of application for the job of Artistic Director of the Royal Shakespeare Company. A month later, he had to face the resignation of Caryl Churchill from the Court's Council over the issue of proffered funding by Barclays Bank. For Churchill, company sponsorship 'means the theatre and those involved with the show endorse not only the product but also the government's policy of privatising the arts, along with medicine and water' (resignation letter, 3 November).

In between fighting for funds and trying to placate dissenters, Stafford-Clark responded to a request from Timberlake Wertenbaker for a workshop. The material developed from these sessions was to become Three Birds Alighting on a Field. *The workshop took place from 3 March 1990, and the first performance on 5 September.*

The rest of 1990 was characterised by Stafford-Clark as 'inertia'. A mooted production of King Lear *could not be cast. A group of writers commissioned to produce a series of dialogues for a show with the umbrella title of* Maydays *missed their delivery dates, and Stafford-Clark moved into 1991 with the battle for his job beginning to accelerate. Despite what some assumed, he did apply, much to the anger of the outgoing Chairman, Matthew Evans, who had been succeeded by John Mortimer. On 16 September Stafford-Clark was interviewed for his own job. After a great deal of negotiation, Stephen Daldry was appointed Artistic Director Designate, with Stafford-Clark as Artistic Director, from 1 April 1992 to 30 September 1993. On 1 October, 1993, Daldry became Artistic Director, with Stafford-Clark as his Associate, for the succeeding two years.*

By November, Stafford-Clark was looking for a name for the new company he hoped to create. On 10 November, he listed: High Ball, Main Drag, Last Gasp, and Home Straight. Meanwhile, he accepted an offer from the RSC to direct Richard Brome's 1641 play, A Jovial Crew, *in the Swan Theatre, Stratford-upon-Avon. He asked Stephen Jeffreys to become involved in some rewriting:*

🔊 STEPHEN JEFFREYS: He got *A Jovial Crew*, which he asked Caryl to work on, and he then asked me to rewrite about 10 per cent of it. And we sat in his house on four consecutive Sundays, going through the script. And each Sunday my heart sank. It wasn't going to be 10 per cent. We were going to rewrite the play.

🔊 LLOYD HUTCHINSON, *actor*:   It was the first time that Max had worked with anything more than eight or ten actors, and he suddenly found himself in a room with twenty-six actors, and a four-man stage-management team. This wasn't a tiny Nissen hut out the back of Sloane Square with ten actors slumming it. I don't think he had a measure of it. And he was totally honest with us from the start. He said, 'Look, I've never done this before and I'm not sure how I'm going to find this.' To begin with, it was almost like being with a schoolmaster. He would get a little bit narky and angry. But it slowly all started coming together. By the end of it, we didn't want it to end. We didn't want to be going off and doing rehearsals with another director.

🔊 RON COOK, *actor*:   *A Jovial Crew* was an absolute joy to do with Max. What happened at the Court was obviously a great drama for him but there is a world beyond, and it's difficult, but going to the RSC and doing *Jovial Crew* was a sort of release.

At the end of 1991, Stafford-Clark received a copy of Caryl Churchill's The Skriker.

✍ 4 Dec   What she depicts is chaos, which is so hard to present on stage, but the wordplay is so loony and the associations so clever it strikes me you would wish to focus and listen to it. Basically, it's wonderful. How can frogs or money come out of someone's mouth? Some of it is just not worked through, like 'a monstrous creature invisible to the others'. How can we possibly know that? A horror story. It could be a film.

[*He returned to it the following July.*] She's been working on it for eight years. I really can't get into it . . . but I can see that there's a powerful theatrical vision there.

[*At the end of July, the two clashed.*] Caryl: 'There are people to whom it [*The Skriker*] means an awful lot.' 'Who?' 'Almost everybody except you.

A feeling you weren't really behind the play . . . a choreographer you did not see the point of . . . A play that's disproportionally important to me . . . Other people excited and moved . . . Each time I've talked to you about it I've come away rather low and drained. Perhaps I do need you to say "Wonderful, wonderful".' I am a bit of a pudding at the moment. Caryl upset that I don't appreciate it.

King Lear, *Stafford-Clark's last production for the Court, with Tom Wilkinson, Adrian Dunbar, Lia Williams, Jason Watkins, Hugh Ross, Saskia Reeves and Andy Serkis, opened on 21 January 1993. By this stage, the new company had a name.*

12 January   David [Hare] said he would write a play for Out of Joint. So will Caryl. How extraordinary.

Case Study

RITA, SUE AND BOB TOO
Andrea Dunbar

Rehearsal: from September 1982

First Performance: 14 October 1982

Cast: Paul Copley, Alan David, Gay Hamilton, Lesley Manville, Tracey Ullman, Joanne Whalley

Published: Rita, Sue and Bob Too (Methuen, 1988)

Cloud Nine was to be my last proper involvement with Joint Stock: by early 1980 I was running the Royal Court. All theatres draw from a pool of professional writers. Any theatre takes pride in presenting new work by Harold Pinter or Caryl Churchill. But its focus on people who haven't previously considered themselves professional playwrights is arguably the Royal Court's most important function. One way of becoming immediately involved in the grassroots was through the annual Young Writers' Festival. This was a national competition open to any aspiring writer up to the age of eighteen. Plays by younger writers made particularly strenuous demands on the actors' versatility. Talking cabbages featured in one play, and neurotic guinea pigs in another, while adolescence provoked a flood of gloomy dramas that invariably ended in suicide or unwanted pregnancies. Every year there were twelve-page bloody sagas on the death of Mary Queen of Scots, as well as vicious satires about eccentric schoolteachers.

But in 1980 there was one outstanding play: *The Arbor*. Written boldly in green biro on pages ripped from a school exercise book, it told the story of a Bradford schoolgirl who became pregnant on the night she lost her virginity. A family argument was depicted with brutal authenticity, and the final scene was heartbreakingly affecting and bleak. The principal character, just called 'Girl', had lost her baby and by accident meets the boy who had made her pregnant. The innocence of the mutual recriminations revealed how young the protagonists really were. I tried to get in touch with the writer, whose name was Andrea Dunbar, but she was in a Battered Wives' Home in Keighley and communication was difficult. In the event, I was to know Andrea for the next thirteen years – and to be involved with her work for even longer: her best known play, *Rita Sue and Bob Too,* which I directed for the Royal Court in 1982, was revived with Robin Soans's *A State Affair* by Out of Joint in the autumn of 2000.

The Arbor was a misleading title. A pack of abandoned and feral dogs roamed the centre of Brafferton Arbor, the crescent on which Andrea lived. But pastoral it was not. It was bleak. Some houses were boarded up, and some gardens were a tangled mess of grass and weeds, often featuring rusty bits of car engine mounted on breezeblocks; like the occasional battered caravan that also blossomed in some gardens, they were dreams of escape – hopeless male fantasies doomed to remain for ever in a state of stagnation. There were a lot of single mothers, but Andrea's own father had stayed with his family, and his violence and feckless drinking had been the dramatic centre of Andrea's childhood. In 1980 this was unusual: in most families the father had fucked off. With no work and no possibility of being a provider, men had become re-dundant in every sense of the word. Families scratched by on benefits, on the occasional odd job, on petty crime and on dole fraud. The poverty was shock-ing. So were other things. A friend of Andrea's on Brafferton had had a baby by her uncle, and it had been born with a skin disease. Andrea related the details with an amused horror. Correct political thinking would have it that male violence and abusive uncles are as common in middle-class as in working-class families. After working on Andrea's plays I don't believe that any longer.

In fact, I first met Andrea in her social worker's house in Haworth. Haworth is everything the Buttershaw Estate is not. Cobbled and fragrant, it is straight out of a Hovis advertisement, and even on a dull November afternoon tourists were ascending the steep hill to the fabled Parsonage. Andrea was taciturn and ungiving. She had watchful eyes and a strong chin. She received the news that we were to produce her play at the Royal Court with no particular enthusiasm. 'No,' she'd never been to London before. 'No,' she'd never been in a theatre. 'Alright,' she'd be prepared to come down, but we had to get the money to the post office for the fare, don't send it to her home. I learnt that it was a culture where you didn't give yourself away. Admitting to pain or showing enthusiasm were both equally undesirable. You had to be hard. And Andrea had developed stoicism and a stubbornness that were imperme-able and particular.

Above: The formality of the production is clear from this photo of *Fanshen*.

Below: Epsom Downs. Left to right: Tony Rohr with Will Knightley up, watched by an admiring Simon Callow, Cecily Hobbs, Gillian Barge and Bob Hamilton.

Antony Sher and Julie Covington in the one moment in *Cloud Nine* where the two time scales meet.

Rita, Sue and Bob Too. Joanne Whalley as Rita avoids looking at Paul Copley's bottom or Lesley Manville's right knee.

Above: Serious Money. Gary Oldman and Burt Caesar on the floor of the Futures Exchange.

Below: Left to right: Lesley Sharp, Alphonsia Emmanuel, Nick Dunning, Jim Broadbent (above), Ron Cook, Linda Bassett and Jude Akuwudike in *Our Country's Good*.

But she enjoyed rehearsal and was amazed to find how much she laughed at the scenes she had written. 'It weren't so funny when it were happening,' she commented wryly about a neighbourhood row that escalated into a riot. Somehow the alchemy of theatre often turned her scenes into something that was hilarious as well as brutal. Humour co-existed with anger and desperation. Andrea and a friend came to stay at my home in Camden Town while the play was being rehearsed. It was a long way from Brafferton Arbor to Gloucester Crescent and both of us had to adapt. She didn't like the food much and found mange-tout particularly disgusting. (Disraeli writes: 'Two nations; who are formed by a different breeding, and are fed by a different food.') And I found it strange to cope with a writer who was more enthusiastic about going to Buckingham Palace or Madame Tussaud's than about coming to rehearsal. But her comments were apt and incisive: 'He weren't sitting down, he were standing up when he said that,' she would say. Or, 'She didn't laugh then, but she did laugh when she said that.' The autobiographical nature of the play and Andrea's gift of total recall meant she could add lines or develop an argument as we were rehearsing. I badgered her for more detail, and invariably she provided it.

The play did well. Kathryn Pogson as the Girl was compelling and vulnerable, but she also captured Andrea's toughness and stubbornness. By the end of the Young Writers' Festival, the word about the quality of the evening had spread and performances were packed out. I asked Andrea to add a second half to the one-act play which would take the story of the Girl further, and we planned the full-length play to open Downstairs immediately after Richard Eyre's production of *Hamlet*. 'To some this appeared a wilful piece of programming. To us, still piecing together our first season as a regime, it felt like a declaration of intent,' wrote Rob Ritchie, the Royal Court's Literary Manager, in his introduction to Andrea's plays.

Programming a play which isn't yet complete is always giving a hostage to fortune. Unbalanced by rushes of hope and despair, it's hard to assess the newly written scenes with any degree of objectivity. Sometimes it works triumphantly. *Serious Money* by Caryl Churchill was programmed before a word had been written. A full-length version of *The Arbor* existed in my head, but I wasn't altogether certain the same play occupied Andrea's thoughts. When she had written the first part of the play she was a fifteen-year-old Bradford schoolgirl writing a CSE exercise for a sympathetic teacher; now she was a seventeen-year-old single mother living in some chaos being asked to complete a play for 'Europe's most interesting theatre'. (This is what the *New York Times* called the Royal Court in 1992: in the same year the *Sunday Times* called it 'a dump'. There was an element of truth about both statements.)

But that's to state the dilemma from my point of view. Andrea wasn't particularly bothered by our middle-class expectations. She had her own problems.

Andrea's world had no agents, no telephones and no bank accounts. Occasionally a few pages would arrive, but the norms of communication with a writer couldn't be taken for granted. Sending cash to her home was impossible as her father would nick it, and sending £2,000 to be drawn in cash from the post office placed Andrea in the position of a local millionaire. Getting her to a friend's flat where I could phone her was a logistical nightmare. And life kept taking priority over art: there was a row with her boyfriend; her daughter Lorraine was poorly; there was a court appearance for assault; the windows had been put out after a row with some neighbours.

When we did speak I would suggest scenes to move the play along. We had established that the principal character, still called 'Girl', worked as a French comber in a mill. What was that? Could there be a scene set in the workplace? And in due course a lively scene with two girls having a fag break in the toilet arrived. But Andrea was nobody's fool, and as she became more engaged in writing her standards became higher. It was consoling to hear her say on the phone one day: 'I've writ you a scene, but I'm not sending it down because it's crap.' Immediately before rehearsals restarted she came down to London to finish the play. Rob Ritchie writes, 'She was given a desk in a tiny office and encouraged to write. "How are you?" I asked on day three. "Knackered," she said, not looking up. "Shut the door." ' My Diary for Sunday 24 May 1980, the day before we started rehearsal, reads, 'After three painful hours, procrastination, and a bit of a sulk, Andrea wrote the last scene.'

The move from Upstairs to Down was bold, and the critics were not prepared to be taken by surprise a second time. What had appeared vibrant and real in the intimacy of the Theatre Upstairs quite rightly had a more searching examination Downstairs. But audiences were double the size, and I felt it was a heartening debut that justified taking Andrea's work out of the context of a Young Writers' Festival and placing it where her talents warranted . . . on a major public stage. Not everyone agreed with this assessment: Michael Billington in the *Guardian* questioned the wisdom of the whole enterprise.

It is always difficult to decide how to respond to critical dismissal. Like everyone else I have suffered in dignified silence, but on occasion I've felt it was more worthwhile to respond. At least you then feel as if you're part of a dialogue rather than the recipient of a mugging. Part of the health of English theatre is that there is no abject dependence on critical response as is the case in New York. In general terms I accept the critics as part of a supportive intelligentsia, but it's never easy when they dismiss four months' work in four paragraphs written within an hour of the curtain coming down. So I wrote this letter to Michael Billington:

> Your analysis of Andrea's shortcomings as a playwright is perfectly correct: there is clearly a missing scene in the second half. The one where she is splattered round the walls by her Pakistani lover. And without it the second half is indeed gap-toothed. Why she can't write it is because she is still too emotionally close to the experience. I find your grudging reaction to *The Arbor* bitterly disappointing. Its achievement is not that it measures up to Eng. Lit. standards of a well-made play, but that it is an articulate record of life in the lower depths recorded not, for once, by an outsider but by someone still passionately involved in that life themselves. I find your casual questioning of the work done for Andrea infuriating. The first part of the play was written three years ago for her CSEs. Since that time she had ceased in any way to see herself as a writer. Our encouragement has given her the opportunity to pursue her talent should she so wish.

Well . . . yes . . . but. My defence is a bit shrill. Undoubtedly my enthusiasm for *The Arbor* and for Andrea's work is because it was authentic. A first-hand report from a world so puzzled over by journalists and sociologists seemed then of enormous importance. It still does.

But authenticity without ability is not enough. I was really angry because I thought Michael Billington was dismissing an outstanding talent. Maybe I was too ready to overlook Andrea's rawness and the juvenilia of her writing. The middle class have always taken pleasure in discovering artistic excellence in the lower orders from the eighteenth century onwards. The *Guardian*'s response to the initial production of *The Arbor* had been to dismiss it as *nostalgie de la boue*. Ben Nicholson had discovered Alfred Wallis in St Ives when the latter was a rag-and-bone man painting on a biscuit tin and scraps of cardboard. But when I first saw Wallis's marine paintings in Kettle's Yard in Cambridge I was stunned by their power and authenticity. Was Andrea's work really so good? How does it stand up now?

Here's an extract from the second scene of *The Arbor*. Sister has just revealed that Girl, aged fifteen is pregnant. Father and Mother are trying to find out the identity of the father. Remember Andrea wrote this when she was fifteen too.

FATHER: Who is the dirty bastard?

GIRL: I'm not telling you who it is.

SISTER: I bet it's a dirty fuckin' old man.

MOTHER: Will you shut your fucking mouth.

SISTER: You must be proud of her, the dirty slag, she's nowt else.

GIRL: You've no room to fuckin' talk, you go out with anybody.

FATHER: All we fuckin' want to know is who the father of it is.

MOTHER: Surely you must know that I'm only concerned about you. You are my daughter you know.

FATHER: She's no fuckin' daughter of mine.

SISTER: She's nowt else but a slag if you ask me.

GIRL: Oh go fuck off will you.

MOTHER: I can't fuckin' understand you two, you're both as fuckin' bad, yet you'll sit there and pull each other down.

FATHER: They're all the fuckin' same in this house.

MOTHER: Yeah! Including you.

SISTER (*to Father*): Yeah! You're nowt but a dirty bastard yourself.

FATHER: You shut your mouth or do you want a punch in the teeth?

GIRL: That's all you're fuckin' fit for isn't it? Yes, belting women.

MOTHER: For crying out fuckin' loud, will the lot of you shut up.

SISTER: I'm not fuckin' stopping here much longer. I'm sick of all this arguing.

FATHER: Yeah! Go on. Piss off.

SISTER: Aye, you an' all you bastard. (*Exits.*)

FATHER: Fuck off then and don't come back.

MOTHER: Oh will you shut up and go see to your sisters.

FATHER: Fuckin' shut up you. I don't like dirty or cheeky fuckin' children.

GIRL: And I don't like drunken fuckin' men either.

FATHER: You fuckin' shut your mouth, I'm not talking to you. Only open yours when I tell you to.

MOTHER: Just leave her alone. Anyway you want to go see your sisters, they've all got kids to different fathers and not one of them is married.

FATHER: I hope it's born dead. The dirty bastard.

GIRL: You should have been born dead as well, and you're a dirty bastard! I've heard about you and that woman.

FATHER: You mind your own business, what I do or where I go, who with is nothing to do with you.

GIRL: Yes and it's nothing to do with *you* where I am or who I'm with is it?

FATHER: It fuckin' is. I'm the one that gets in trouble for you, as soon as you earn enough money for you and that baby you can get out.

GIRL: Fuck off! It's you that wants kicking out!

FATHER: Fuck off! Get out of my sight before I kill you.

GIRL: If you hit me I'll hit you back *and* you'll get it off our David when he comes in.

FATHER: That fuckin' David won't get in to hit me. And if you don't shut up you won't be here long.

GIRL: I'll go now if you want me to. *The Arbor*, Act 1, Sc. 2

And so on. The Father goes off to the pub leaving the Mother to try unsuccessfully to discover the paternity of the child. I can't think of a scene that captures better the chaos of a dysfunctional family, and the excitement and power of violence is as vividly depicted as Dickens's scenes between Bill Sikes and Nancy. The Father's curse ('I hope it's born dead. The dirty bastard') is as shocking as Lear's curse of Goneril. The language is rough but it has its own rhythm, while the writer's ear for dialogue is acute. The family are both violent and vulnerable because the balance of power is shifting. A crisis has arisen because Father's authority is waning, while David, the offstage eldest son, is becoming more powerful. And the hierarchy between the sisters is also changing. The Sister is two years older than The Girl, but her seniority is challenged both by the Girl's force of personality and by her pregnancy, which is in itself an assertion of independence.

The dialogue keeps four well-developed characters alive, and all of them have very clear objectives. The Sister's is to invoke family values and get the Girl punished, while the Girl's is to assert her toughness by preserving her independence. The objectives of the Father and the Mother are impeccable: they are to find out the identity of the baby's father and preserve family life. Only the Girl achieves her objective, and her tenacity in the face of both the Father's brutal threats and the Mother's insistent cajoling, once he has left for the pub, mark a particular coming of age. A psychologist might add that if you're a young mother you can no longer be treated like a child, and that escaping a bleak childhood might be a superobjective for all young women in Andrea's plays. Her observation is exact. The Father is the focus of attention, and it's his approval that the Sister seeks. She is outraged when she doesn't get it: 'Don't tell me. Tell her. I'll kill her in a minute.' The Father's ineffectiveness doesn't have to be played. It comes from the fact that in the end nobody responds to his threats.

In a more structured society the Sister might even be rewarded for revealing information vital to the family and its position, but here everything is reversed and it is she who is first forced out of the house. The moral code is not a stabilising force: on the contrary it's a cause of tension because of the gap that exists between life as it ought to be lived and the grim reality. There is no 'new' morality on offer, and Andrea's characters can't make the old morality work. The writer gives us a world where it's impossible to be a good mother just as it is impossible to be a good daughter. The past is constantly invoked as a time when there was some kind of order:

> MUM: We're no longer living in those times. Things have changed.
>
> FATHER: They were better in those days than it is today . . . Trouble with people today is they're not strict enough. I couldn't turn round and say I'm not doing this and that. If I was told to do something I had to run.
>
> MUM: Oh shut up.   Rita, Sue and Bob Too, Act 1, Sc. 2

But it's a mythical past, and the gap between memory and reality confounds the characters. The Father remembers an ordered childhood, but the Mother exposes this fiction: 'you want to go see your sisters, they've all got kids to different fathers and not one of them is married.'   The Arbor, Act 1, Sc. 2

We have to hark still further back to find a persuasive dream of working-class order. In the opening scene of D.H. Lawrence's play The Daughter-in-Law (1912) we also see a working-class family dealing with an unwanted pregnancy. But rather than unheeded advice offered in *The Arbor* ('You want to get maintenance money off him', says Mother), Luther's family in Lawrence's play rally round and decide to pay Mrs Gascoigne £20 now and £20 in a year's time as long as the scandal is hushed up. In a nice touch both families agree to lay the blame for the unwanted pregnancy on one of the engineers laying the new gas mains. Lawrence's working-class family have unions, the chapel, adult education classes, employment, Delft on the sideboard, and a close family structure, all of which reinforce a sense of morality and a sense of self. On Andrea's estate the shame and hypocrisy have gone, but so has the morality and so have all the other buttresses that created a sense of self. The seventy years between the two plays reveals a slide from working class to underclass that could have been illustrated by Hogarth.

After *The Arbor* Andrea went back to Bradford and began to write a second play. She had no desire to move away from Buttershaw and had little curiosity about life elsewhere. *The Arbor* ends with the Girl holed up in a Battered Wives' Home. 'I'm glad we got away from that dump,' says her friend. Girl responds: 'It may be a dump but I quite miss it myself, funny ain't it? . . . Well, I miss my Mum and the kids and funnily enough, I miss my Dad. And all my mates. (*Pause.*) It's very quiet here.'(Act 2, Sc. 9) These were certainly Andrea's own views. She rejected any life much removed from her own experience. After *The Arbor,* Andrea phoned a couple of times and asked, 'What can you do on stage?' She wasn't seeking advice about Brecht but was asking how sexually candid it was possible to be in the theatre.

Rita, Sue and Bob Too was Andrea's second play, and it became notorious for the hilarious first scene in which two schoolgirl babysitters take it in turns to have sex with Bob, their employer, in the back of his car. There's an increase in confidence, and, although there's never much political analysis in Andrea's work, there's an awareness of life getting grimmer. Bob reveals the good times will have to end because he's going to have to sell the car, and he gives the two girls a political seminar: 'There's no hope for kids today, and it's all Maggie Thatcher's fault. She'll bring total destruction. Just you wait and see . . . It'll take years to get the country back on its feet again.' (Sc. 6) But the hardness of the life is mitigated by the sheer priapic vigour of the two girls, who certainly don't see themselves as victims. 'I hope he brings us here again,' says Rita anxiously at the end of their first sex session. 'Oh he will. Make no mistake about it,' says Sue with confidence. It's the one certainty in a fickle world.

'Sex is plainly central', writes Rob Ritchie, 'but it is the unlooked for consequences, the unwanted pregnancies, the family rows, the broken friendships
that provide the real dramatic interest.' Men provide the fun, but in the end
they bring trouble. Each of Andrea's plays ends with a quieter moment of
pre-feminist reflection. In *Rita, Sue and Bob Too* Michelle, who has been
deserted by Bob, and Sue's Mother, who is a tough but bedraggled figure,
meet in a pub. They've last met during a steaming neighbourhood row:
antagonists then, they arrive at a slow understanding. 'Anyway, all men are
no good. They want shooting for all the trouble they cause,' advises Mother.
'All fellas do the dirty on you sometime or other. Only let them come on
your conditions and stick to them. Don't let them mess you around.' (Act 2,
Sc. 10)

Andrea died of a brain haemorrhage at the age of twenty-nine. She had
written three plays and had had three children. All her plays are written from
a young woman's perspective, but as her technique sharpened she began to
move away from the simple autobiographical stance of *The Arbor*, and in *Shirley*,
her final play, there are several scenes written from the point of view of the
older woman character, who in previous plays was just called 'Mother'. Her
plays as a girl showed an extraordinary talent; the tragedy is that she never
lived to write the plays of her maturity. Script meetings at the Royal Court
throw up lots of ideas which aren't always followed up. One was a season of
work entitled 'Dead Young'. It was to have been devoted to the work of
playwrights who had died under the age of thirty. Andrea, dead at 29, would
have taken a place alongside Büchner (24), Farquhar (29) and Marlowe (29).

The success of her work and of the film of *Rita, Sue and Bob Too* didn't make
life easier. She didn't like the film much. It had an upbeat ending with the
ménage between the two girls and Bob continuing in frolicsome mode. 'That
would never have happened,' said Andrea. You didn't go back with somebody
who had rejected you. The film infringed Andrea's particular moral code.
She knew that life was rarely that easy; and sometimes it was impossible.
Telephone calls to Andrea were constantly upstaged by the domestic crises
that made existence on the Arbor so dramatic. On one occasion one of the
kids had set fire to the curtains, and on another, one had stuck their fingers
in an electric socket. For the interviews that followed the film Andrea would
only consent to be filmed from one side. She had scars down one cheek that
she said she had got through a fight in a pub. I learnt later that she had fallen
through a glass door when she was drunk and had needed sixty stitches and

plastic surgery. Often it seems the middle class can only endure working-class stories when they chronicle plucky triumph over adversity, as in *Educating Rita*. We need the working class to succeed in getting that play on (*Our Country's Good*), or getting to the Royal Ballet (*Billy Elliot*). But the qualities needed for survival are often brutish, and I came to learn that Andrea's hardness was a smart choice. She was always suspicious of middle-class interest. 'They'll forget all about us by tomorrow,' she said. And of course there came a point at which my involvement in her life ceased.

On my first visit to the Arbor I had met Andrea's family. I had been to the pub, been up to the moors and seen her old school. I was about to drive off in my MGB when I felt a firm tug on the seam of my trousers. It was Andrea's younger sister, Catherine, aged thirteen. 'Tek me wi' yer,' she said. 'Tek me wi' yer.' I explained it was impossible. And I went. Eight years later I met Catherine again. It was after Andrea's death, at a benefit the Royal Court had organised to raise money for her children. Politely I explained that although she had probably forgotten we had in fact met on a previous occasion. 'Oh no,' she said staring at me unforgivingly, 'I remember you.' She now has six children of her own and lives in Bradford. Lorraine, Andrea's eldest daughter, now aged twenty-six, is a heroin addict. She has two children of her own, the youngest of which was also born a heroin addict. As I write, the two children have been taken into care by social services.

But they remember their writers in Bradford. Outside the Central Library is a fine statue of Priestley. His face is turned towards what is left of the elegant Victorian square, and the brass coat tails of his raincoat fly behind him. Inside the Library a small room is named after Andrea. The Andrea Dunbar Room provides a word processor and a quiet space for writers who can't get any peace at home. It's an appropriate memorial, although I don't suppose Andrea would have used it much. She remained suspicious of middle-class institutions and was more in the Dostoyevsky mode, scrawling at the kitchen table while the bailiffs were at the door. Upstairs in 'Local History' there's a scrapbook that has carefully been put together about Andrea's life. There is stuff on the plays and on the film and on local people disapproving of the grim and disreputable picture that her work gives, but the final clipping is about dole fraud.

Award-winning playwright Andrea Dunbar told today how she was considering giving up writing after being prosecuted for claiming social security without revealing her royalties. Dunbar, who won acclaim for her plays about down-to-earth Bradford life, was fined £75 with £50 costs after admitting receiving £5,400 she was not entitled to. Dunbar, 27, said she had faced a series of blows throughout her life – most recently this summer when she needed sixty stitches in her face and plastic surgery after she fell through a glass door. Dunbar of Brafferton Arbor, Buttershaw, said she regretted ever starting to write for all the trouble it had brought her. People thought she was rich, but she wasn't. She still lived with her parents and her three children. Dunbar was ordered to pay back the £5,400 at £3 a week. The court heard that, like her characters, she was living in poverty.   *Bradford Telegraph and Argus, 15 December 1988*

It would have taken Andrea over thirty-four years to have paid it off. She would have taken satisfaction from the fact that the state only got a couple of years' worth out of her.

There is a postscript to my involvement with the Andrea Dunbar story. In 2000 there was an opportunity to visit her world again. Mrs Thatcher had famously denied there was such a thing as society, and she had denied the existence of an underclass too. The term was distasteful to both left and right in the eighties. But by the time of the Labour administration, its presence was unavoidable. 'Tony Blair knows that vast numbers live outside mainstream society, and he openly called them "the underclass" when he came to power,' wrote the *Sunday Times* (18 January 2000). Most of the time the crime-ridden council estates that ring our cities slumber sulphurously, but an occasional event propels them into prominence. In the summer of 1992 council estates from Oxford to Newcastle erupted in violence. And in 1993 the abduction and murder of two-year-old James Bulger by two ten-year-old boys in Liverpool caused widespread horror and incomprehension. In the spring of 2000 a Norfolk farmer, Tony Martin, shot at two burglars in his house, killing one of them. They had driven to the farm from a council estate outside Newark. All this aroused comment and concern: a number of books presented England as a country that had become a stranger to itself. Nick Danziger's *Britain* (1996) or Nick Davies's *Dark Heart* (1997) investigated England's heartland with the curiosity of an anthropological quest up the Amazon. In May 2000 a television series called 'Fergal Keane's Forgotten

Britain' undertook to reintroduce us to ourselves. Appropriately enough, Fergal Keane is a foreign correspondent.

On 9 May 2000 the *Sunday Times* organised a debate called 'The Growing Threat of the Underclass'. It was the culmination of a series of articles by the controversial right-wing sociologist Charles Murray. Security measures were formidable: a team of blazered security men with 'News International' written discreetly on their pockets awaited student disruptions that never came. The audience were middle-class, middle-aged and middle England. They were there to be reassured. Jack Straw blamed the Thatcher years. Sue Slipman, an ex-Communist and now social director of Camelot, blamed 'economic and industrial changes which have met with an inadequate social response'. She said that 'the victory of capitalism over socialism' carried with it 'a responsibility that the corporate world must accept'. Melanie Phillips of the *Daily Mail* blamed 'the disintegration of family values . . . the emergence of children who were simply unsocialised . . . appallingly low social expectations . . . girls who have no greater expectation than to be a hairdresser . . . what children get now is wall-to-wall sex education, what has gone is morality' (big applause).

The government 'is desperate to avoid being judgmental'. Charles Murray, who was introduced by the Editor of the *Sunday Times* as 'possibly the most dangerous right-wing thinker in the United States', had a smooth and pleasant delivery. He blamed the huge increase on illegitimacy, now running as high as 70 per cent in inner cities. He said this was 'a unique departure from the norms of Western society. Communities without fathers are vicious places to live, and people who have money choose not to live there.' But, he added, 'I have a solution. Get rid of the Welfare State.' It is only because of the Welfare State 'that young men can sire children with no responsibility'. He was passionately applauded by couples in front of me and to my right. Basically, his assertion is that there are three principal indices that reveal the presence of an underclass: the growth rate in violent crime, the increase in male unemployment and the increase, not just of illegitimacy, but of single women bringing up children alone.

Twenty years earlier in 1980 the Buttershaw Estate outside Bradford could already demonstrate all three characteristics in fruitful abundance.

When faced with this world there's always an inclination to blame people rather than circumstances. Dr Johnson advised Boswell: 'Resolve not to be poor. Poverty is a great enemy to human happiness. It makes some virtues impracticable, and others extremely difficult.' In the Bradford Central Library I found the *Bradford Report of the Work of Female Sanitary Inspectors*. It is dated 1907: 'One of the most serious sins of the lowest slum inhabitants is that of laziness. We constantly find men and women in bed at eleven a.m. or just down eating breakfast at midday. And when children aren't trained in self-control, one constantly finds lack of moral backbone. The gratification of desire, the fleeting pleasures of the hour, seems to be these women's only thought. The more serious side of life, the realisation of God-given duties, never occurs to them.' Following the sentencing of Tony Martin, the *Sunday Times* hosted a vigorous correspondence which featured similar philosophy in this letter from a JP in Somerset: 'There is usually a whole battery of skilled and assiduous apologists for these offenders. Every conceivable factor is blamed for their offending except their own weakness, cupidity, immorality, fecklessness and sheer malevolence' (30 April 2000).

So in the summer of 2000 I revisited Buttershaw and the surrounding estates with Robin Soans, an actor and playwright, and with a group of actors. For three weeks we talked to people who live on the estates where Andrea had grown up. The stories they told us and the words they spoke were to make a new play: *A State Affair*. Two principal events had changed the Buttershaw Estate in the twenty years since *Rita, Sue and Bob Too*: in the early nineties a heroin epidemic had begun which continues to ravage the lives of many of the estate's young people; and in 1994 a Single Regeneration Budget of £31 million had been given to Buttershaw and two neighbouring estates. A massive rebuilding programme had seen many houses either knocked down, or rebuilt with security fences and with specially designed burglarproof doors and windows. People were under no illusions that they had stopped crime: they had merely moved it elsewhere. On the Arbor itself there was less evidence of extreme poverty, and there were a few more tended gardens than there had been in the eighties, but the centre of the Arbor was still a jungle of wild grass, waist-high, through which kids had pioneered the occasional trail. It was a tough place in 1980, but to it had been added, by 2000, the chaos, criminality and desolation brought by heroin.

The people we talked to gave us their stories with great freedom and willingness. Many were coping with grim situations. I had expected that. What none of us had anticipated was the charisma and commitment of the care workers. We met police, health visitors, youth workers, drugs rehabilitation officers, midwives, hostel wardens, housing officers, probation officers, vicars and teachers. They are the infantry dealing on the ground with the massive problems created by poverty, crime and addiction. To say they were impressive is an understatement. We also met Lorraine Dunbar, Andrea's daughter, who told us: 'If I wrote a play, I'd do it about the Buttershaw Estate. I'd show some people getting their lives together with a lot of courage and determination. But it would show others going down a big steep hill, into a black hole.'

Andrea Dunbar was a formidable personality and a prodigious talent. She had seemed promising in 1980 and from the retrospect of 2000 nothing had occurred to diminish that judgement. The full-length version of *The Arbor* had opened on the Royal Court's main stage following Richard Eyre's seminal production of *Hamlet* with Jonathan Pryce. Rob Ritchie wrote: 'We didn't know if Andrea Dunbar was going to be able to write a second act to make it into a main-stage play. It just seemed fantastic to be able to say, look here's Shakespeare and here's a sixteen-year-old mother of three from Bradford, and this is what we're about.'

PS. Incidentally, *Rita, Sue and Bob Too* threw up a problem that often faces contemporary directors, and that is at what point to assay the candid scenes involving nudity and sexual contact. I often think that drama schools should remove swordplay and fencing from the curriculum and replace it with sex. After all, in most contemporary plays, the penis is both mightier and more frequent than the sword. Not long before *Rita, Sue and Bob Too* I had had some success directing *A Thought in Three Parts* by Wallace Shawn, which contained more orgasms per page than any other play in theatre history. We confronted the question of nudity fairly early in rehearsal and we had done a number of rehearsals where the actors were naked. We had even rehearsed the comparative vigour of each orgasm, of course by drawing cards at random from a pack. So it was with some confidence that I told the cast and stage management of *Rita, Sue and Bob Too* that the afternoon's rehearsal would be held with everybody in the rehearsal room naked . . . The stage management team made their excuses and left, but my assistant, the young Simon Curtis, manfully took his clothes off and has dined out ever since on the story of how he spent an afternoon in rehearsal with a naked 22-year-old Joanne Whalley and a naked 23-year-old Lesley Manville. I believe that this story has been instrumental in many young people deciding to make their career in theatre.

Case Study

SERIOUS MONEY
Caryl Churchill

Workshop: from 27 September 1986

Rehearsal: from February 1987

First Performance: 21 March 1987

Cast: Linda Bassett, Burt Caesar, Allan Corduner, Lesley Manville, Alfred Molina, Gary Oldman, Meera Syal, Julian Wadham

Published: Plays 2 (Methuen, 1990)

My first involvement with Andrea Dunbar was as I began my fourteen years as Artistic Director of the Royal Court. *Serious Money* came halfway through that tenure and was to be the most commercially successful play of my regime. It went on to run for a year in the West End and for a brief but unforgettable time on Broadway. It appeared in London at the same time as Tom Wolfe's novel *Bonfire of the Vanities* and the film *Wall Street*. All three pieces focus on the workings of the financial world. The Wall Street broker Ivan Boesky had memorably asserted that 'greed is good'. He was later imprisoned for insider dealing. It was exhilarating and exciting to be at the centre of this world. But my memories of the play are inextricably linked with the crisis over *Perdition* and the beginning of Matthew Evans's attempts to remove me as the Royal Court's Artistic Director.

Matthew Evans was appointed Chairman of the Board of the English Stage Company in December 1984. At this point the Royal Court had recently survived a calculated attempt by William Rees-Mogg, Chairman of the Arts Council, to eliminate its subsidy. For three months Rob Ritchie, the Court's Literary Manager, and I had effectively stopped running the theatre and mounted a successful campaign to prevent the demise of the Royal Court. Our staunchest allies had been David Hare and the critic Nicholas de Jongh. With some help from the Royal Court's Council we had reversed the momentum of Rees-Mogg's manifesto *The Glory of The Garden*. The aim of this had been, amongst other things, to remove funding from the Royal Court, whose purpose in presenting new writing, it was argued, was now being served by the Cottesloe at the National and at the Warehouse by the RSC. The intention was to devolve this money to the regions. A central plank of our counter argument had been the historic importance of the Royal Court in giving a first hearing to regional writers.

In 1984 this campaign was over.

Letter to The Times
Too many senior officers of the Arts Council share a passionately held and dangerous indifference to new writing. Their tastes lie elsewhere. The new play is often arrogant, usually opinionated; sometimes it is subversive and bites the hand that feeds it. They have little sympathy for it and, for all their acquaintance with horticultural imagery, little understanding of how the new play is nurtured and cultivated. The proposal to cut the Royal Court emanated from a small group of senior Arts Council officers. The proposal was seen to be wholly out of step with professional and public opinion about the theatre's function and was hastily withdrawn. This in itself is an indictment of the wilful ignorance of those responsible for framing the proposal in the first place.

1 September 1984

Matthew Evans had little knowledge of these events, which had served to weld the staff together and which had doubtless also made us over-protective, battle-scarred, self-involved and suspicious of outsiders. We started off at odds with each other. He came to see *An Honourable Trade* by G.F. Newman. This was about corruption and was neither as successful nor as deft as his earlier *Operation Bad Apple*.

◀) Matthew came in and he clearly had some disdain for the rather hybrid form of consultation with the staff that we'd arrived at. And his disdain was probably the wrong tone to strike at the beginning. At the same time I think I was over-defensive. I remember him coming to see *An Honourable Trade*. And he thought it was not very good. I remember defending the play over-vigorously. This got us off on the wrong foot, and we never really recovered. And he's not a theatregoer. I couldn't fucking well forgive him for that . . . I wanted him to be in love with it the way that all the rest of us working there were. And he never was. So I regarded him, I suppose, as an obstacle rather than an ally.

🔊 MATTHEW EVANS: It was a mess because it was run by Max as a fiefdom, and if you didn't agree with Max, forget it. He's a clever chap, no question about that. He had neutralised the Board . . . and the Board really had no role at all . . . And what Max wanted was a neutral, castrated Board, and not a heavily interventionist Chairman who had some idea of where things should go . . . So we met after *An Honourable Trade*, and Max said, 'What do you think?' and I said, 'Max, I thought it was absolutely terrible, all obvious, and naive for the following eight reasons.' And he went berserk. He got very, very upset, and it was clear to me that he didn't want this discourse . . . I just felt there was a siege mentality there.

It didn't help that Matthew and I were much the same age. Pete Townshend's description of Matthew, which Matthew himself passed on with some pride, was that he looked like a seedy geography teacher with patched elbows to his sports jacket.

Over the course of the next six years things got progressively worse between us. The crisis over *Perdition* fuelled the bad feeling, but once the momentum of ill-will had started it became hard to reverse. When I was at school I remember hating a boy called Cummins. He had arrived at the school one term earlier, and this was accompanied by various futile privileges of rank and superiority. One afternoon after games we had a fight in the changing room. He was a skilled boxer but had the disadvantage of being completely naked. I got in one good blow before we were separated. Next Sunday in chapel I watched him blinking slightly from the bruise over his eye and rubbed my own skinned knuckle with some degree of happiness. I hated him with a purity that I have never felt for anyone before or since until I met Matthew Evans.

It wasn't as if we didn't both try. I recall one evening in the Groucho Club where we both drank whisky till the early hours, and he talked movingly about his collapsed marriage and the effect on his two sons. The effort at reconciliation nearly killed me: one evening David Hare, who was the nearest to a mutual friend we both had, invited me to dinner by myself to advocate that Matthew Evans and I should both grow up. He opened a bottle of claret, and we sat down to talk. At that moment the phone rang. It was the *New York*

Times for David, clearly an interview that couldn't be postponed. An hour and a half later David had finished the interview, but I had finished the claret. We had two more bottles over dinner, and I was unsteady as I drove back from Notting Hill. On the slip road up to the M40 I realised I was going far too fast and braked sharply. The Jensen spun in a complete circle, and I ended up facing the oncoming traffic. It was a matter of pure luck that it didn't lunge over the parapet, or that I didn't have a head-on collision. I drove home shaking.

At least our relationship ended with me in pocket. Matthew's animosity cut loose in an interview with *GQ Magazine*. He stated that I had canvassed other directors persuading them not to apply for my job, thus securing the position for myself. This was totally fictitious. Peter Murphy, my agent, put me in touch with Mishcon de Reya, later to be Princess Diana's lawyers. After a brisk exchange of correspondence *GQ* printed a retraction, and I settled for £10,000. I was delighted to discover that legal settlements are tax-free.

✍ *15 March 1985*   Of course we are paranoid, entrenched, defensive, suspicious. One visit to Matthew's gracious, spacious office at Faber and Faber in Queen Square tells why. We're overworked, overcrowded and underpaid. The syndrome is clear. We'll end up with one Artistic Director, one General Manager and a Youth Opportunity Person. The attempt to perpetuate standards, and the staff that maintain those standards, will have failed.

Royal Court Council minutes, 13 June 1985
The question of the Artistic Director's contract was discussed. It was due to expire in March 1986. The Artistic Director asked for five years, the term to include a sabbatical year. Mr Stafford-Clark did not view the Court as a 'stepping stone to a larger ambition. He wanted to be at the Royal Court, and he saw much that he wanted to achieve and felt willing and able to undertake it'.   *Royal Court archive*

◀) MATTHEW EVANS: I thought it would be in the interests of the Court to get rid of Max. I told this to Max . . . I wanted to get rid of him, and he obviously didn't want to go. I think what we were all afraid of was that the Court was just a sort of fragile entity and that if we really went to war with Max the whole thing might collapse. So he was at that time, at the Court, all-powerful, and had the support of most of the staff.

This was the atmosphere in which the first discussions about *Serious Money* took place. At the end of 1985 my Diary records my asking Caryl Churchill a crucial question.

✍ *7 Dec*   'So if we did a workshop then when do you think is a realistic date for the delivery of the first draft?' The longest silence in theatre history follows.

In early 1986 I watched the technical rehearsal for a production of *Women Beware Women* directed by Bill Gaskill and freely adapted by Howard Barker. Twenty years later it looks as if it may have been Bill's final production at the Royal Court. If so, it's the theatre's loss.

✍ *27 Jan*   Watching Bill. The staging is so exact, and the set is nothing – just a black box with rust-coloured red dripping down the sides – but the images are etched against the light, and you see him working away at it . . . The costumes are all black, but they have texture, and even though they have elegance and style, they evoke a world of sex and money with such clarity that you think that must have been how it was. The focus is on the actors and the text. And the play brings you the truth of that world as surely as any contemporary production. I would have done *Women* in modern dress and staging. Wrong.

THE WORKSHOP

It was this world of sex and money that I was keen to explore further. The Royal Court was accustomed to researching plays about the deprived, but to give a whole picture of society it's also necessary to look at the people who are making lots of money. In September 1986 I began a two-week workshop with Caryl Churchill that investigated the City. The acting team was formidable and included Gary Oldman, Alfred Molina, Lesley Manville, Julian Wadham, Meera Syal and Linda Bassett. The working title was LIFFE. These were the initials of the London International Financial Futures Exchange. Two of the actors got jobs on the floor of LIFFE, where they were objects of amused concern because they earned so little. During the two weeks of the workshop we met stockbrokers, traders on the Metal Exchange and on the Baltic Exchange, financial advisers and also someone from War on Want who explained some of the consequences of international financial practice for the Third World. Ian Dury agreed to write the music and the lyrics, and he joined in the research too. Ian was a god to the Essex boys and girls who worked on the floor of LIFFE, and, when he visited, the stunned traders stopped working. He was immediately banned from the trading floor. LIFFE was pretty tolerant about unorthodox behaviour, but the one unforgivable crime was to stop making money.

The first session of each day would be a group rehearsal. One exercise was for each of the actors to pursue a story from the *Financial Times*, which meant that we all became involved in comprehending the financial world and its jargon. But the main purpose was to report back to Caryl. We would set up improvisations replaying the interviews with the people we had met the previous day. If two or three actors had interviewed a person they would simultaneously re-enact and impersonate the character, while the rest of the cast became the interviewers. This is a technique I have employed a lot since. It makes the actors prompt each other so the effort at recall is not dependent on any single person, and it makes the characterisation firmer and bolder.

The discussions and the run-up to the workshop of *Serious Money* had been accompanied both by an increase in admiration for the breadth and scope of Caryl's work and an increase in frostiness with Matthew:

✍ *2 June*   Saw *Top Girls* last night at a pub theatre in Tufnell Park. What a fine play . . . It still emerges as the finest play I know from the eighties. Good idea to revive it when the new play is written and finally establish Caryl Churchill's reputation, but in the absence of work of that stature we have to create our own. Debbie Horsfield's new commissioned play about Club 18–30 holidays in the Mediterranean is relentlessly apolitical . . . Somehow I should push her feminist instincts.

Letter to Matthew Evans, 6 August 1986
Thank you for your letter of 1 August. Although I'm still not quite accustomed to the intemperate nature of your correspondence, Janie's letter is alarming. [Jayne Rayne, Council Member, had written about the

difficulty of interesting prospective patrons in the Court's programme and the lack of a hospitality structure to support the scheme.] By the time you receive this I will have met her and responded to her reservations about the Patronage Scheme: I trust I will also have resolved what are clearly misunderstandings between us . . . I have absorbed your homily about pulling together as a team, and, as I hoped you were already aware, I support its sentiments entirely.
Best wishes,
As ever, Max

At the same time the exhilaration of discovering another world was matched by concern about how much we could find out in the limited time we could afford on the workshop itself.

✍ *23 Sept*   A good day in the workshop yesterday [for *Serious Money*], but it's not gonna crack easily. How can we think that in two weeks we can become whiz financial analysts, and expose the antics of experts who've spent their lives with it? . . . Visited Futures Market and Stock Exchange. Saw a lot of hanging about. Came back and set up impros of people's behaviour. Terrified by the subject, but we laughed a lot.

Part of the exhilaration was caused by discovering just how much money people in the city were earning. We did an exercise where each member of the workshop had to spend £200,000 in a year. We divided neatly into selfish Hedonists (me, Julian Wadham, Meera Syal), who would go for Porsches, manor houses, swimming pools and flying lessons, and a Politically Correct group (Linda Bassett, Lesley Manville), who declared they would 'give gifts to the ANC. Buy a street in London and rent houses to friends. Help niece who wants to go to RADA.'

People in the city were dismissive about our ability to unravel the complexities of the financial world in two weeks. And of course Caryl read more widely once the workshop had finished. But we had all found the buccaneering spirit of the financial world intoxicating, and a certain admiration mingled with Caryl's inherent disapproval of so much money swilling about.

And in some ways we were progressing quicker than we realised. The actors' first task each morning was to read the *Financial Times* and to endeavour to follow through the intricacies of a particular story. Allan Corduner had been following a story about the price of chocolate in the Ivory Coast. A large portion of the world's chocolate is grown in Africa but is processed in Belgium or France. The French Transport Ministry had determined to phase out transport subsidies to francophone ex-colonies. Allan asked a stock-broker we were interviewing if this didn't mean that inevitably the price of chocolate would rise. The broker looked shocked. It was the early days of mobile phones, and he extracted a telephone the size of a house brick from his immaculate briefcase to phone his office with Allan's tip about chocolate futures.

But this exhilaration was countered by the extraordinary row about *Perdition* which was beginning to appear over the horizon.

Royal Court Council minutes, 20 Oct
Mr Evans reported that Lord Weidenfeld had expressed concern regarding *Perdition*, a play being produced in the Theatre Upstairs. Ms Sonia Melchett reported that concern had been expressed to her. Mr Stafford-Clark reported that reports had been commissioned regarding the accuracy of the play and had been shown to Jim Allen [the author]. He believed the play to be very serious if provocative. Both he and Mr Curtis [Director of the Theatre Upstairs] supported the play. Mr Evans concluded that, given this commitment to the play and its historical accuracy, and since the expressed concerns appeared not to be based on a reading of the play, criticism should be resisted by the Council.

Royal Court archive

At Michael Hastings's suggestion we had commissioned a play by Jim Allen that Ken Loach was to direct. It seemed a great coup to have Ken Loach at the Royal Court. The subject of the play was the behaviour of a group of Hungarian Jews in Budapest in 1944. The play suggests that the deportation of Jews from Hungary in the last months of World War Two was expedited by a group of Zionist Jews who collaborated with the Nazis in order to pursue the creation of a Jewish homeland. At the same time we had commissioned a report which was used as a means of getting a second draft and of placing some further research at the disposal of the writer. I had naively expected that Loach and Allen would welcome that. It was also true that this same report signalled the problems that the play was going to have;

it said the play would be accused of anti-Semitism. I noted this, but didn't believe it was of great significance; the Royal Court had staged many controversial plays in its history. I didn't think this was going to be enormously difficult. I had no idea of the furore that would erupt, and I certainly didn't signal that there would be a huge problem to the Council or to anyone else. This was later seen as culpable.

At this point Triumph and Disaster were jogging along quite happily together. I was oblivious to both.

   ✍ *8 Dec*   Should we involve fifteen Activists [the name given to members of the Court's youth group] in *Serious Money*? It would be an inexpensive way of both providing a *coup de théâtre* at the end of each act and increasing cast size. They could do one scene which would be on the floor of the Futures Market and which would probably be a first-half closer. The only problem – well, apart from Equity – would be in getting them to repeat performances night after night.

In fact there was a cast of eight, supplemented by a Junior Eight who appeared in the two scenes that took place on a trading floor at the end of the first half and at the beginning of the second. Sophie Okonedo was in the Royal Court Company and Julianne Moore was in the Junior Eight in New York, so we attracted distinguished younger company.

   ✍ *6 Jan*   Extra £200 on *Perdition* set.

15 Jan   *Perdition*. What's missing is a speech which gives a proper defence of Zionism.

16 Jan   Matthew says the Israeli Government will make representations, and the Israeli Ambassador is involved.

18 Jan   At 4.30 p.m., the invitation comes to go to Sonia's [Melchett] house at 6.00 p.m.

The meeting appears to have been convened by Lord Weidenfeld, a self-appointed leader of the Jewish community, rather than the Council, and the purpose is to hear the historian Martin Gilbert rehearse a catalogue of the play's inaccuracies. Since I have already spent three hours with him earlier this week hearing his reservations about *Perdition* I feel no need to attend . . . But clearly this is turning into a full Council meeting. I wonder how long it will be before news leaks out.

My absence from the meeting was later characterised as 'unforgivable arrogance'.

It was at this point that the British Board of Deputies sought a meeting. They represented the Jewish Community and ostensibly their objective was to ask for a disclaimer in the programme that made it clear the play was an interpretation of events and not a factual account. Ken Loach vigorously resisted, and Matthew advised against a disclaimer, but with hindsight it would have been a relatively simple compromise. There was no meeting with the British Board of Deputies, but the Institute of Jewish Affairs was not so easily put off. We met the Chairman of the Institute, Dr Stephen Roth, in my office at the top of the Royal Court late one night. There was no play on in either theatre, so the building was both deserted and freezing. The central heating had been turned off. Dr Roth was elderly and kept his coat on. Also present at the meeting were Ken Loach and Jo Beddoe, the Royal Court's General Manager.

A key issue had become how many trains to Switzerland the Zionists had been able to prevail upon the Gestapo to arrange as part of their agreement. Apparently there had been three trains, but at this point Jim Allen's play made mention of only one. It was a civilised if fairly fruitless discussion because there was little sense of either Ken or Stephen Roth giving ground. However, with no particular provocation Dr Roth burst into an impassioned rage. He screamed at us, his frail body quivering beneath his mac. The purport of this tirade was what he was not going to do but could do if he wished . . . He detailed this as cutting off the Royal Court's funding, and making our supposed anti-Semitism clear to Joe Papp and the American funding bodies to which the Royal Court was supposedly beholden. He stopped shouting minutes after he had begun, and although the conversation resumed on polite terms his extraordinary outburst lingered in the air.

The meeting closed, and I conducted our guest out of the darkened building. The only route now open was down through the circle, past the stage door, up the backstage staircase and out on to the fire-escape; three steps down, four steps down, turn, five steps up, a landing, then thirteen steps down an icy fire escape all in complete blackness. It was a perilous journey in the dark for an old man uncertain of his steps. We made it safely down the fire escape and were heading across the frozen alley to the safety of sodium-lit Sloane Square when he slipped on a pool of ice. I just caught his body under his arms and prevented a nasty tumble. I put my arm round the old man's skinny ribs as we progressed towards the taxi rank. I could feel his gasps come and go within his ribcage.

His frailty and passion demanded some attention, but back in my office Ken Loach was dismissive and was later to suggest that I had set up this meeting having calculated the likely outcome. We had also naively circulated the text to the critics so they could read the play beforehand. This was Royal Court practice, but Loach was later to see this too as an attempt to undermine him. Rather it seems evidence of how little we had anticipated the trouble that was to come.

On the evening of 20 January 1987 an Extraordinary Council Meeting was held to debate the controversy. At lunchtime Simon Curtis, the Director of the Theatre Upstairs, where *Perdition* was scheduled for performance, had come back in tears from lunch with his father. He came from a Jewish family; producing *Perdition* seemed to his father a spectacular act of betrayal. Meanwhile the relationship between Ken and me had begun to break down. He made it clear that I would not be welcome at a run-through. Years of negotiation with the BBC meant that any discussion with him turned into protracted arbitration. It was agreed that the script would acknowledge that there had been two trains of escaping Jews. It seemed likely, according to Martin Gilbert, that there had been three, but mention of further trains would begin to dilute the polemical stance of the piece.

My Diary reflects the dilemma I was becoming involved in but shows little recognition of the serious issues of free speech with which the play would also become involved:

> ✍ *18 Jan*   Clearly someone on the Council is leaking every phone call
> and discussion to the *Daily Telegraph*. Above all, I feel I'm involved in a
> quarrel between two opposing factions neither of whom I feel
> particularly aligned with. To be caught between the Zionists and the
> Trots is truly to be between a rock and a hard place. The ferocity of the
> lobbying has to be experienced to be believed . . . and meanwhile is the
> play, poor thing, worth the trouble?

> *Royal Court Council minutes, 20 January 1987*
> Extraordinary Council Meeting . . . Jocelyn Herbert was aware that the
> Council's role was not to interfere in artistic decisions but she . . .
> found it incredible that things had gone so far. She also asked whether,
> in fact, the play was of artistic merit. Mr Stafford-Clark said that the

deciding factor was the combination of Jim Allen and Ken Loach . . .
Caryl Churchill said that she had read most of the play and felt there
could be no possibility of seeing the play as anti-Semitic. She felt an
enormous amount of compassion came through. She would hate to think
that the fact that the play was a polemic would go against it. She felt
the Council should respect Jim Allen's reputation and his right to his
position . . . Bill Gaskill felt the play to be partial, polemical and
strongly anti-Zionist. If a play is put on, the theatre is seen to be behind
that play. He felt that the position should be clarified: that the theatre
stands by *Perdition*, or washes its hands of it. He asked Max Stafford-
Clark if he went along with the anti-Zionist stance . . . we must not
evade the issue. The Council has to stand behind Mr Stafford-Clark, and
Mr Stafford-Clark has to stand behind the play. Matthew Evans asked
whether Mr Stafford-Clark and Simon Curtis were one hundred per cent
behind the play. Mr Stafford-Clark confirmed that he was not as anti-
Zionist as Jim Allen, but that he felt as Artistic Director there was a
need to broaden one's own tastes. Simon Curtis said that he could not
reassure Bill Gaskill that he was as anti-Zionist as Jim Allen, but he felt
that passion makes great work . . . Mr Gaskill felt that not to do the play
would be dishonourable to the Royal Court . . . Matthew Evans put
forward the following proposals: that simultaneously the following
happen:

- Check for libel with Anthony Burton [Vice Chairman and a solicitor].
- All Council members read the play.
- An impartial historian's view is sought.
- The previews are postponed.   *Royal Court archive*

The meeting was dreadful because I could see no way forward. As might
have been anticipated, Bill Gaskill spoke with most clarity and passion. He
asked if I was committed to the anti-Zionist stance of the play. If I wasn't I
had no business putting it on. I was silenced. Of course I should have told
Bill I was as committed to anti-Zionism as he had been committed to the
Marxism of Edward Bond when he had presented Edward's plays at the
Royal Court. That is: not very much at all.

I could see no way out. I had no faith in 'an impartial historian'. Matthew was
suggesting Norman Stone, whose views were anything but impartial. I had
got the Royal Court into this mess, and I felt I had to get us out. After the

meeting I sought a private word with Anthony Burton and Matthew Evans. I told them I would withdraw the play. Anthony called the decision 'brave'. Within twelve hours it would be called one or two other things. Dame Mary Warnock said I was in 'a fascinating moral dilemma'. It didn't seem so fascinating to me.

The decision to withdraw the play was more controversial than a resolution to proceed would have been. I have said on several occasions since that I think I got both decisions wrong. I was wrong to programme a play I wasn't able to defend, and I was also wrong to withdraw it under pressure.

✍ *21 Jan*   The meeting with Ken Loach last night and the meeting with the actors this morning, in which I told them that I would withdraw the play, were both agonising. 'Disgusting' and 'craven' are two of the words used about me today.

23 Jan   This has been the worst week of my life. An Artistic Director has no business programming a play which in the end he cannot defend.

3 Feb   I learn that there's to be a Council meeting on Monday. Jo [General Manager] hints that I may not be invited to it. If she hopes to undermine me, she succeeds. I feel so demoralised, it's going to be hard to get on with *Serious Money*. Bill said on the phone on Sunday: 'I'm afraid you don't come out of this well.' He also said: 'I think you should have fought for it.'

7 Feb   *Serious Money* – start rehearsal on Monday. First draft seems a bit breathless. Caryl's bravery and boldness to the fore: she's written it in rhyming couplets. I mean, in verse of all kinds, which sometimes doesn't give it much room to stop and be serious. It's caricature and it's funny. Doesn't show the real feelings of characters like Durkfeld and Morrison, but that's not the point. Jacinta's feelings about her own country could possibly have more weight. The merit of the lunchtime run that we did at the end of the workshop was the sniff of authenticity which the Metal Market or the LIFFE improvisations gave us. We should not blow all that away. So the final image I have currently of the play would be nuggets of serious money linked by frenetic and rhymed activity.

So much else is happening.

Once I had withdrawn *Perdition*, Ken lobbied against the decision and a debate about freedom of speech hit the correspondence pages of the *Guardian*.

✐ *8 Feb*   Break down the monologues, so that the information may be given in scenes. Less plot. More serious moments of the financial world could be seen. Make the murder more mysterious.

THE REHEARSAL PERIOD

As rehearsals were about to start a Council meeting was convened as a post-mortem to the *Perdition* affair

Royal Court Council minutes, 9 February

Extraordinary Council Meeting. Max Stafford-Clark would be present for the first half of the meeting only as he was attending a reception at Downing Street . . . Max Stafford-Clark acknowledged that a mistake had been made. He said that to select a play and then take it off was an enormous mistake, and he must take full responsibility . . . The decision to withdraw the play came twenty minutes before the end of the Council meeting [of 20 Jan.] . . . Matthew Evans reported that he felt that the situation was a complete mess. He felt it was bad for the Royal Court, for Max Stafford-Clark, for the Council, for the staff, for the author. He felt that what was under discussion was the attitude to Max Stafford-Clark . . . He felt that the time had come to confront the issue of whether the Council felt this was a dismissal issue . . . Matthew Evans asked if the Council would accept that any other matter of a similar nature be immediately referred to the Council. This was agreed. Matthew Evans asked if Council accepted that Max Stafford-Clark's contract would finally end in April 1989. This was agreed. It was further agreed that a sub-committee be formed to be responsible for implementing replacement procedures. Robert Fox, Jocelyn Herbert, Derek Granger and Stuart Burge agreed to be members.   *Royal Court archive*

Later there was some confusion over whether I had agreed that my contract would come to an end in April 1989. Some people seemed to think I had: certainly that was Matthew's intention, but I had already left to go to

Downing Street by the time the matter was discussed, and nobody saw fit to relay the discussion to me. In fact it was only when preparing this book that I read the Council minutes for the first time and realised the full sequence of events.

Number 10 Downing Street is an illusion; behind the façade of the Georgian town house is a series of corridors and meeting rooms that stretch on and on. The reception was already well under way by the time I ascended the famous staircase with black and white photographs of every serving Prime Minister from Campbell-Bannerman to the present. At the top of the staircase they had ventured into colour and there was a primitive and fading colour photograph of Jim Callaghan. A flunkey gestured in the direction of the reception, but the butler whose job it was to announce people as they entered the elegant drawing room had long gone. I stood nervously in the doorway: it looked like the sixth-form common room thirty years on; portly men in suits with pukka accents were barking in friendly fashion at a roomful of assorted artists. A woman in a blue suit turned from a nearby group and made her way towards me; it was Mrs Thatcher. 'Max Stafford-Clark from the Royal Court Theatre,' I said with no expectation that it would mean anything to her at all. 'Oh dear what a terrible time you must be having,' she said, 'but it is a *very* difficult part of the world.' We talked for several minutes on the difficulties of Israel and Palestine. 'Now,' she said, 'have you met my minister?'

The same day had been the first read through of *Serious Money*:

✍ *9 Feb*   *Serious Money* seems alive . . . I think I've ironed too much verse out of it. The actors do get to play an awful lot of characters, and it will test their powers of characterisation.

11 Feb   Agonising hours where actors say how good the play is but just that their own particular parts are underdeveloped. The play is an epic account of the financial worlds, and it doesn't go into the psychology of the characters in any detailed manner. Normally, of course, these conversations take place between actors and their agents.

12 Feb   Good day's rehearsal. Only did the first scene. Burt [Caesar] is a bit slow and hardly conjures the immediate image of a patrician Boston banker, but I think he'll be OK. Some of it is quite broad, and once you've found the stroke that makes it work, it comes alive. Our big problem will be getting the play finished enough to rehearse it.

17 Feb   Kind of get stuck on the 'Take-over Song', which still sounds a bit operetterish and should be much more funky. Second half still a bit too much unknown territory.

20 Feb   Cast not happy with Colin's [Sell, the composer] music in general and 'Big Bang Song' in particular. Must urge Colin to try again with it. Otherwise going well. I can't block it very easily. Too many scenes split into general comedy, but 'actions'are working well in giving the text muscle and strength. Some of the writing is extraordinarily wonderful.

Perdition still going. Ken Loach has written a long open letter to the Council in the *Guardian*, and apparently a two-page article in the *New Statesman*. I must write my own account over the weekend.

The article I composed in response appeared in the *Guardian* on 13 March.

WHY I AXED PERDITION

Ken Loach's open letter to the Royal Court Council suggests undeclared Zionist pressure led to the 'banning' of the play *Perdition*. This is not the case. It should be made clear that as Artistic Director the constitution of the Royal Court entrusts me with responsibility for the selection of the theatre's programme. As Artistic Director, I lost confidence in the play's credibility.

Jim Allen's play *Perdition* was first sent to the Royal Court in the summer of 1985. Loach comments that eighteen months is a long time 'to assess the play's worth'. He forgets that for many months the play was withdrawn by the writer, who wished for a larger theatre.

From the beginning it was clear the play would be provocative, but controversy wasn't unknown in Royal Court history. We had deliberately commissioned a report from David Cesarani, a Zionist historian, so as to ensure that the facts contained in the play would undergo the most vigorous analysis.

The report was hostile but Jim Allen, a most straightforward and persuasive advocate, had convincingly rebutted some points while accepting others. He had rewritten and edited the play to half its former length. And, in any case, I believed a playwright was free to loot whatever facts from history suited his thesis. As Jim Allen had written in the margin of the Cesarani report when accused of partiality and lack of balance: 'This is a play, not an essay . . . what do you expect?'

The first time I realised how difficult things could become was in early January when Dr Stephen Roth from the Institute of Jewish Affairs asked to meet me as he had criticisms of the play he wished to present. I met him on Tuesday 13 January with Simon Curtis, the Royal Court Deputy Director. Jim was not available and the meeting began without Ken as he was delayed. For 20 minutes Simon Curtis, Dr Roth and I discussed *Perdition* amicably enough.

As I recall, Roth made three main criticisms: firstly that the work of the Zionist Resistance Organisation wasn't mentioned; secondly that efforts of the Jewish leaders had saved not merely the 1,684 mentioned in the play but a further 18,000 who had been sent to work-camps in Austria; and thirdly that the sheer nightmare and agonising confusion in Budapest in 1944 was not represented in the play. He didn't deny that terrible mistakes had been made.

Dr Roth also indicated the powers he could use to remove the play. He could picket. He could contact 'the Royal Court's friends' in New York. He could influence funding bodies in London. On Ken's arrival exchanges between the two men became alarmingly heated. Loach was provocative and Dr Roth was intemperate. He brandished a sheet detailing, he said, 24 major errors. He declined to reveal them as he wished to discredit the play when it was produced.

The meeting had passed the point where it had any useful purpose. His threats could be dismissed, but he had an authority in his rage that both Simon Curtis and I found impressive. Ken Loach found him absurd, but it seemed important to pick any relevant points from this torrent of condemnation. If in fact 18,000 had been saved, and if there was an active Zionist Resistance movement, then shouldn't that be included in the play too? I argued that the play would be more dramatically viable if the accused Dr Yaron mounted a more vigorous self-defence.

But this was dangerously close to asking for balance, and besides, I couldn't present this as advice on aesthetics if it was really a political point. Ken warned me off: this would be asking for a different play and wasn't the one Jim wished to write. We talked further and agreed on the inclusion of the 18,000 and on some reference to the Zionist Resistance Movement, but it was clear that further pressure would lead to a breakdown of trust between us.

Ken Loach asks what pressure was put on the Court. He writes, 'it is simply not credible that the management changed its mind . . . without overwhelming and undeclared pressure from the censorship lobby.' Certainly the pressure on me was intense, but Loach himself was present at the only occasion when a direct threat was made.

I spoke to Joe Papp [of the Public Theatre] in New York some time over the following week, making it clear that we were presenting a controversial play and that he would probably be contacted about it. He replied that his relationship with me contained no element of control over choice of plays and that if he were to read the play and find it repugnant this would still remain the case.

I understand he was lobbied intensively but in fact we did not speak again until after I had withdrawn the play. It is ironic that throughout its history, the Royal Court has received generous help from a number of Jewish trusts and prominent Jewish families. In the course of this affair, none of them put any pressure on me. As for any other 'undeclared pressure', there was none. Much of the pressure put on the play was unacceptable, but because some condemnations could themselves be dismissed as distortions, it didn't mean that all criticism could be dismissed.

In the middle of the same week, Martin Gilbert, the historian, who had claimed the play was 'a travesty', rang saying he would like to meet. Against the wishes of Allen and Loach I agreed. It seemed irresponsible not to listen. It was at this meeting, on Saturday 17 January, that the claim to a list of '64 errors' was made.

Many of these points were Gilbert's own opinion about what the principal character might have said. He even suggested some alternative lines. He argued that for some months the Jewish Councils must have believed they were negotiating with Eichmann to save one million Jews from the camps. His objective was to prove the Jewish Councils had done as much as possible to preserve lives.

Jim Allen's thesis was the opposite. There was no meeting point. But again, the horrific situation facing Jewish leaders became clearer to me. I grouped Gilbert's major points together and relayed them to Ken and Jim later that day. Jim didn't dispute the facts but didn't wish to expand the play to encompass them. It was very late in the day.

On Sunday 18 January some Council members were invited to Sonia Melchett's home to hear Dr Gilbert rehearse his criticisms. Having spent the previous morning with him, I did not go. However, Simon Curtis described to me that notwithstanding the emotive representations of a heated Lord Weidenfeld, who asserted that the play was anti-Semitic and the measured observations of Rabbi Hugo Gryn, the Council members remained firm in their resolve to support the theatre's artistic policy.

Over the same weekend I had begun to re-read the books myself and to read others. I became more and more uneasy as I realised the extent to which Jim Allen had selected the evidence for his case and for the first time it didn't seem so clear that a writer making accusations of this gravity led to the artistic licence a playwright could normally depend on.

It became harder and harder to have much enthusiasm about fighting on the side of a piece which was so selective and so certain about such a confused and uncertain period of history. For the first time I saw the possibility that *Perdition* was a dishonest piece of writing; both because it was so half-hearted in including any mitigating factors, and because its passionate conviction led it to a picture of these horrifying events that seemed less and less authentic.

On Thursday 20 January there was a four-hour Council meeting at which the whole issue was discussed. At no time did a single Council member suggest either that the play should be withdrawn or that it was anti-Semitic. At the same time, I was quite unable to give the passionate defence of the play that the occasion demanded.

The Council decided on a two-day postponement of previews so that the question of libel could be assessed, the historical accuracy reviewed by a neutral historian and every Council member given an opportunity to read the play. The Council were keen to meet Jim Allen to hear his point of view . . . and had the proposed scrutiny by a neutral historian taken place a meeting with Allen would have followed.

However I didn't believe the facts contained in the play were any longer the issue. I remained convinced that Jim Allen had sources for any material he had used. But many facts were clearly in dispute, and it was the facts omitted that were my principal concern.

I was in what Mary Warnock was later to describe as 'a fascinatingly complex moral dilemma'. To withdraw the play would be damaging not just to Jim Allen and Ken Loach but also to the fine and committed acting company . . . also accusations of censorship would follow . . . but to defend a play which I now thought both distorted and distressingly incomplete was impossible. I thought *Perdition* fell within a spectrum of work whose views I could support. I now found it did not.

On returning to the Court, I sought out Matthew Evans (Chairman) and Anthony Burton (Vice Chairman) and told them I thought I should withdraw the play. They supported this decision fully. As Ken Loach knows, Burton offered to meet the company with me, but I thought it better to face them with this awful decision on my own . . .

Within 24 hours this action had been called both 'craven' and 'courageous'. Without doubt, it was the hardest decision I have ever had to take. The Royal Court's reputation as a champion of new writing is an enviable one. In 99 cases out of 100 of course an Artistic Director must protect the work he has chosen. In the hundredth he must admit he has made a mistake.   *Guardian 13 March 1987*

The debate raged on in the letters pages of the *Guardian*. On 18 March Jim Allen responded:

JIM ALLEN: Sir – with straight-faced solemnity, Max Stafford-Clark assures us (*Arts Guardian*, 13 March) that there was no pressure put upon him to take off my play, *Perdition*.

We are asked to believe that five days before the play was to have opened and eighteen months after he first read *Perdition*, he spent the weekend 're-reading the books'. Then, like Paul on the road to Damascus, came the revelation: 'For the first time I saw the possibility that *Perdition* was a dishonest piece of work.'

That is a serious allegation to make against a writer, and I read on hoping to find some evidence that would prove my 'dishonesty', but no proofs were offered. Not one single quotation from the play to back up his allegations. Obviously his courtship with the Zionists has not been entirely unprofitable . . .   *Guardian Letters, 18 March 1987*

I couldn't let this particular allegation go unchallenged:

> Sir – Jim Allen complains (Letters, 18 March) that I give not one single example of my doubts about *Perdition*. In fact these paragraphs were cut by the *Guardian* from my article:

> ' . . . There are two accounts of a party given by the leaders of the Skalat Ghetto for the Gestapo on the eve of the trains arriving to take them to Auschwitz. Obviously the party was a reassuring signal to the Jews waiting for the cattle trucks. One account shows this as a deliberately organised and perfidious betrayal . . . while another portrays families shot until a measure of complicity was achieved.'

> 'Jim Allen used the story to discredit Zionist leaders. There was expert evidence to support both views. But which version did I believe? The latter view seemed more likely. It no longer seemed so smart to rely on experts.'   *Guardian Letters 21 March 1987*

Against this backdrop of recrimination and accusation over the *Perdition* affair, rehearsals for *Serious Money* were in full swing. Linda Bassett (who coincidentally had been offered a part in *Perdition* but had turned it down and was in *Serious Money*) commented some years later: 'He never brought any of it in to the rehearsal room. He always left his troubles at the door.' Which is comforting to know. There was, however, already enough to deal with in the rehearsal room.

📝 *21 Feb*   Did LIFFE scene with Activists. They're a bit raw but on the whole it went well. I'm not sure how long a trading scene should be. At the moment the audience doesn't know what the fuck is happening. Important not to let it all become high comedy.

4 March   Near crisis with the music today. Actors losing confidence in Colin's music and starting to panic.

5 March   Should try and run first half by the end of the week.

7 March   First run-through of first act. Very far from definitive; in fact, a mess. Some of the acting was poor. The music and the songs by Colin Sell still meet with universal disapproval from the company, and will probably have to be dropped. In addition, the structure of the first half is most peculiar. We begin with Burt. Then a monologue. Then a scene where the actors are being horses. Then a scene from Shadwell [which Caryl had incorporated from Thomas Shadwell's late Restoration play *The Stockjobbers*, 1692]. Then a song. And it's not until the scene in the Greenhouse bar [a bar in the City where we had conducted much of our research] that you actually meet the characters from the play. After a reflective weekend Caryl came in with a completely restructured first act. She moved the extract from *The Stockjobbers* to the start, where it became a kind of prologue. Most of the music was cut – it seemed to hold up the action – and we were left with Ian Dury's magnificent and obscene anthemic numbers to end each half.

Rehearsals continued against a background of recrimination as Matthew kept on rallying support for a change of Artistic Director.

Letter from Matthew Evans to Jocelyn Herbert, 19 March
. . . Would you consider not resigning from the Council? Many members of the Council are upset that you are leaving, because of the contribution you make . . . When Howard Newby asked me to do the job, I said I'd do it for three years which is up in September this year. I feel I ought to stay on until we get a new Artistic Director, as I do anticipate – even at this stage – some reluctance on Max's part to let go of the reins. I am totally convinced that he must, and the more people I have on the Council who have a background knowledge and support this view unequivocally, the happier I would feel . . .   *Royal Court archive*

Ken Loach is on record as saying that *Perdition* was the most unpleasant incident in his career. That's one sentiment of his that I can support whole-heartedly. In the years afterwards I relived the debate many times in my head, justifying both sides of the argument. It caused a damaging and long-lasting rift with Bill Gaskill, who resigned from the Council because I had withdrawn the play. He had been an inspiration and a friend, and I felt the loss keenly.

Serious Money went on to be a triumph.

✍ *21 March*   Obviously a highly successful First Preview. In fact the first First Preview I can ever remember which was full and which was a real occasion. The first half was superbly played – real ensemble playing – and what a wonderful writer she is.

Serious Money transferred and played in the West End for a year; it also had a successful run at Joseph Papp's Public Theatre in New York. It transferred to Broadway, but by this time there had been a Wall Street collapse and finance was no longer a matter for satire: nor did the triumphant obscenity of Ian Dury's lyrics slip down very easily. The chorus at the end of each verse went:

> 'Out! Buy buy buy! Leave it!
> No! Yes! Cunt!
> 4! 5! Sell!
> Quick! Prick! Yes! No! Cunt!'

The accents were difficult for a Broadway audience to fathom too. In the interval of an early preview I heard one lady say to her friend, 'Margaret, I didn't understand a word, not one word of that entire half. (*Pause.*) And the one word I did understand I couldn't possibly repeat to you.'

Back in London I had a conversation with Matthew Evans.

✍ *23 April*. At some point in the evening, [Matthew] made it clear that he did not expect me to re-apply for the job in two years' time. I said I had never given any such undertaking. He seemed a bit caught, and turned the conversation to emphasise how much some members of the Council wanted me out. He said some would have expected my resignation after the *Perdition* affair.

Matthew seemed to think I had been present at the meeting when the committee had been formed to find my successor. But I had a perfect alibi . . . I had been talking to Mrs Thatcher.

Case Study

OUR COUNTRY'S GOOD
Timberlake Wertenbaker

Workshop: from 11 April 1988

Rehearsal: from 6 June 1988

First performance: 6 September 1988

Cast: Jude Akuwudike, Linda Bassett, Jim Broadbent, Ron Cook, Nick Dunning, Alphonsia Emmanuel, David Haig, Mark Lambert, Lesley Sharp, Mossie Smith

Published: Our Country's Good (Methuen, 1991)

Running the Royal Court is the most demanding and the most exhilarating job I can imagine. So much so that it's hard to find the time to think. The imperative is to keep the theatre open, to make the books balance, to secure the funding, to commission the writers, to find the work. When I began directing in Edinburgh, the chairman of the Traverse had been a charismatic property developer called Tom Mitchell. He had also been the manager of the Great Britain Rugby League team touring Australia, which impressed me no end. He gave me a lift one night and expansively offered me cash if I wanted backing to produce a show. I had no particular play in mind at that moment. 'Never mind, son,' he said. 'It takes thirty-five seconds to have a good idea.' His remark has stayed with me. It's just finding the thirty-five seconds.

So it's no coincidence that the idea for *Our Country's Good* came when I was, comparatively, at leisure. I was directing *Serious Money* on Broadway. The play had already been triumphant at the Royal Court and off-Broadway at Joseph Papp's Public Theatre, but the mood had changed. So had the cast. Americans had replaced the English cast, and the sense of an ensemble that we had so laboriously endeavoured to create inevitably had been lost. The cast was led by Alec Baldwin and Kate Nelligan. They were all on different salaries but had also committed to varying lengths of contract; the more prestigious the star, the shorter the time they would commit. They compared notes furtively in the coffee breaks.

The play was previewed endlessly because Joe Papp had a hunch that the moment it opened it would close. The time I was allotted to give notes was restricted to an hour and a half call per day, otherwise stringent overtime regulations would be activated. Under no circumstances was I permitted to rehearse the music. This would have involved calls for electricians, musicians and stage management. However, as a great concession the local union lodge permitted us to rehearse with one working light on a stand in the middle of the stage and a battery-operated tape-recorder. Under these stygian circumstances I wasn't making much progress. I was staying at the Algonquin Hotel in mid-town, which was a treat, but I had run out of reading material. It was thus that I was browsing through the fiction section in the huge Barnes and Noble store on Fifth Avenue.

There I picked up *The Playmaker* by Thomas Keneally. I had always known somewhere in the back of my mind that there had been a convict production of *The Recruiting Officer* in the early days of the Australian penal colony. Farquhar's play was also the first European play performed in the American colonies. Little wonder, perhaps, as it had been the most performed play of the eighteenth century. This couldn't have been much consolation to poor George Farquhar, who died in poverty in an attic in St Martin's Lane before reaching thirty. But I turned the pages of Keneally's book with increasing interest. Keneally is a cracking storyteller, and back in the Algonquin I had to prevent myself from reading the novel too fast . . . Halfway through the story the good idea began to dawn. Back I went to Barnes and Noble and found a copy of *The Recruiting Officer* in a collection of Restoration plays.

It was a play I had read once. Bill Gaskill had directed a definitive production twenty years before in the early days of the National Theatre, so I had never read it with the serious intent of undertaking a production. All classics are a message from the past, and most have to be decoded, but I was stunned by the directness of Farquhar's play. It is the straightforward story of a hero of Blenheim who returns to Shrewsbury on a recruiting mission and, against expectation, marries the daughter of a local landowner and justice of the peace. It had a freshness and exhilaration that seemed to blow off the Welsh mountains, and a directness about sex and its consequences that is absent from earlier Restoration plays where the superobjective of the hero is invariably to get laid and to obtain a fortune without working for it. Captain Plume is a working officer and although he too is a fairly feckless fellow out for a good time, he has redeeming qualities; certainly Justice Balance, his prospective father-in-law, sees them. Turning back to the Dramatis Personae, I wrestled with the casting. What was the minimum number of actors that *The Recruiting Officer* demanded? Could it be done with a company of eleven? Yes, possibly, if Bullock could be doubled with Brazen. Late Restoration theatre was also going through an economic crisis and cast sizes had correspondingly shrunk.

Why not commission an adaptation of Keneally's novel and produce it in tandem with *The Recruiting Officer*, involving the same company of actors? At least we would be actively pursuing the elusive idea of an ensemble. With fresh purpose I finished reading *The Playmaker*. Thomas Keneally's novel imagines the convict production of 1789. It is explicit about the hierarchy in the Sydney convict settlement and clear how the women could be upwardly mobile by becoming the concubines of the officers. It details the relationship between the liberal Governor Phillip and the aboriginal Arabanoo. It dwells on the sweaty agonies of the apprentice hangman, Ketch Freeman, and on the burgeoning love affair between Ralph Clark, the nervous young officer charged with directing the production, and Mary Brenham, the traumatised young convict who plays Silvia. The book made use of contemporary accounts of the convict colony such as Watkin Tench's encounters with aboriginals and with kangaroos. It also draws widely on the lesser known journals of Ralph Clark published by the Library of Australian History. These extraordinary diaries cover Ralph Clark's four-year posting to Australia and Norfolk Island. He emerges as a fearful, dream-haunted subaltern anxious about money and promotion and worried about his young wife's ability to manage household finances in his long absence.

I had had my thirty-five seconds. And it was a good idea. Of all the plays I have been involved with, *Our Country's Good* has been the most widely performed. Its presence on the A-level drama syllabus ensures regular revivals. My daughter, Kitty, is studying it at school now. She has to address all kinds of questions about whether it was influenced by Stanislavsky or by Brecht, which concerned us not one whit when we were working on the play. I'm sure part of the reason it's so widely embraced by drama teachers is because the final scene provides such a triumphant proclamation of the theatre's emotional power. I often feel that the demands of the school timetable don't do the play much service. Why can't it be studied as a joint project between the history and the drama departments? The first task of anyone directing the play is to make history come alive; the convicts were very much a product of the particular cruelties and yet finally the humanity of eighteenth-century England and the Age of Reason. I recall our efforts to engage with the eighteenth century and how seminal the reading of Robert Hughes's *The Fatal Shore* was to the whole enterprise. His great book begins, as does the play, with the brutality of the beatings. Robert Hughes quotes from a convict's account of life in the penal colony:

> There was two floggers, Richard Rice and John Johnson, the Hangman from Sydney. Rice was a left-handed man and Johnson was right-handed, so they stood at each side, and I never saw two threshers in a barn move their strokes more handier than those two man-killers did . . . I was to leeward of the floggers . . . I was two perches from them. The flesh and skin blew in my face as it shook off the cats . . . During the time [Fitzgerald] was getting his punishment he never gave so much as a word – only one, and that was saying, 'Don't strike me on the neck, flog me fair.'   (*The Fatal Shore, Harvill Press, 1996, pp. 88–9*)

From a flogging to a first night: it seemed a journey full of promise.

It astonishes me now how quickly and with what momentum the project was put together. Back in England, I approached Timberlake Wertenbaker in January 1988 to work on a dramatisation; we did a two-week workshop with eight actors from 11 April and went into rehearsal on 6 June. I had committed the Royal Court to a ten-week season of both plays before Timberlake had finished her first draft. There are occasions when such reckless and irresponsible confidence fails to pay off. There were to be moments when this seemed it could be one of them.

THE WORKSHOP

The purpose of any workshop is to stimulate the writer: a by-product is that it invariably begins to stimulate and enthuse the actors too. There were exercises that aimed to give Timberlake specific information. For one, Mark Lambert had the grisly task of reading and reporting back to us on Albert

Pierrepoint's book. He was Britain's last hangman and apparently took great pride in the expeditious and efficient manner in which he dispatched his victims. It was a matter of assessing the weight of the client and matching that to the length of the drop. Timberlake eventually used these details in the scene where Ketch Freeman visits Liz Morden in her cell. For another, Nick Dunning, who was to play Robert Sideway, the London pickpocket who is a theatre buff, was dispatched to the far end of London Bridge. He was armed with a map of eighteenth-century London. He was asked to recount the story of a journey only 'seeing' the buildings and the streets that would have been there in 1789.

Reading is a key part of any history play; we turned to Mayhew's accounts of London life in order to catch the characters' own voices. Mayhew was a pioneer of the 'verbatim' method, and although his was not exactly the right period it helped bring a semi-criminal underworld alive. Each of the actors presented a Mayhew character to be interviewed by the rest of the group.

✍ *22 April*   This arvo Mark Lambert was turned into character as James Mahon, a lock-picking burglar who had been transported to Australia, done his time, got his ticket-of-leave and had returned. The rest of the actors interrogated him as his character. He was about to start thieving again but was worried that technology had moved on and a new type of lock introduced in his absence. Mark explained in detail how to break through a fanlight and how he had been recruited as a small lad to do just that. Alphonsia was Nancy Jenks, a child prostitute already hooked on gin. After a bit I got all the actors to do it jump-cutting so sometimes it was two voices, sometimes all eight at once and sometimes just a solitary voice. As always it's the detail that's interesting.

The overlapping gave a great drive and energy to the session and prevented the actors either from being too self-conscious or from planning too carefully. It meant they began to work more from instinct. I always use playing cards in rehearsal to determine the specific element of a scene; and I used this to address the scene which Timberlake called 'The Authorities Discuss the Merits of Theatre'. This takes place in the officers' mess, where in most regiments the colonel is simply called Colonel and junior officers are addressed by their Christian names. It gives the opportunity for hierarchy to be semi-suspended and for a relatively informal discussion to take place. Debate was, Timberlake reminded us, a great eighteenth-century pastime.

The particular subject was the proposal for a play in which the convicts would perform. Governor General Phillip is in favour of rehabilitating the convicts and looks on the production as an interesting liberal experiment. The Senior Marine officer, Major Ross, is vehemently opposed to the scheme. His rage prevents him from marshalling a coherent argument. It's always easy in a liberal, left-wing play to ridicule the right-wing argument. Timberlake wished to prevent this and gave another character, Watkin Tench, sensible and coherent reasons why the play should not go ahead. The whole company were given playing cards at random. A red card indicated you were a supporter of the play and a black card indicated opposition. The higher the card the greater the strength of feeling. The actors had to learn to marshal arguments to which they may well have been opposed. I don't think we ever came up with arguments that were particularly inspired by the Age of Reason or any that impressed Timberlake, but it was of great value in focusing the actors' energy and imagination.

One day in the workshop we met a woman who had done time in Holloway prison:

✍ *27 April*   'I dreaded the Muppet House [the psychiatric wing] . . . It's full of women shouting and screaming all the time . . . That gets to you. So does the person you're banged up with. I was with a woman who dreamed she was going on a picnic and fucking her solicitor. She did my head in.' She talked of her time in an earlier prison. 'This screw she hated me . . . One afternoon she confiscated my guitar . . . She didn't fucking need to do that . . . She was just trying to get one over on me.' It's clear how incarceration turns minor grievances into monstrous injustices. 'Some lifers are brutal . . . That's how they cope, but others are broken from within . . . You can become obsessed with gardening. Or you can really get into scrubbing and cleaning . . . In some ways people become comfortable in prison . . . Men outside appear like a threat, and even women who aren't gay become prison-bent.'

🔊 TIMBERLAKE WERTENBAKER: Max asked me to read *The Playmaker*. And I read it rather quickly, and then met with him, and that was the beginning, and then he suggested the workshop in April. I felt that what I wanted to write about was this humanising aspect of the theatre. That was very personal too, because of John being an actor [Timberlake Wertenbaker's partner, John Price, had died on 23 October 1987]. I arrived, and there were Nick Dunning, Linda Bassett – they were all there. We must have started discussing the project, and read bits of the book . . . Max said, 'The actors will not be telling you what to write. No one will tell you what to write. No one will interfere with the script [but] the actors will do a lot of research for you.' He put no pressure on getting a play at the end because I didn't think I could do a play. I'd pulled out of the workshop at some point before we had started. I didn't think I could do it. I'd panicked, and I was in quite a state, and that's when he said, 'Just come and try it. Just spend two weeks.'

Max came to me each evening, and we would meet very often after the rehearsals of each play, and say 'What interests you?' It was really like that. And I would say anything that came into my mind, for example, brutalisation; or what was the style of acting in those days. He would then have specific things he was interested in . . . It was all thrown into the pot. I would tell him what interested me. He would try to find a way of representing that theatrically. So that when I said, 'How do I understand brutalisation?', he used status games about how you avoided being punished. I remember that one very clearly because I used that later on.

✍ *27 April*   Day 3. Arguing for and against the play. You fancy somebody in rehearsal. Political cartoons of the eighteenth century. Eighteenth-century acting – show the different elements. How do you transmit emotion over a distance in a big theatre? Scowl, gasp, etc. Body language – swearing – invention in swearing. Stage the flogging scene. We turn some Mayhew into dialogue.

28 April   Not a very good day. Couldn't get anything off the ground. The improvisations didn't have much weight behind them. We haven't touched the rage or the brutality of these people.

29 April   Last day of workshop.

◀)) TIMBERLAKE WERTENBAKER: On the final day [the actors] all had a thing of saying what bits we had improvised that they had really liked.

That was Max's idea – writers not being very keen on that one. I stood there rigidly, but in fact they were so open and they suggested all of these things. I can't tell you what I took and didn't take because I was sort of blanking it out . . . because they were so involved in the material themselves, they were saying, 'This is what I experienced in the work-shop.' That's the difference – the difference between an actor who has experienced the workshop with all the imagination of an actor, and then says, 'This is what moved me. This is what I remember', and an actor slightly coming out of their experience and saying, 'I think you should write about this' . . . It's not the drafting, because I wrote twenty drafts of the play, but the feeding process. It's riches, these imaginative riches, and then you begin to scan it and say, 'I can use this. I can't use this. This is fine but it doesn't say anything to me because of who I am.'

What the workshop does is throw infinite amounts at you which, instead of controlling the material from the beginning, comes at you like all kinds of surprises. It's a little bit like you're travelling, and you're not deciding where you're going, so it is an adventure in which everybody participates. So it is very enriching when it works. When it doesn't, it's absolute hell.

In the two weeks of the workshop we had moved from collective ignorance to mass enthusiasm for the project. We had digested a huge amount of information, and the actors had begun to focus on an assortment of char-acters drawn from Keneally's novel. The next week I went straight into rehearsal for *Bloody Poetry* by Howard Brenton with Nigel Terry as Byron and Mark Rylance as Shelley . . . and Timberlake got on with the script.

THE REHEARSAL PERIOD

When we started rehearsal in June for *The Recruiting Officer* the copy of Ralph Clark's journal published by the Library of Australian History had arrived from Sydney. It's a day-by-day account of the five years spent by Lieutenant Ralph Clark, Royal Marines, in Australia and was written to show to his young wife, Betsey Alicia, on his return from abroad. From other sources we know that he had a relationship with a young convict woman, Mary Brenham, who bore him a daughter. Of course the diary makes no mention of this. Or of the fact that, with what seems to us extraordinary insensitivity, the child was named Betsey Alicia.

Through June and July the initial scene of *Our Country's Good* began to arrive; and we began our dual rehearsal period with an early appraisal of Timberlake's first draft before turning to *The Recruiting Officer*.

> ✍ *6 June   Our Country's Good*: Timberlake wants more precise history of characters. Where she needs help is on the details of characters. Harry Brewer: The obsession of an older man for a younger woman. Liz Morden: Gin. Prostitute. Steal. Rough, rough. How you lose self-value as a prostitute. Dabby Bryant's history: Charting her life. She escapes from Sydney Cove the night after the play has been put on. Duckling: Harry Brewer's girl. More passive. I realise we should cast it very young. She should be a child. Beyond anger. An abused child. Mary Brenham: Village life. Could be middle-classish background? She's been a servant in a middle-class household, so she has acquired some manners. The real Mary Brenham was transported for stealing a tablecloth from her employer. Ralph Clark: Shy. Not very authoritative. Desperately wants to get promoted. John Wisehammer: Eighteenth-century Jewish background. Wrongly accused of stealing snuff. Sideway: Sophisticated character. Skilled pickpocket. Thinks of himself as an artist. What is the hierarchy of the criminal world? Black Caesar: Research should be about Madagascar. Attitudes towards black people in eighteenth century? Ketch: Hanging. Pierrepoint's book. Exiled within the community. The women hate him because he's a working-class traitor. He had little alternative because he would have been hanged himself if he had not agreed to become the hangman.

> *17 June*   We have a lot of scenes, but not a through line. Is Ralph and Mary romance vibrant enough to bear the whole story line? Or is it the different love stories?

After two weeks we changed horses and left *Our Country's Good* as we started rehearsing *The Recruiting Officer*. It was at this point that we had the opportunity for our own experience of prison drama. It was a sobering event and proved beyond question the validity of Timberlake's belief in the redemptive power of theatre.

9 July   During the course of last week all of the cast have been to Her
Majesty's Prison, Wormwood Scrubs, to see a performance by the
prisoners of Howard Barker's *Love of a Good Man*. I went tonight for the
final performance. The prisoner/actors had been supplemented by two
professional actresses, and by one professional actor, who had been
drafted in to replace a member of cast who was transferred to Wakefield
high-security nick. It was an instructive occasion. We waited outside the
prison gates in a kind of airlock. We were counted again and our passes
examined. We were a strange collection. Howard's play had been
deemed unsuitable for consumption by fellow-prisoners, so the
audience was stuffed with theatrical potentates invited by ILEA. Half the
audience seemed to be casting directors. There was Mary Selway, hello
Patsy Pollock. I learned afterwards that the professional actors were
rather overawed by this unanticipated event. From being a rather
peculiar fringe gig, this job had become a major showcase opportunity.
I'd never been in a prison before. Evelyn Waugh once said nobody who
had been to an English public school would ever feel out of place in a
prison. How right: through the second airlock and it was immediately
familiar territory. It was like playing an away match at one of the rather
rugged schools, like Sedburgh, where they all wear shorts the whole
time. It smelt of disinfectant and bottled male misery. The performance
took place in the classroom block next to the kennels, where the prison
dogs were kept. So the play was accompanied by howling dogs. Very
Howard Barker.

The production was clear and simple, with a minimum of props and
lights. I spent part of the time wondering which the prisoners were and
what they had done. All of them were Lifers from the Scrubs' D-Wing.
The prisoners weren't exactly hard to spot. Two of them were very
striking indeed; tall, thin and incredibly pale, they looked like great
skinny plants forced to shoot up to find light. They performed with
varying degrees of skill but with intense focus and commitment. Clearly
the performance was of great importance to them. Its sexuality was
tangible. The play didn't have the frequent references to dripping
genitalia that characterise most of Howard's work, but it wasn't lacking
in robust sexual expression either: 'I'd like one of her muff hairs to put
in my tobacco tin' was one gem, or 'I'd crawl across half a mile of
broken glass just to sip her dirty bathwater.' There was no kissing in the

play, but there was one tantalisingly close moment. 'I'd like to kiss your white arse,' murmured the gangling, pale prisoner as he clasped his hands on the neatly suited buttocks of the extremely attractive actress (Eve White). As his mouth hovered close to hers the charge was tangible. It was difficult to watch.

The actors' pride in their work and their pleasure in the achievement was thrilling. Above all, the evening was heady confirmation of how sexy plays are. Keneally spotted that and, of course, he's absolutely right. In an atmosphere of repression and constraint where sex is forbidden, the play becomes a conduit for sexuality. In *The Recruiting Officer* most of the characters are horny most of the time. Given that it remained one of the few expressions of independence for the prisoners too, the rehearsals in Australia must have been crackling with sexual energy.

The actors' exit from the classroom where the performance took place was into a corridor patrolled by two porky screws, who watched the performance with intense disinterest. One of them left his radio on, and the occasional crackle from it mingled with the howling dogs to provide atmospheric background noise. There were three more warders behind me at the back of the room. One of them, the youngest, clapped at the end.

After the performance there was an opportunity to meet the actors for about ten minutes before they were led back to D-Wing. They were eager to talk. There was no shyness or hanging back. Joe, clearly the star of the evening, had killed his best friend when on an LSD trip. I asked him if he wanted to be an actor when he go out. He said he did. I was about to introduce him to Patsy Pollock when I thought to ask when he got out. 'Ten to fifteen years,' he said. There didn't seem such a hurry for him to meet Patsy after all. Colin had been a contract killer. The price had been £300. I thought I could afford one or two if that was the going rate. The part of the effete Edward had been played by a chunky, black cockney who had been a bodybuilder before he came in. He had killed a bloke who had been harassing his sister. Onstage, he seemed charming, witty and rather camp. Offstage, I realised this had been character work of a high order. He was still charming, but definitely not the kind of bloke whose drink you would want to spill in the pub. The men said things like 'Rehearsing is the only time you're not in prison.' They had clearly been obsessed with rehearsing, and wholehearted approval from professionals gave them huge pleasure. They could rehearse for an hour and a half two or three times a week. But rehearsals were often cancelled as screws declined to volunteer for the extra duty, or there simply wasn't sufficient prison staff.

I asked when they were going to do another play. Joe didn't know; he said he could be transferred at any time. He expected to go to Wakefield, and there were no drama facilities there. It seemed heartbreaking to awaken this talent and then deny him the possibility of using it. Up close they had a real prison pallor; that's how convicts must have looked when they landed at Sydney Cove after the eight months in the hold. They were very emotional. It was, after all, their final performance, and they had been rehearsing since just before Christmas. Joe made a very moving speech thanking the director, Alan McCormack. As they were led away we applauded again; their commitment seemed courageous in this context.

Afterwards we met the professional actors and the director in the prison officers' bar just outside the gates. This was a shock too. It was Saturday night, and a country-and-western band was playing. The lead singer was dressed as a scantily clad cowgirl. Somehow the sound of this jollity drifting back to the men, now locked in their cells, was disturbing. The actors were keen to tell us everything: 'They approach everything like the SAS. It's their one chance to prove themselves. They never forget a line; and if you lose your lines they prompt you.' Alan McCormack said, 'It's the screws that make the prison terrible; they don't think the prisoners should get applause. They're there to be punished. If the prisoners enjoy themselves that's not on.' Exactly the same arguments have been used in the officers' mess in *Our Country's Good*. He said the sense of achieving something provided tremendous therapy for the cons: 'It is a total liberation for them.' One problem of directing them was getting to play anger: 'The last time they lost their temper they probably killed somebody.' Eve White told me she and her fellow-actress had been treated with extraordinary care and consideration by the prisoners, as if they were china dolls. They had all received first-night presents that the prisoners had made themselves.

An hour or so later I left to go home. As I walked to the car I could hear the prisoners shouting from cell to cell through the warm night. I stopped and listened. Theatre is a savage god, which, year by year, takes more from you than it ever gives back, but it can be potent and thrilling. And it rewards you when you least expect it.

The whole background to *The Recruiting Officer* and *Our Country's Good* was one of financial despair. Through the eighties, the Royal Court's subsidy had been continually cut back. By the end of the decade the Royal Court was able to produce about half the work we had been able to do fifteen years earlier. The year after *Our Country's Good* was produced I dramatised our distress by closing the Theatre Upstairs for forty weeks.

✍ *10 July* The agony of survival freezes the soul. So determined do we become simply to endure that we forget what it is we really wish to say. At the moment there's enough going on in our greedy, child-abusing, football-hooliganing society to provoke comment, reaction and discussion, but I'm fucked if I know where the big plays are coming from. We live in an epic age, but we're producing domestic plays.

On 3 July *The Recruiting Officer* was previewing and I was able to read Timberlake's rehearsal draft. My Diary records anxieties about the importance of Ralph's role and the difficulty of doubling parts. In rehearsals for *The Recruiting Officer* Ron Cook had been reluctant to double the roles of Bullock and Brazen. This debate was to be captured in Act 2, Scene 7, 'The Meaning of Plays'.

✍ *12 Aug* First day yesterday. Read through very confident. Overwritten, but funny and moving. Actors pleased. Some of the characters — Ralph, Harry, Mary, Wisehammer — still underdeveloped, but Timberlake's work is impressive: witty, humorous, moving. Second day: Morning OK, but afternoon quite ghastly. Got stuck with the dream sequences, which she is very keen on. I must stop resisting them quite so much. We worked or read each scene and then discussed it. The trouble is that we cannot do much without Timberlake being there, and we cannot really rehearse until some rewriting is undertaken. I feel so tired. Two plays back to back is a killer. Scene 1: Some doubt in the actors' minds. Will it sustain, will the image sustain the scene which is otherwise dramatically inert? The scene is called 'Identity' — they are clinging on to their sense of themselves. Couldn't we start with a flogging, and then they debate whether there should be a hanging? [The first scene is rather different in style to the rest of the play and covers the eight-month voyage. It is a poetic meditation on hunger, guilt and sex.]

Philip Howard, the assistant director, also kept a journal. It was his first involvement with a production of this kind and he records the vigorous but fractious nature of early rehearsals with ill-concealed alarm:

PHILIP HOWARD: *Tuesday 2 Aug*   Max asks Timberlake to justify Scene 10 ('Ralph Dreams of His Beloved Wife') – he's made no secret of disliking it!

After tea: Max thinks we've done enough going through the play; time to do some rehearsing, so he picks on what is rapidly becoming the old chestnut of Act 1, Scene 10. Max's motive appears to be to show that it's unstageable – but how can you put on a scene without wanting to do it? Alicia is to be alarming, maternal and sexy. Max corners Timberlake into giving the scene *one* main function. Answer is to show Ralph as a disturbed young man. We rehearse the scene. Max wonders whether the function couldn't be carried out more dramatically by a monologue. David (Haig) reads out one of Clark's monologues from latter's *Journals*. Timberlake says that when she hears a monologue from a diary she tunes out. Max says the same thing about dreams on stage. This isn't going well – everyone is talking and giving opinions (especially Nick Dunning). Everyone knows that Max isn't happy – perhaps it would be better if he were more authoritative and just cut it now. Trouble is, he feels so much pressure with this project anway, he doesn't want to do anything so cavalier.

This is a kindly rationalisation on Philip's part. However, he was inclined to mistake healthy scepticism for dislike, or a degree of wary silence on the part of the actors for unanimous approval. In fact, our efforts to stage the dream scene had almost persuaded me of its possibilities. Nor should a director be too authoritarian, particularly in the early days of rehearsal. If you proceed by argument and debate it's important to know which arguments to lose as well as which ones to win. When we had worked through the play and arrived at the dream scene some weeks later, its purpose seemed accomplished elsewhere and it was quietly dropped without much further discussion.

Philip Howard's journal records an early debate on 'The Authorities Discuss the Merits of the Theatre'.

> PHILIP HOWARD: Mark (Lambert) feels that Major Ross's personal status is too low. He and Captain Campbell (Jim Broadbent) are too jokey. But his status among other officers was a paradox: a major and yet a laughing-stock because he was so extremist. Max says Ross *is* written as a comic role in this scene but that doesn't mean he can't take tragic weight elsewhere. Mark thinks the scene is too long and so does David (Haig). Max won't let them cut it till we've been through it again.

Part of the actors' resistance to the scene was their lack of excitement at what seemed a dry, intellectual discussion. Timberlake pointed out that intellectual debate would have been a major excitement to a group of eighteenth-century gentlemen. Timberlake, who would have been at home in Madame de Staël's salon, has a pellucid intelligence which never let us down. Part of the difficulty of the scene was that Timberlake was trying to write three characters of equal intellectual stature: Watkin Trench, the conservative; Davy Collins, the cynic; and Governor Phillip, the radical humanitarian. I recalled Wally Shawn saying that it was impossible for a writer to create a character more intelligent than himself. And very nearly impossible to write a character as intelligent who held views to which the writer was antagonistic. Through the five weeks' rehearsal we returned to 'Authorities Discuss . . .' again and again; cutting and honing it. It set the intellectual premise from which the emotion in the play would spring in the second half. Governor Phillip believed that the most loathsome, foul-mouthed convict had the possibility of redemption. The scene was the mainspring of the first half.

Philip Howard wrote in his journal:

> PHILIP HOWARD: *8 Aug* Methuen [who were publishing the play alongside the opening] will have to wait for more rewrites – if we only have 3+ weeks to get this show on the road they can wait to print the playtext. Whole mornings spent in hot-off-the-press rewrite of 'Authorities Discuss . . .'. Changes dictated, actions clarified, moves worked out. David [Haig] is frightened of Clark being depicted as too weak. He shouldn't always equate theatrical viability with aggression. In fact, he's not really being humble enough in front of largely antagonistic superior officers.

This was quite true. In the hierarchy of the officers' mess, Clark was insignificant. But as director of the play he was a central figure in the audience's perception. Also, in this particular scene, he surprises his brother officers with unexpected eloquence. This sets up a fascinating and complex scene but inevitably it involved more changes.

> PHILIP HOWARD: *17 Aug*   7.45 p.m. Max has received proofs of Act 1, Scenes 1–6, from Methuen – all wrong of course, but it's no use getting in a panic about it because this is going to go on and on and on and on. As usual, Max just doesn't understand how much time has been spent upstairs trying to get this right.

Governor Phillip, my Diary says, teaches the Officers' Mess in this scene by the Socratic Method. I compare him, ironically, to a Joint Stock director: superficial encouragement of democracy, followed by autocratic final decision-taking. It was not a comparison that went unnoticed.

The first scene changed shape continually through rehearsal and didn't arrive at its final form till the second preview. Philip Howard's journal records our attempts to wrestle it to the ground:

> PHILIP HOWARD: *Wednesday 3 Aug*   Afternoon. Timberlake brought along rewrites of the first two scenes, in effect just drastically cut versions of old ones. Max comments that these monologues shouldn't be introverted; there must be a reason for saying all this. A thorough going-over of Scene 1 with hundreds of changes. Oh dear. Next, an ORGY, recreating the tableaux where, for the first time, we try a sheet over the heaving company with them crawling out from underneath – as they land on the beach – 'rutting'.

The night after the convicts had been finally landed in Sydney Cove, there was an extraordinary and terrifying orgy in the middle of a ferocious storm with the rum-maddened sailors slithering through the mud in pursuit of the women convicts. In the middle of this a sheep was struck dead by lightning. The vivid description in *The Fatal Shore* is compelling: but our attempts to bring this event to the stage were doomed. With Joint Stock in the seventies it would have been fine, but, in the eighties, actors just wouldn't take orgies seriously. Our rehearsals ended with everyone in a giggling heap on the floor.

Philip records the moment when at last we began to find structure for the first scene.

PHILIP HOWARD: *Saturday 13 Aug* 4.20 p.m. Attempt to sort out that old chestnut, the first scene of the play: whole company are now either going to be beaten or do the beating, except Ralph, who is to count the number of lashes. Max splits up Jim's hunger speech between all of them. A chorus of starved ranting. Next we practise flagellation. Mark, Nick and I disappear into the Stalls Bar for a warm-up. They both complain that this is like drama school, which isn't giving Max much of a chance. What is then worked out is a sequence from start of play into Scene 3, and it is *good*: first the sound of slow, calculated, counted lashes, which are then overlapped by the 'hunger' and 'cunt' speeches. Victim faints, is cut down and, as he is brought downstage, lights will go up on the huddle of other prisoners, who split to avoid him. Linda (Bassett) announces Scene 2 title, and Jude (Akuwudike), on high, does the few lines of 'A Lone Aboriginal Australian', and straight into Scene 3, 'Punishment', a scene in which Governor Phillip leads a discussion on the first hangings. But unlike previous occasions Max is very anti anyone pondering over theatrical difficulties. We run it twice and it is *good*.
Dare I send this to Methuen now?

The answer was: not quite. The speech went through further changes, and John Arscott's speech about hunger was not cut till after the first preview. But I learned to love the first scene. In performance, it was one of the scenes I enjoyed watching most. It had a filmic quality, with the images emerging slowly from the mist. David's red-coated officer, bewigged, erect, still, counting the lashes; Nick stripped to the waist, strapped to the triangle motionless. And the huddle of convicts downstage like a Doré print. Mark, with the cat, emerged from the wings moving like a fast bowler, the delivery point Robert Sideway's (Nick's) back. The scene pulled us into the eighteenth century and set brutality firmly on the agenda for the evening.

Meanwhile, the actors were still performing *The Recruiting Officer* four times a week. Their concentration began to drift round 4.00 p.m. every afternoon as they preserved their energy for the evening performance.

PHILIP HOWARD: *Saturday 13 Aug* Punishingly hot afternoon.
The actors found performing last night very stifling. So now the air conditioning is going to be switched on at select intervals.

Frayed with fatigue, always aware that we were fighting against the time factor, we kept at it, but something had to give. Philip wrote:

PHILIP HOWARD: *Monday 15 Aug*   These days of rehearsals are different to those of *The Recruiting Officer*: a constant tension, which *never* seems to be released. We do not relax – everything is a rush. How spoilt we were with *The Recruiting Officer*. Today Max decided to postpone the opening of *Our Country's Good* by four days. Administrative side of building are furious that they weren't consulted about this. Attempting to co-ordinate rewrites for Methuen is very difficult – they haven't received any of Act Two yet. Whole afternoon in the photocopying room.

Poor Philip. I sense the peace of the photocopying room become a haven away from the heat and oppression of rehearsal. But I think there were moments when we all panicked.

✍ 16 Aug   I can't even stage things. Set appears to have no focus. I think we're sliding towards a disaster. I can't see my way through it all. Even with the postponement there just isn't enough time. Feel knackered.

But I have to say that this despair is customary. It's lucky that we have such limited ability to retain the memory of physical and mental exhaustion. Or I would never direct again. Timberlake would write in the morning and come in after lunch. We would show her the scene we had worked on that day, then read through the new scene. There was no production in the Theatre Upstairs at the time so this became our rehearsal room. On the wall, we chalked a chronology of the scenes in the play from 26 January 1788, the day the First Fleet landed, to 4 June 1789, the date of the convict performance. Every scene was given a specific date.

I can't remember the moment when it all began to seem possible rather than impossible, but gradually Philip Howard began to spend more time in rehearsal than he did in the photocopying room. I've emphasised the scenes that were the hardest to crack, but there were also ones that slotted sweetly into place, like 'The First Rehearsal', when the convicts hilariously have their first acquaintance with *The Recruiting Officer*, or 'A Love Scene', where Ralph's passion for Mary is reciprocated through the text of Farquhar's play. Some of Timberlake's finest writing emerged in this period. And then there were scenes that we chipped away at, making gradual progress each time we rehearsed, consolidating the through-line of the characters and clarifying the scenes.

One evening, at about 9.30 p.m., we made a breakthrough with the penultimate scene, 'A Question of Liz'. The foul-mouthed and brutalised Liz Morden (Linda Bassett) had been condemned to hang for stealing food. She's probably innocent, but sticks to her convict vow of silence and stubbornly declines to clear herself. Collins, the colony's Advocate General, is concerned that the law will be discredited if there's a miscarriage of justice. He and Governor Phillip are also reluctant to hang a woman. It had taken the latter part of the afternoon and all of the evening to sift through the different lines of argument, and to clarify the objectives and powers of this tribunal. Was Collins seeking a retrial? If Phillip had a power of veto why was it necessary for Liz to speak?

As we became tired it became natural to hit the stale and irritable tones of people who had been arguing for four hours and were at an impasse. Linda had no lines till the end of the scene, and we had rehearsed since tea without reaching this point. Each time we neared it something else would go awry. We would work it out and go back. When we broke again, Linda moved away and sat by herself. I realised she hadn't spoken for over three hours. After the break I ran the scene. When we reached the point where Linda spoke, the moment was electric. Our own anticipation and anxiety paralleled the characters in the play. In the final lines of the scene Ron Cook as the Governor says, 'Liz, I hope you are good in your part.' Timberlake has Linda respond, 'Your Excellency, I will endeavour to speak Mr Farquhar's lines with the elegance and clarity their own worth commands.' It was a thrilling fusion of heart and intellect. The thesis behind the play was illuminated with enormous emotional power.

It was equally thrilling to reflect, as I drove home, that there remained only one more scene to broach. This was 'Backstage', the final scene of the play, where the convict actors are preparing for their performance. The scenes of debate in the play are alternated with scenes of rehearsal. It was really a Royal Court work scene where the rhythms of a very ordinary activity reveal a secret world. There were moments when the whole group focused on one moment together, as when Ron Cook as Wisehammer recites his prologue from which Timberlake had taken the play's title. Other moments showed backstage activity as actors went over lines, made each other up and got into their costumes. This was one scene the actors didn't need to research. I enjoyed bringing first one moment and then another into focus. We looked at Hogarth's 'Strolling Actors Dressing in a Barn', and some of the grouping in our scene was based on that wonderfully evocative picture. Since there was no problem in clearing the stage for another scene we were able to accumulate an evocative pile of props and costumes during the course of the scene. Midway through the afternoon, I caught Neil O'Malley's eye. He was supposed to be on the book, prompting, but I could see that he was fascinated and visibly moved by the eighteenth-century equivalent of the backstage life so familiar to him. In the course of the afternoon, Jenny Cook, the wardrobe mistress, came to drop off some costumes. She stayed too. And by the end of the afternoon, I had come to see how moving Timberlake's final scene would be. We had learned from our evening at Wormwood Scrubs, and there was no apology for the passion and commitment with which the actors prepared for their performance. David Haig, as Ralph Clark, the director, was trembling with excitement and emotion as he made Ralph's final speech thanking his actors and acknowledging the experience they had been through together. In the hushed pause that follows, Lesley Sharp as Mary Brenham whispers, 'I love this'. Her journey from cowed and brutalised convict to Australia's first leading lady was complete.

The public response and critical reception of *Our Country's Good*, by no means always the same things, were universally favourable. It wasn't a huge hit to begin with, but through September and October audiences built steadily, and the final weeks played to packed houses. Not the least of the play's achievements was the resonant chord it touched in London's beleaguered theatrical community. A play that proclaimed the power and enduring worth of theatre, and that celebrated its centrality to our lives, was of importance in the third term of a government which deemed 'subsidy' a dirty word. Perhaps it was a turning point for the Royal Court too. The success of *Our Country's Good* in London and, later, in Australia made it harder for the Arts Council to overlook the erosion of funding which had so afflicted the Court through the previous decade. In 1980 funding from local and Arts Council sources placed the Royal Court just behind Manchester Royal Exchange as the second best funded theatre company in the country apart from the National and the RSC. Truly we had been the third jewel in the Arts Council Crown, but the decade saw a deliberate withdrawal of funding. By 1990 Mrs Thatcher was finally ousted by her own party, and in 1991 an Arts Council Appraisal led to the first substantial increase in the Royal Court's funding for years. We had only once been in deficit during my fourteen years at the Royal

Court, but when I handed over to Stephen Daldry in 1993 there was an operating surplus of £350,000.

Success transformed our exhausting rehearsal experience into a shared Amazonian adventure that we had had together. We all felt very close. Timberlake's first-night card to me said simply, 'I cherish every argument.'

The actors were under considerable pressure. They had become an articulate ensemble through the work we had done together. They were performing *The Recruiting Officer* for four nights a week and rehearsing a new play which was far from complete. But hindsight made them wise too.

◄)) RON COOK: We didn't know what we were playing. I think I knew I was playing Wisehammer, but that's all. Some of the parts were still to be cast, so when we started the workshop, it was an act of faith. We didn't know what it was going to be. I didn't know I was going to be playing Governor Phillip. I didn't know what John Wisehammer was going to be . . .

It was a difficult process. We had a lot of rewriting, right up to the wire, and during the preview we were still changing it. It was like being in the tube – you come up to street level to find out where you are. Because we all played different parts in it – you can have a bit on, and then you get off – but when you're off, you're changing, usually, to come on to play somebody else. So we didn't know how it linked. We knew some scenes, but we didn't know how it worked as a whole. The morning after a preview, Max always says, 'Right. Spouses' notes', because your partner always comes to see it first. On the first preview of *Our Country's Good*, we were just going, 'What's going on?' because we had no idea. At the curtain call, people were just in tears.

◄)) TIMBERLAKE WERTENBAKER: So, I would rewrite in the mornings. They would rehearse in the mornings. I would come in at 1.00 p.m. with whatever rewritten scenes I'd done that morning. And Max would then say, 'Look, we've done this and that scene, and we'll show it to you.' And so they would have done some work, and they would either see problems, or we would talk about it . . . I remember

I was getting up at six every morning and writing . . .

There was one improvised scene which I actually used in the play, but that's the only one. It was the hanging scene. Max kept saying, 'I'm interested in the details of hanging,' and I was not interested, I have to say, and he said, 'Just let me do this.' And he had the hangman measuring Liz (Linda Bassett), and she didn't say anything. She refused to talk, so it was almost as it is in the play. Linda then called me at two in the morning, that night, and said, 'You know, I would have talked if the improvisation had gone on,' so I used the whole thing. It was wonderful. I used the silence, and I used the fact that she told me that she would have eventually talked . . .

Max was very responsive, but what was wonderful – and I think he doesn't even admit it to himself – is that he was totally open to writers, to their imagination and passion. He was incredibly clear about what he felt just didn't work, was sort of mush. He never interfered with content. He would either say, 'I don't understand the scene.' Or he would say, 'I think it's OK,' but he never said, 'What about this or that?' It's why it was wonderful working with him, especially for me, because I'm quite defensive, and he's quite ruthless about cutting, and this is where we did have a lot of fights. He was very clear about what didn't work.

Part Three

OUT OF JOINT THEATRE COMPANY, 1993—

Part Three

OUT OF JOINT THEATRE COMPANY, 1993—

As his time at the Royal Court came to an end, the issue facing Stafford-Clark, as it had been with Joint Stock, was that of finding a context within which his own theatrical taste could flourish. As his Diary records, he was approached by the RSC, but, although he had done a production with the company in 1992, he was initially worried about the implications of working formally within the Royal Shakespeare Company.

✍ *24 May 1993*   I enjoyed *A Jovial Crew* at Stratford, but unless I'm able to come to some arrangement with Stephen [Daldry]/Royal Court about a company, I will have to approach the Arts Council and start my own. As of last week I have a name: Out of Joint. My fear about Stratford had been that I would not be able to reproduce my own work, my own signature, under foreign circumstances. Certainly this was not the case, and the production was the most fulfilling and most challenging I've done since *Our Country's Good*. Adrian [Noble, Artistic Director of the RSC] has asked me to have dinner and discuss plans for Stratford next year.

At this point, Sonia Friedman, then working at the National, and looking for a change, wrote to Stafford-Clark, and went to see him at the Court. She was to become the co-founder and first producer of Out of Joint.

🔊 SONIA FRIEDMAN: I had an hour and a half to pitch to him why I thought he should set up a touring company for new writing. And at the end of that hour and a half, we as good as shook hands and agreed to do it. The pitch was that British theatre needed him: that new writing needed him, and that the regions needed him. And that I believed profoundly, and I still do, that Max's energy was just what the regions needed. And that to go to the RSC would not be the right move for somebody of his distinction and experience and level of contact, and wouldn't help him to develop further as an artist.

Stafford-Clark and Friedman then approached the Arts Council for funding to get the new company off the ground.

From the submission to the Arts Council
The name, Out of Joint, indicates the philosophy of the company. The
point of departure is the work pioneered by Joint Stock in the 1970s
and, to a certain extent, carried on during Max Stafford-Clark's tenure
as Artistic Director of the Royal Court in the eighties and early nineties.

25 May 1995

◀) SONIA FRIEDMAN: We went along to the Arts Council with no
plans at all, just between us an interesting set of experiences. Obviously,
I'm from a younger generation, but it was a good marriage in terms of
what I could bring to the company: fresh, young energy, really, married
to his extraordinary gifts. And our timing was pretty perfect. They only
gave us project-by-project funding for the first three years, but we were
never turned down [except for *The Steward of Christendom*, see p. 182 – 95].
And the project funding was generous; it allowed the company to survive
. . . It was an incredibly fertile period for the company, because we had
to tour everywhere; take the work everywhere; take every opportunity
we could in order to survive . . . We had lots of debates in the early days
about whether we brought in other directors; we did flirt with the idea
and offer a couple of directors projects, but people didn't want that.
They wanted Max. They wanted Max's identity and that was clearly
what was working for the company.

*Once the project was funded, Stafford-Clark explained the modus operandi of the new
company:*

The company will offer a six-month period of work to a group of actors
during which time a new play will be workshopped, rehearsed and
produced alongside the revival of a classic play . . . By enticing venues
with a new production of a classic play, they will be encouraged to show
a greater commitment to fresh writing. The company's first double
venture will comprise *The Queen and I*, a stage adaptation of the Sue
Townsend novel, and a revival of *Road* by Jim Cartwright.

Stage, 25 November 1993

*Early and important decisions were taken at the 16 February 1994 Board meeting,
namely that 'The programme should not always be classics driven. [Max Stafford-
Clark] should direct every show. We have to plan at least twelve months in advance'.
Setting up the company involved difficult choices, and a degree of re-education:*

. . . Touring is hard, and all the reasons why I left touring and went to the Court fourteen years ago are vividly clear. It's hard to get an audience for new work . . . The difference between touring now and fifteen years ago is that you could go to somewhere like Cheltenham, and the audience would have seen [say] Snoo Wilson's new play two weeks before and *Fanshen* was no shock to them, whereas the audience in Warwick last week had not been trained and sustained on a diet of new plays at all, so that makes it both harder and more important.

Plays International, December 1994

At the same time, the worry was about recruitment. Early on, Stafford-Clark knew that 'it will be hard too to get senior actors to go on the road' (Diary, 29 August 1992). By September 1993, however, a pattern began to emerge:

✍ Out of Joint will take some thought. I can't just slam into it. The nature of the first two projects already seems rich and diverse. In the second year we should do two studio projects with two relatively unknown writers. Exciting, because the pressure to produce volume has gone. It's the time of my life.

And Stephen Jeffreys recalls a telephone call from Stafford-Clark:

◀)) STEPHEN JEFFREYS: After his first full day at work he phoned me up and said, 'Ask me how I feel.' I said, 'How do you feel, Max?', and he said, 'I'm as happy as a pig in shit. No one has come up to me today to ask me about the state of the men's lavatories.' He was really in seventh heaven, like a kid with a new toy.

After The Queen and I *opened at the Haymarket, Leicester on 25 March 1994, both it and* Road *played in repertory at the Court from 9 June. This first project was not felt to be an unqualified success:*

Out of Joint Company minutes, 5 February 1995

The Director reported that *The Queen and I* and *Road* had proved to be an ill-yoked project. On tour, it had been hard to get houses for *Road*. In retrospect, it would have been easier had *The Queen and I* been a solo project. The Director felt the principal reason for this was that it had been too early to revive (this particular) modern classic [i.e., *Road*].

🔊 SONIA FRIEDMAN There were times when we did marriages which, as producer, I felt were bad decisions, like *The Queen and I* and *Road*. Max perversely wanted to do *Road* with a hugely commercial venture like *The Queen and I*, in order to set down the rule for the company very clearly, which was: we may be very successful, but we're also going to do the sort of work which is challenging and difficult, and won't necessarily fill theatres.

Out of Joint's next project was Stephen Jeffreys's The Libertine, *about Charles II's favourite, the Earl of Rochester, together with the Restoration comedy,* The Man of Mode. *The former opened on 20 October 1994 at the Warwick Arts Centre, while Etherege's play opened in Bury St Edmunds on 22 September.*

🔊 STEPHEN JEFFREYS: I think I must have met him around 1990, and we sat down and said, 'Let's do a play,' and about ten days later he phoned me and said, 'We've got a job here [at the Royal Court] called Literary Associate, and you'd have a desk and a phone. Come to the theatre one day a week.' Never seen either the desk or the phone . . . A few months into that, there was a discussion about a play commissioned from another writer [Heathcote Williams] about the Earl of Rochester, which was never delivered. And I said, 'This is my subject, Max,' and he said, 'Let's do that, then.' And then I suspended writing *The Libertine* to write *A Jovial Crew*.

Towards the end of 1995, the pressures of creating back-to-back productions for Out of Joint were shown painfully with the combination of Three Sisters *and* The Break of Day, *a new piece by Timberlake Wertenbaker. The shows opened in September and October 1995 respectively. In the middle of the year, Stafford-Clark revealed some of the looming problems in a seminar for Sheffield students:*

🔊 Timberlake was asked to write the play in parallel with *Three Sisters*. And, although I tried to discourage her, because *Three Sisters* has a cast of at least thirteen, she stuck to her guns. Now, again, you can see that we're heading for crisis because she has to write thirteen parts, and the engagement for the actors is six months . . . Timberlake fucking well *has* to write the parts for those people. For an actor, it's a huge leap of faith to commit for six months, for very little money, to a job where they haven't even read their part. She wanted to do the play in parallel with *Three Sisters* because she has a similar end-of-the-century feeling. So, if

Three Sisters is written in the shadow of the failure of capitalism, Timberlake's play is written in the shadow of the failure of socialism. Of course, there's also an autobiographical element because, as it happens, both Timberlake and John [her second husband], and Ann [my wife] and I have each adopted a baby from Bulgaria, so it's also a story about that. It's going to be quite hard.

🔊 TIMBERLAKE WERTENBAKER: It was not a happy experience. The actors did a brilliant production of *Three Sisters*, but they didn't want to do *The Break of Day*, that's for sure. They were fine for *Three Sisters*, and, actually, they were all specifically cast for it. I wanted three older women, so there was a problem right there. My idea of *Three Sisters* was to have three fabulous actresses in their late thirties or forties, which is what *The Break of Day* is about. These were supposed to be women who were reaching the end of their fertility. If it's played by a twenty-three-year-old, they just couldn't bring their own experience to it.

Olga is twenty-nine and Irina is twenty-one, with Masha somewhere between the two. My inclination was to cast three rather younger women, as is customary, all in their twenties.

🔊 SONIA FRIEDMAN: *The Break of Day* was unfortunate for everybody involved, and this goes back to being forced into producing at that point. We should have pulled it. We should have held it. We should have honed it. We shouldn't have put anybody into that position, particularly Timberlake, of having to produce a play because we'd scheduled it. But we were still at a relatively early stage in the company's life. We needed the play. And I think that we put the writer under too much pressure to deliver.

It was during 1995 that a new contact was made with Caryl Churchill. Board minutes for 15 February record Stafford-Clark's statement that he was 'Not at liberty to discuss the project further [but] he stressed that she was working with a sense of purpose.' And Sonia Friedman wrote to the Arts Council in May to say that 'Caryl is set to write an epic and satirical piece for ten actors, dealing with "freedom". It aims to look at how the word and notion of freedom has been exploited and misunderstood through the ages'. By July, Stafford-Clark was writing to a potential venue to report . . .

Letter to Ruth Mackenzie, of Nottingham Playhouse
. . . with qualified optimism on a meeting I had with Caryl last week.
The play now has a title, *Britannia and the Bad Baby*, and Caryl has very
clearly got an epic subject in her sights with the work she has already
done. At the same time, she has not been enormously well over the
whole spring period, and this has undoubtedly affected her appetite for
the work. It hardly needs saying that this kind of project is hazardous,
but I feel positive. I think it would be good to leave Caryl for as long as
your dates and timing permit, and then seek a clear answer.

*By November, he was telling the Arts Council that 'at the moment, Caryl is not
writing, though the expectation is that she will still deliver the play'. The epic play
was not delivered. Instead, as the Board minutes for May 1996 record: 'The Director
was looking to open Caryl Churchill's double-bill,* Heart's Desire *and* Blue Kettle,
*in June 1997. Sonia Friedman felt that the double bill [eventually staged under the
title* Blue Heart] *was 'the most fantastic response from a writer who couldn't write
the epic. It was all about a writer's journey, and I felt we were completely blessed to
have just those two pieces'. Rehearsing the play was a challenge, as Max recalls:*

🔊 Caryl and I were finding out how to do the play. I mean the
particular problem she set was that every moment you said a particular
line in the various different versions of the script you had to, say, have
your hand picking up the cup of tea, and so, if you only did the half-
line, was your hand stretching for it, or did you actually pick it up on
the second half-line? All the technical problems that she set, and the
rules that governed that, were things we discovered in rehearsal. She
didn't know any more than I did quite how to do it, and so it was how
to do it that was fun.

A major event of 1996 was the production of Mark Ravenhill's Shopping and
Fucking, *which opened at the Royal Court Theatre Upstairs on 26 September.
The title did raise the odd eyebrow. As reported at the Board of 8 May, the legal
consequences of using the title were being investigated. It was confirmed that the full
title could be printed in the programme, providing the programme was bought inside
the theatre. Though it was asserted that the full name of the play would be used
where possible, it was also the case that the company must consider the views of the
venues.*

1997 saw Stafford-Clark's production of Sebastian Barry's The Steward of Christendom *(see Case Study, pp. 182–95), and, in 1998, the same author's* Our Lady of Sligo *opened on 26 March at the Oxford Playhouse. In June, Sonia Friedman left Out of Joint, and was succeeded by Graham Cowley, who had previously worked with Max as General Manager for both Joint Stock and the Royal Court from 1988.*

◀)) SONIA FRIEDMAN: I'm ambitious. I love producing. I will never have a working relationship again like I did with Max. I put a proposal to Max after five years, once we were secure, that we set up an independent commercial arm, whereby I would take on other projects. And we talked about it at great length, and we both decided that it would perhaps be the wrong decision for the company. And the right decision therefore would be for me to go . . . Max is my mentor. What Max taught me was that to be fashionable is a very dangerous place to try to be, because you're only going to go out of fashion. And therefore always try to take the surprising route.

In September, 1998, Stafford-Clark directed a revival of Wertenbaker's Our Country's Good, *which opened at Bath. His reaction to revisiting one of the great successes of his time at the Court was that he 'enjoyed doing [it] again but it doesn't have quite the same toxic mixture of thrill and terror provided by a new play' (letter to Philip Roberts, 21 September, 1998). In the same month, he took delivery of part of a play commissioned from Mark Ravenhill. This became* Some Explicit Polaroids *(see Case Study, pp. 196–216). The completed piece finally opened on 30 September 1999.*

The long-standing collaboration between Stafford-Clark and Caryl Churchill came under pressure in December.

✍ I spoke to Caryl in the course of the morning. She has written a half-hour play which she has sent me. Later, she rings to tell me she wants Stephen Daldry to direct it. She says she's lain awake worrying about telling me. Certainly I feel a cold hand on my gut. I ask if she's bored with me. She says the play is not realistic. I'm not sure why this makes it more suitable for Stephen, but I'm pissed off and upset. Of course she's entitled to have whom she likes, but I feel unreasonably angry. She tells me she doesn't like to be pestered, but, if you don't happen to call, it gets sent somewhere else. She always wanted to wander off and have other directors from time to time, but it is not good news. Oh, for fuck's sake. I should console myself by thinking that someone as unremittingly inventive as Caryl needs to be reinvented by her director as well. What a day.

🔊 Absolutely, it did upset me. What particularly upset me was the manner in which it was done. We went out for dinner, and Caryl said, 'Oh, I have written a play.' And I said, 'Send it to me,' and she said, 'Yes. Well, I've sent it to Ian Rickson [Artistic Director of the Royal Court], and I've sent it to Stephen [Daldry].' Then the next day, when she said she wanted Stephen to do it, Ian said, 'Hard luck. You know we've all been trying.' And I realised I was part of a competition. They had all been pursuing her for a play, and I was part of that competition.

On 11 December Stafford-Clark read the new play, Far Away. *He thought it 'an elliptical, political fable ... surreal and powerful. It would have formed a good double-bill with* Mountain Language, *or another of Pinter's directly political short plays'. He resolved on 13 December to write to both Churchill and Pinter to suggest a programme of political shorts. Pinter replied on 21 December to say that he was fully engaged for the moment. Churchill, according to the Diary for the same date*

✍ . . . doesn't want to upset me, but doesn't want this one to tour if Stephen doesn't want to. I don't think I have much to offer her at the moment. She doesn't want to feel she's on a treadmill of work which has to come to me . . . well, I do see the point.

At a Court script meeting the following March, attended as usual by Stafford-Clark, Far Away *was discussed.*

✍ I say she's developed her own response to a political agenda which she has discovered she cannot effectively address directly any more. The play is compressed and surreal but epic, and also functions like an installation. We disagree about whether it should go on Upstairs or Downstairs. Apparently, Caryl doesn't want the focus of Downstairs. I understand, but she's evading her own significance. Katie [Mitchell] admits she would kill to direct it. I think the same but opt not to admit it.

At the end of 1999, Out of Joint's Arts Council grant increased from £280,000 to £420,000, the biggest percentage increase Stafford-Clark had ever known, and a recognition of the success of touring new work. What had begun as a gamble in the early nineties had been vindicated, and Stafford-Clark set about planning the forthcoming programme. If Spring 2001 were to be occupied by Rebecca Prichard's new play, and the Autumn by April De Angelis, Stafford-Clark needed to programme for 2002. However, Rebecca Prichard's play did not materialise.

◀) She wrote and wrote. The play was partly based on Ibsen's *An Enemy of the People*, so it concerned a scandal about water, and how that touched people. And she got more and more confused with it, and it became a crisis in her writing, because it's not as though she's not written that play and gone on to write other plays. We never received a draft which was able in any way to go into rehearsal, so I've left it for a bit . . . and I may well pick it up again when Rebecca says she's ready.

On the other hand, April De Angelis delivered a first draft of what became A Laughing Matter, *described in the Diary for 1 September as 'a work in progress, but it's eccentric and lively. It certainly could be wonderful.' On 4 September Stafford-Clark suggested to De Angelis that 'we should take a liberty with history, and get Garrick's unacknowledged illegitimate son to play the role of Tony Lumpkin in the rival theatre's production of* She Stoops to Conquer'. *Two days later, he wrote to Trevor Nunn at the National to say that he had seen 'the first eighty pages of April's new play, which is provisionally entitled* Garrick. *I think it's terrific: fresh, witty and engaging. Sixty pages are scenes in first draft, and twenty further pages sketch in the rest of the play. I would hope to have a complete first draft with you in the next three months.'* A Laughing Matter *eventually opened in September 2002, playing at the National Theatre at the end of the year.*

At the same time, Stafford-Clark was rehearsing a double-bill of a revival of Rita, Sue and Bob Too *and a new piece written by Robin Soans,* A State Affair. *The double-bill opened in October 2000. The principal concept was to juxtapose Dunbar's original account of life on a 'sink' estate in the 1970s with an up-to-the-minute account, based on the Hyde Park Estate in Leeds (see pp. 109 – 23).*

Prior to that, Stafford-Clark directed Judy Upton's Sliding with Suzanne *(August 2001), and Sebastian Barry's* Hinterland *(January 2002).*

✍ *8 Sept 2000*   See Judy Upton and become more enthusiastic about *Sliding with Suzanne*. The weird and wacky world of Judy Upton bears some examination. Principal character is a thirty-five-year-old foster-mother who is fucking her foster son (aged sixteen), who tries to make her more responsible. Her world is peopled with characters who have been pushed to the edge, whose expectations and qualifications are not matched by the jobs on offer . . . I'm not sure what appeal it has, except that there's a great part for a thirty-five-year-old. Katrin Cartlidge?

Hinterland *went through five drafts, and Stafford-Clark became concerned that his suggestions to Barry were too many:*

✍ *8 Oct*   Is my input becoming too great in *Hinterland*? There was a moment in *Shopping and Fucking* when Mark [Ravenhill] said, 'The trouble with this scene is I'm just writing to please you.' But Sebastian seems to relish the contributions, and I have to say the play has steadily got better.

In June 2003, Stafford-Clark continued a partnership with David Hare when he directed Hare's The Breath of Life *at the Sydney Theatre Company in Australia. This new phase of their partnership had already begun in February, the result of which was* The Permanent Way. *Before that came* Duck, *by Stella Feehily, which was first performed in Summer 2003:*

Stella Feehily sent me a smaller play, a twenty-minute play. I thought it was very striking . . . so when I was here [Dublin] doing *Hinterland*, I met her, and she gave me eight scenes which were the progenitor of *Duck*, and said, 'I'm writing about violence, I'm not sure how far to go.' I thought that was very striking. We spoke on the phone, had a correspondence, and the play kind of grew from eight scenes to its current twenty scenes . . . And obviously, working on *Duck* with Stella Feehily, who's a first-time writer, you could win every debate, and you have to resolve not to. She was very vigorous in standing up for her interpretation of the play . . . So you're more nudging them . . . having them write scenes rather than saying what scenes should be written.

The Theatre Shop, tenth anniversary conference, Dublin, 3 October 2003, 9–10, 14–15 (www.theatreshop.ie)

The Permanent Way, *like* Serious Money (*Royal Court, 1987*) *and* Three Birds Alighting on a Field (*the Court, 1991*), *began with a two-week workshop. It followed a familiar pattern in Stafford-Clark's work.*

> BELLA MERLIN: . . . The actors set out to interview a host of people who had been involved with or had encountered the railways since their privatisation in 1991. The interviewees included union leaders and heads of train-operating companies from the four major train crashes that had occurred since 1997 . . . On our return from the interviews and encounters, we fed the information back *in character* to Max, David and the other actors.
>
> *National Theatre Education Workpack* (*www.nationaltheatre.org.uk*)

The play opened in York in November 2003.

Three years earlier, the Diary records a conversation with the Artistic Director of the Royal Court, Ian Rickson, about the decisions of the Court's script meetings as to what plays to schedule, and what to discard. It led Stafford-Clark to reflect on the vagaries of his profession. A life spent directing new work is crucially dependent on the quality of what scripts appear:

> ✍ *5 November 2000*   How many dodgy projects do I take on? And, more to the point, how many of them do I bring off? Well, the script meeting certainly thought *Rita, Sue and Bob Too* was dodgy and, in fact, *Our Lady of Sligo* and *Our Country's Good* were actually turned down by the Royal Court, so we have to go back to *Blue Heart* to find a project acceptable to the script meeting. On the other hand, how many of them were brilliant plays? It's time I did a classic again.

He did just that in 2004, with a site-specific Macbeth, *which he had considered early in 2000 (see Case Study, pp. 217–50). It became the tenth-anniversary production of Out of Joint, opening at the Red Brick Mill, Batley on 10 September 2004.*

Case Study

THE STEWARD OF CHRISTENDOM
Sebastian Barry

Rehearsal: from February 1995

First Performance: 31 August 1995

Cast: Kieran Ahern, Tina Kellegher, Cara Kelly, Donal McCann, Maggie McCarthy, Aislin McGuckin, Rory Murray, Jonathan Newman

Published: The Steward of Christendom (Methuen, 1995)

The Steward of Christendom was commissioned towards the end of my time at the Royal Court, but wasn't produced until Out of Joint was well into its stride. It was to be a co-production between the two organisations so dear to me. I had commissioned Sebastian Barry having seen his *White Woman Street* at the Bush and had been struck by its quirky originality. I had also had a tip from Donal McCann: mindful that it would be impossible to lure McCann to London without a substantial part, I had asked the great Irish actor and tipster what young writers he would recommend and he had talked warmly of *The Prayers of Sherkin*, an earlier Sebastian Barry play about a religious community on a small island off the Cork coast. Several drafts of *The Steward of Christendom* had arrived at the Court while I was still there, but Sebastian's lyrical gifts had commanded limited support at the Court's weekly script meeting.

I had had several phone conversations with Sebastian, but we had never met, so I encouraged him to come to London for the day so we could talk through the script. We had a great time together. We met in the morning, talked, had lunch, then walked through Sloane Square to Ranelagh Gardens behind the Chelsea Hospital, founded by Charles II at the prompting of his friend Nell Gwynn. Sitting on the grass amidst the nannies, the kids and the Chelsea pensioners, we talked about the play and about how Sebastian's own ancestors had provided him with a lens to examine the past. The particular ancestor in

The Steward of Christendom is Thomas Dunne, a superintendent in the Dublin Metropolitan Police. A Catholic, but fiercely loyal to the Queen, he had been ordered to clear Sackville Street in the General Strike of 1913. He had done so, but at the cost of four strikers being killed. In the play Thomas Dunne, now in the county home, looks back on his life. Almost the whole of the action takes place in his cell-like room where he is visited by his eldest daughter and by various ghosts from his past. After my conversation with Sebastian I saw the story more clearly, and how the production had to move seamlessly from the present to the past. Thomas Dunne is onstage throughout: it was a mammoth task, but also a huge opportunity for an actor.

A further version of the script reached me at Stratford later that summer where I was directing *The Country Wife*. Happy to take time off from the endless and punishing task of unifying a large and diverse company of actors, I read it while watching a game of cricket at the Recreation Ground across the river from the theatre. I didn't know the teams and I didn't care about the result, but it was a peaceful way to spend the afternoon and gave me the space to recognise the emotional heft of Sebastian's story. In a few months I was to leave the Court, and my objective was to find a director for Sebastian, but I was being drawn in. I had various conversations with Sebastian, in one of which I suggested that Thomas Dunne's story of his attempts, when he was a little boy, to save the life of his dog should be used to conclude the evening. The dog had been condemned because he had savaged a ewe. One evening Thomas walks him over the hill to a neighbour who catches rabbits, but he too won't take in a dog that has killed. At a loss, the boy and the dog spend the night alone in the wintry wood, and as they walk home at dawn they meet the search parties sent out to find them. The boy experiences 'the mercy of fathers' and is forgiven as he realises fully for the first time that his father loves him. 'And the dog lived till he died.' Graham Greene writes of fallen priests; in Chekhov the writer's disapproval is reserved for doctors and for teachers who don't accept the responsibilities that their office confer; and in Sebastian Barry's world there is no irresponsibility more culpable than that of the careless father.

Two years later I started rehearsal. *The Steward of Christendom* was a hard one to get together. I had wanted to put it Downstairs at the Court on the main stage, but Stephen Daldry, my successor as Artistic Director, had not been persuaded and had offered a production in the Theatre Upstairs for three and a half weeks. Michael Colgan of the Gate Theatre, Dublin, as he would now readily admit, had also been less than wholehearted. He offered us two weeks at his theatre, subject to casting approval. In 1994 Out of Joint was on a project-by-project grant from the Arts Council. Each play had to win their approval and they too were unenthusiastic. It was the only play of Out of Joint's that they ever turned down. Sonia Friedman and I were in despair. Sonia phoned Kate Deevy, then Head of Touring at the Arts Council, and she came up with a personal grant of £12,000 from some touring budget. Without that unexpected patronage it's difficult to see how the production could have happened. The only person who showed no hesitation at all in committing to the project was Donal McCann. I first sent the play to Donal in Yorkshire, where he was on location. Two days later he rang. He didn't actually say he would do the play, but I knew we had his commitment when he said, 'I don't want to wear slippers. I'll wear socks, then I don't have to be putting them on and off each time when I get out of bed.' He was visualising his performance already.

I had first worked with Donal in *Tea and Sex and Shakespeare* by Tom Kilroy at the Abbey in 1976, and again in 1978 in *Prayer for my Daughter* by Thomas Babe in the Theatre Upstairs. At that particular time Donal's tactic was to go off the drink during the rehearsals and the run of any play he was involved in, but this period of restraint would be preceded and followed by 'monumental batters, during which he would vanish for weeks on end', recalls Garrett Keogh, a fellow actor. I was unaware of this, so it was no concern to me when his agent, Peter Crouch, phoned a few days before rehearsals began for the Thomas Babe play to say he couldn't return a signed contract because Donal was nowhere to be found. He arrived in the Theatre Upstairs for the first day of rehearsals of *Prayer for my Daughter* with one minute to spare. He looked terrible. The read through was a strange affair. They are often circumspect occasions, when the actors tentatively grope towards the outline of a performance, but Donal went for the emotion in the play full tilt. He had clearly thought the character through in some detail, but it was a distinguished cast and Antony Sher, Kevin McNally and John Dick matched Donal's ferocity and energy. It became a disjointed but highly energised performance piece; as the morning wore on, the sweat poured down Donal's face.

I enjoyed rehearsals, and Donal responded well to direction and to the other actors, none of whom he knew. But total restraint didn't last long and two vodkas at lunchtime made him markedly less tolerant in the afternoons. One morning rehearsal dragged on past the customary one o'clock lunchbreak.

I was endeavouring to make some point no doubt, but it must have been nearly half past when we broke. That afternoon Donal was particularly tetchy. At the end of the day he pulled me aside. 'Don't you ever do that to me again, you cunt,' he said. I was at a loss. 'But I showed you,' he added. 'I ordered two vodkas, I put them on the bar and didn't touch them for ten minutes.' After this abrupt revelation of his dependence I stopped for lunch promptly at one.

THE REHEARSAL PERIOD

By the time we came to *The Steward of Christendom* Donal had conquered the drink and was well on his way to becoming a national icon. The responsibility of the artist in Ireland is a peculiar one; particularly so with theatre. The theatre is to Ireland what rugby is to New Zealand, a means of national expression and a matter of national pride, subject to huge praise when successful and rancorous abuse when anything less.

The absence of socialism and the decline of religion in Ireland mean that the theatre can assume near spiritual significance. The writer or actor has the possibility of becoming the spokesperson for the nation; the play or the performance transcends itself and becomes an object of wonder and worship itself. Equally, if expectation is not matched by performance, abuse and rage can follow out of all proportion to the offence. Sebastian Barry was to have each of these experiences in turn with *The Steward of Christendom* and *Hinterland*. This extraordinary pressure has always seemed to me to be the metaphor behind Brian Friel's *Faith Healer,* which was also to be one of Donal's most extraordinary performances. Faith healer Frank Hardy, his cockney manager, Teddy, and girlfriend Grace are touring church halls on the Celtic fringes of Scotland and Wales. Occasionally Hardy has, it seems, the ability to effect miraculous cures. At other times this power is absent and at the play's chilling final moment he is killed for his failure to produce a miracle. *Faith Healer* was directed by that fine Irish director, Joe Dowling, who writes about the last performance at the Royal Court:

> JOE DOWLING: As Frank Hardy made his way downstage for the final moment of epiphany, delicately removing an imaginary piece of fluff from his coat, certain that he was going to his death, the focus of the

entire audience was on his every tiny gesture. The stillness in the theatre was palpable. In that moment, I understood the nature of his theatrical greatness. A complete concentration on the character, [Donal McCann's] ability to hold our attention fully and the magic within him to communicate his feelings clearly to the audience, made it a moment to hold on to for ever.

Donal had total emotional recall, and if he approved of a note or suggestion he had the ability to play it back to you that second. Like a dancer choreographing a role, he would find a specific moment, movement or gesture, and, once found, there was no particular necessity to rehearse it over and over again: that brick was lodged in the architecture of his performance. I recall talking to him rather tentatively about a scene: I had half an idea and I wasn't being very clear . . . Donal listened with his head on one side and then said: 'I'd do it Max, exactly as you wish, except I can't understand what the fuck you're talking about.' There was one gesture in repose he used as Thomas Dunne with his linked hand resting on top of his head. I asked him one day where it came from: 'It was an old Terenure player,' he told me, 'who went on playing when he should have retired . . . He came to each lineout and stood like that getting his breath back.' (Donal was a student at one of Dublin's great rugby playing schools, Terenure College.)

✍ *7 Oct 1994*   Dinner with Stephen Daldry, who is certainly not persuaded by the idea of Sebastian's play. He's alarmed at the lack of drama. He tells me he's having a hard time at the Court. I'm sure the Meredith Oakes play he's directing will be a triumph but he says he hates coming into rehearsal at the moment. 'I'm not like you,' he says. 'I'm a success junkie.' I like him.

12 Nov 1994   Another meeting with Sebastian. I urge more clarity for the present storyline as opposed to flashbacks. How did Thomas get into the asylum? Who signed the papers that committed him? It would have been Annie, the eldest daughter, which would argue for her being a more forceful character. Who is Thomas talking to? Is it friends? Is it the audience?

That was a significant question: there are many passages in the play where Thomas is re-examining moments from his past. A key decision we arrived at was that he was recalling it to himself, neither reliving it nor talking directly to the audience. If it were a film much of the dialogue would be in voice-over, which is of course why there was never a film. Sebastian and I had three days' preliminary rehearsal with Donal in Dublin in the middle of February 1995. The Samuel Beckett Centre at Trinity College Dublin gave us a room. Out of the side window there was a view of a dark corner of the rugby pitch in College Park where I had spent so much blood and sweat some thirty years earlier. I think I was complaining about the inconvenience or the cold or both: 'Ah go on,' said Donal. 'This country gave you your education; it's time you gave something back.'

23 Feb 1995 Donal begins to relax and Sebastian is grateful but vigilant. I haven't embarked on actions yet, not wanting to raise Donal's hackles, but it lies ahead.

In the course of the week I learned how much of a history Donal and Sebastian had in common. Both had grown up amidst the grim restraints of de Valera's Ireland ('the most cunning old shite that ever lived,' said Donal), and both had spent their summers on farms in the country, as I had in Buckinghamshire.

Donal said later, 'I recognised huge chunks of it, having spent a lot of my childhood down in County Wexford, ten miles from Kiltegan in County Wicklow . . . My mother was born there, and I knew that Thomas Dunne had been born on a farm, and his subsequent life was always spent thinking of returning to that . . . I did think, unworthily, for a while, that Sebastian had found out how my formative years had been spent, but it turned out that he too had spent the whole summer with his aunt, and of course, "a city kid" on a farm, well, he thinks he's discovered all these things, that he's the only person in the whole world who knows where a certain hen lays and things like that . . . I loved it.'

The next week we began rehearsal in London:

27 Feb Not a bad first day. Essayed actions with Donal. Bit of a workshop. We pool childhood memories. It broke the ice. Quite fun. The play reads well and it seems to break down into sections easily. Sebastian cheerful.

28 Feb   We struggle with the history of Ireland. I learn Fine Gael was pro-treaty and Fianna Fail was an anti-treaty party. 'The Irish civil war was as frightening as Rwanda,' says Sebastian.

1 March   Try to supplement the information about Thomas's daughters. Who is the best cook? Is there a competitive spirit? Who has the mother role? Does Thomas 'remember' them accurately or are they his nightmares?

2 March   Bit stolid. Got Thomas's dream of his daughters going a bit surreal. Sebastian approves. Donal got tired and then it was hard to make out the shape of it. I gave up working with actions, or rather I gave up using them directly. Donal resists it, although in fact a) he always plays an objective, and b) he's extraordinarily consistent. I just note them down and talk to him if they change.

7 March   The actors begin to appear more like a family. 'Family' is the one experience all actors have in common. Yet the experience is so diverse. Portraying a convincing family on stage, and one without a mother, requires more detail than we can muster as yet.

9 March   Bad day. I was uninspired. Donal cranky.

10 March   Make Annie, the daughter, improvise a monologue that justifies certifying Thomas. How violent do they think he had been? Why is Thomas so afraid of his anger?

13 March   Donal tetchy. He feels Tina Kellegher as Annie isn't strong enough with him. But it seems good to me.

15 March   Run-through. First half stolid, but potentially extraordinary. Donal feeling his way through the material. There are isolated moments where he allows the emotion to flow through him, and there are moments where simple insecurity with the lines prevails. What do I do next? In the afternoon we do a ten-minute run-through of the first half, condensing the play and moving Donal through the stations of the cross, from bed to mantelpiece to door. He resists the idea at first but then launches himself into it. He says afterwards it has given him great security. He knows the route through the first act better than he thought.

17 March   Today I am fifty-four. Donal brings in an untidy brown paper parcel into rehearsal and slams it down. It's an Irish rugby shirt. 'You're the only Englishman involved in this operation,' he says, 'so you'd better join our side.'

20 March   Donal wants to work today. Donal fretting at any halt to the flow of the rehearsal. But we're still not clear what are the mood changes of the second act.

24 March   Donal at his worst, barking, tired and paranoid. At the end of a long day he walks out slamming the door behind him. I know he's only gone for a pee, but I have to pretend to lose my temper too. Donal calms down: 'This is not a moment for us to lose faith in each other,' he says cryptically.

28 March   Run-through. Notes are all about containing energy and how much time he has when he draws us in. Sean Davey's music was added for the first time. It made a powerful conclusion. 'Well, it's a five-Kleenex ending,' said Bo Barton, the production manager, wiping away her tears.

At the end of the play Donal as Thomas tells the story of the condemned dog to his son Willie or rather to his memory of Willie at the age of ten. He then sleeps, and as the lights fade I had directed Willie, played by a beautiful and sensitive young schoolboy, Jonathan Newman, to place his arm protectively across his father's chest. The combination of the story, the music and this gesture made for a moment of almost unbearable tension and poignancy. Laughter is usually the only audible audience response, but with *The Steward of Christendom* as the music died down there were usually four or five people to be heard snuffling in the audience. Towards the end of the two-year run I began to avoid the end myself. I knew that it regularly triggered a tearful response from me too. Why do we weep? A sense of loss? And the loss of a father's love is as sharp as it gets.

✍ *31 March*   The photo call. Donal courteous and helpful to the photographers; and in the technical, too: working people doing a job . . . He likes that.

Donal could certainly be tetchy and cantankerous with his fellow actors; but he had an unexpected generosity with photographers and technicians. He was always alarmed by pretension. He referred to acting as a job, and if the job was to give the photographer a good shot he took pleasure in doing it. That's why there are so many fine photographs of his performances.

The run in the Theatre Upstairs was a success: the intimacy of the sixty-five seat theatre, the dark lyricism of Sebastian's writing and the intensity of Donal's performance made it very special. During the run Donal had a certain routine. Sebastian writes, 'These were happy days, days of meeting Donal at a certain corner in Chelsea in the morning, watching for his slow figure in that black leather jacket to come ambling through the expensive houses.' He had digs round the corner in Chelsea. A mid-morning appointment at the bookies would be followed by a light lunch and a visit to the theatre, where he would walk through selected moments of the play. The important afternoon nap preceded an early arrival at the theatre. Following the performance he would have one, or at the most two, St Clements in the bar before the walk back for the stew which he had prepared before his afternoon nap. It was the life of a monk with the performance as the central act of reverence.

The run Upstairs – to excellent reviews – was followed by two weeks at the Gate Theatre in Dublin. Both the play and Donal's performance had been acclaimed, so I was less apprehensive at the Gate's opening night than per-haps I should have been. Dublin makes up its own mind on these occasions without any help from London. But the Gate was packed and Donal was on top form.

Nudity is always a particularly sensitive issue in Dublin. I remembered *A Prayer for my Daughter* in the Dublin Festival of 1979, where Donal had embraced and enfolded a stark naked Kevin McNally. The tender image crackled with tension, and Festival Director Hugh Leonard, who had looked in on the production in the course of his rounds, was unable to leave lest it be con-strued as a gesture of disapproval. In *The Steward of Christendom* the scene where Thomas Dunne is stripped naked and washed by the warder, Smith, went well. Donal ended the long first half with the wrenching story of his wife's death in childbirth. It was always a crucial moment and demanded as much from the audience as it did from Donal. The first half set up the Dunne family and the situation, while the second half delivered the most moving climax.

The interval arrived and I panicked in the face of the packed bar and the interval chat. I scurried down the steps and out into the faded elegance of Parnell Square where I sheltered behind a pillar. Behind me came two women in their thirties who were keen for a fag. As they lit up I tuned into their half-time verdict.

'Well,' said one thoughtfully in a cultivated Dublin accent, 'he's not a thin man.'

'Ah, go on, Margaret,' said the other. 'I wouldn't say no and neither would you.'

I recounted this conversation at notes the next day. Donal claimed it was an aesthetic verdict based on performance rather than physique. And so it was.

After the Dublin run we had further dates in Brighton, Luxembourg and Liverpool, but it was already clear that the initial run in the Theatre Upstairs had created a huge demand for the play. The arrival of a fully-fledged leading actor and a major new playwright with a distinctive style had taken London aback. Stephen Daldry responded and offered us an eight-week run Downstairs in the autumn of 1995.

Brighton started badly. The company flew from Dublin to Luton, and Donal hailed a taxi at Kings Cross and asked to be taken to Brighton. He explained loftily to Sonia that he had been unable to locate Kings Cross Thameslink which would have taken him to Brighton direct. Sonia was upset and feared that this was an ominous sign of extravagance to come. Donal was repentant and became happily involved in the technique required to conquer the Theatre Royal, which seated over eight hundred people. The Royal was respectably half-full, and it was good to see how Donal's voice and presence were able to command the space.

✎ *10 May 1995* Very pleasant journey from Brussels to Luxembourg with Sebastian; we feel like true Europeans on the Eurostar and on the Luxembourg Express. Luxembourg is a fortress city situated at the junction of two ravines. The Festival that we're part of is a bit haphazard though they're very charming. You don't get to meet the other companies: Polish, Danish, Spanish, Finnish, French and Italian. Not for the first time I realised how out of step with the rest of Europe is our text-based Anglo-Irish theatre tradition. 'Your English theatre is so old-fashioned, so traditional,' says a German journalist to me in the bar. But twenty minutes of a director-dominated, Eurotrash version of *Faust* had me cherishing our values afresh. It was clear that the limited run in the Theatre Upstairs, the two weeks in Dublin and the further two-week tour which Sonia had arranged for Out of Joint wouldn't satisfy the demand to see Sebastian's play and Donal's performance.

11 May   The canonisation of Donal proceeds apace in the Irish papers with everybody else's effort trivialised in comparison. Cara [Kelly, playing Maud] doesn't want to do the run Downstairs at the Royal Court in part because the role is small, but in part because Donal won't allow the other scenes to develop and makes loud harrumphing noises if they get too many laughs in the dinner scene. I'm sure he believes he is disciplining the company, but in fact a few laughs there ease the tension and help him change gear before the end. Cara says she is not the only one who is terrorised by him. The show clearly has a future, but how willing is everybody else to traipse around the world as an appendage to Donal's glory?

A large part of the audience tonight in Luxembourg were Irish exiles and the show was terrific. The second performance was even better, but the audience were mostly diplomatic corps. The British Ambassador gave a reception afterwards. It seems ironic that the English should be laying claim to a new play by an Irish writer with an entirely Irish cast led by Ireland's leading actor. However, without English enthusiasm and backing the play would probably not have been staged in Ireland at all. In fact the run in Dublin was funded in part by the British Council, 'and so it was the first Irish play ever to be toured into Ireland,' wrote Sebastian. 'The new British ambassador to Ireland had opened the champagne for us at the Dublin opening, and there was a great pleasure in the ease and simplicity of the relationship.'

The run back at the Royal Court at the end of August was full, and December 1995 found me back in Dublin rehearsing the play once more for festivals in Sydney, Adelaide and Wellington. Donal was at his most gracious in that bleak week before Christmas, welcoming the new actors on board and at ease in his own city. Sydney was terrific, although we played in a hard, old barn of a theatre. In Wellington they made a theatre for us in a warehouse on the quay. The crew who put the theatre together were friendly Scots, whose expertise took them round the world to festivals and rock concerts. The theatre they had built for us was grand but nobody had realised that the start of the performance coincided with the departure of the evening ferry to South Island. Donal's opening words were drowned by the mighty throb of the diesel engines. The next day the ferry changed its departure point: I couldn't imagine commerce bending the knee to art so gracefully in England.

The most important monument in many Australian or New Zealand towns is the war memorial, and the ambivalent situation of a man who loved both his country and his queen, but had to choose between them, struck a resonant chord in both countries. For many older New Zealanders their first trip abroad had been to join the Allied Forces in Europe in the service of the Crown.

'When I was a young recruit it used to frighten me how much I loved her,' says Thomas Dunne. 'The trains went sleekly through the fields, and her mark was everywhere, Ireland, Africa, the Canadas, every blessed place. And men like me were there to make everything peaceable, to keep order in her kingdoms. She was our pride.'   (*The Steward of Christendom, Act 1*)

So *The Steward of Christendom* lost none of its resonance in Wellington and was hailed as a wonder when it returned to the Gate in Dublin for a ten-week season. Donal's performance took its place alongside his performances as Captain Boyle in *Juno and the Paycock* and Frank Hardy in *Faith Healer* as icons of the Irish stage. One night after the play the barman at the Gate held out a phone to me. 'He wants to speak to someone involved in the play,' he said. It was an elderly member of that night's audience who had surfaced at a bar down the road. He was in tears, and wanted to tell someone what the play had meant to him. His mother and his aunts had always listened to the Queen's speech on Christmas Day, but he had had to keep this a secret from his friends and indeed the rest of his family.

The play affected the President too. I had known Mary Robinson at Trinity. She was the younger sister of Aubrey Bourke, Trinity's rugby captain, and she used to come and watch the matches in College Park. She asked to meet the company after the performance, so the cast assembled backstage in the Gate's hospitality suite: Donal in his shabby, dark-blue dressing gown. We waited for some time before the President arrived. It was evident at once why she had not appeared straight away: her mascara was all over the place and she was visibly overwhelmed by the play. She was gracious and talked of the play's achievement in restoring a piece of Irish history, which indeed it had. The Gate became a place of pilgrimage. Neil Jordan wrote, 'Sitting in the theatre, feeling the almost sacral nature of his relationship with the audience, I began to see elements in his performance that no movie could ever have caught. He could change the moment in so many ways, there was an existential quality to the meaning of his performance that in an odd way needed the transitory nature of a theatrical event. What was happening on stage would never happen again, in quite the same way.'

It had been an extraordinary period for Out of Joint too. At the same time as *The Steward of Christendom* had been playing in Dublin, *Three Sisters* had been touring India and *The Queen and I* was rehearsing to tour Australia. From a small fringe company, Out of Joint had become a mega international touring concern. Sonia handled the extraordinary expansion with equanimity.

Christmas 1996 found me in rehearsal once more. The final leg of *The Steward of Christendom* was to be a season at the Brooklyn Academy of Music in New York. The theatre was big and Donal was already ill, although we were not to know this till much later. His technique and timing in expanding his performance to the bigger theatre was flawless. It was the first occasion we had taken the play outside the confines of the ex-British Empire, and it was with some curiosity that we awaited the verdict of the *New York Times*. Everybody always pretends New York theatre is about something else and that an independent verdict is a possibility. It isn't. It's about the opinion of the *New York Times*, which is why it may be a great show city, but it's not a great town for theatre. But the *New York Times* was good . . . as was the *Irish Echo* ('this astonishing diamond of a play').

The last time I saw the play was the first night in New York, and I was concerned that Donal was beginning to slow the play both to accommodate the larger audience and to allow for a certain cultural slippage. Four minutes had been added to the running time. I was leaving the next morning so I spoke to Donal at the first night party. He was furious: 'Talk to Rory Murray,' he snarled. 'He's the one putting the fucking time on.' Rory must have been on stage during the whole play for all of ten minutes, whereas Donal never left it. I dared to say I thought Donal was reacting a bit unreasonably.

Two days later I was back in London when the stage manager called. Donal would like to talk to you on the phone, he said. 'You were quite right. We took four minutes off,' said Donal sweetly. 'I had a word with Rory,' he added. It was to be the last note I ever gave him.

When people ask who is the best actor I've ever worked with I usually talk about an ensemble and the many fine actors I've been privileged to work with. But if I'm feeling a bit more honest I just say, 'Donal McCann'.

Case Study

SOME EXPLICIT POLAROIDS
Mark Ravenhill

Workshop: from 18 March 1999

Rehearsal: 23 August 1999

First Performance: 30 September 1999

Cast: Russell Barr, Nick Dunning, Fritha Goodey, Sally Rogers, David Sibley, Matthew Wait

Published: Some Explicit Polaroids (Methuen, 1999)

I first met Mark Ravenhill at an evening of short plays at the Finborough, a fringe theatre in West London.

🔊 MARK RAVENHILL: It was an evening about playing with erotic themes, called *'I'll show you mine'*, and I wrote this little play called *Fist*, which Max came to see. We exchanged a few words downstairs, and Max expressed an interest in a full-length play. I didn't have a full-length play, so I decided to write one quickly while his interest was there and before he forgot that we'd met, so I wrote *Shopping and Fucking* in the next four months. He got back to me to say he had read and liked the play, so we met up.

The meeting took place with no particular commitment from Out of Joint, and certainly with no idea that I might eventually be directing the play. Sometimes meetings with writers are laboured occasions when it is impossible to express any reservations about the play without sending the writer into a state of advanced misery. But Mark Ravenhill was open and engaged. The meeting lasted an hour and a half, and he was enthusiastic about taking on a new draft. There was one character who had no lines but who followed the others round with a camera. The point eluded me as did Mark's baffling explanation, but anyway the character disappeared from subsequent drafts. I looked forward to the next meeting, but then Mark disappeared himself. I had become intrigued by the play and the title, so after some difficulty I eventually tracked Mark down to the Salisbury Playhouse, where he had been directing a children's play. We had several further meetings in the course of which I found myself recommending other directors to Mark with less and less enthusiasm. I had become hooked, and it became clear that I was going to direct the play myself.

The shape of *Shopping and Fucking* changed quite a bit in the course of rewrites and particularly as the result of a ten-day workshop at the National Theatre Studio. But through all this the kernel of the play remained the same. It was about two young people adrift in London, and their emotional relationship with a slightly older father-figure, who is struggling with a heroin addiction. They get caught up in a drugs deal that goes hilariously wrong and are given a lecture in market economics by a sinister crime boss. The most comic moment was a long shaggy-dog story, in which the character called Mark, who was to be played by Lloyd Hutchinson, claimed to have had sex with Princess Di and Fergie, the Duchess of York, in the Gents' toilet of a London club, both dressed as policewomen, with Di very much taking the lead. We were performing the play in Leeds on the night after Princess Di's car crash, and I got a panicked phone call from Lloyd pointing out that this material had become well-nigh combustible in the period of national hysteria that followed her death. An instant rewrite was essayed, and the chief protagonist in this subterranean toilet orgy became the Duchess of York.

The play's title was the cause of much discussion and proved a test of manhood for various broadsheet editors. The *Daily Telegraph* and *The Times* opted for the safety of asterisks while the *Independent*, the *Guardian* and, of course, intrepid *Time Out* went all the way with the title. Philip Roberts records Sonia Friedman's worries:

◀) SONIA FRIEDMAN: I was nervous. Max not remotely. We had a lot of serious discussions about it, and I was completely wrong. I thought the problem was that we were a relatively new, young touring company, and I thought we were going to be in legal trouble with it. I recall a lot of discussions with Max, asking if we were going to be laughed out of town, and Max said, 'No, we stick with the title.' And, of course, he was completely right, and I think if it had been called anything else, it would have signalled that the times were different.

But Sonia wasn't alone with her sensitivity; when the play finally transferred to the West End the sign-writers employed to erect the name outside the theatre declined the job on moral grounds.

The journey for *Shopping and Fucking* was eventually to embrace five separate productions, and Out of Joint would tour it to nine different countries. But the play began in the tiny studio arrangement that Stephen Daldry had chiselled out of the Ambassadors Theatre during the Royal Court's exile from Sloane Square. (From 1996 to 1999 the Royal Court was being rebuilt and the theatre occupied the Ambassadors and the Duke of York's Theatre.) In this proximity the play was at its most intense, and on the first night at a crucial moment the *Times* critic galloped towards the exit in desperate need of some fresh air. In Bristol people fainted in the Old Vic's confined studio space. But with success the play moved into bigger theatres where it became much more dependent on the wit and humour of the writing, and the intensity was defused by the laughter.

More than with any other play I can think of, I started or continued a series of relationships during the course of *Shopping and Fucking* that were to be of enormous importance to Out of Joint: with Mark himself, of course, but also with the actors: Lloyd Hutchinson, Kate Ashfield, Russell Barr, Stephen Beresford, Ian Redford, Sally Rogers and Robin Soans. The quality of Out of Joint's work can be traced to this continuity. It's the nearest to an ensemble that you can create, given Out of Joint's touring commitment and economic circumstances.

🔉 MARK RAVENHILL: What I'd anticipated that Max would focus on would be the social aspect of the play, which he did, and actors were sent off to interview drug addicts, rent boys etc., though I didn't really feel it was terribly important to the play, which I'd written as a kind of urban fairy story. But what surprised me was how much Max was interested in the archetypal qualities of the characters, in particular the kind of Jungian archetypes. We did some movement exercises to explore the characters, which you don't associate with Max. We looked at archetypes, like the mother, the hero . . . And we used that quite a lot in unlocking the play. Bad and good fathers, bad and good mothers. Actually, that revealed things to me about the play itself that I wasn't aware of . . . The other thing that I appreciated when I first worked with Max, and still do, is a line which you see through Bill Gaskill, and that is just a real passion about directing the text, really looking at each line, where the stress is, and what the rhythm of the line is . . . There's not much democracy. Max is generally absolutely prepared. When you start actioning, you see that he's actioned the whole scene the night before, so on the whole he'll suggest the actions because otherwise it would take for ever. And if somebody comes up with a much better action, then he'll pencil his out. But if you compare what he started and ended the day with, relatively few actions have been changed.

🔊 I spend the first two weeks of a five-week rehearsal period breaking the play into units and then working on actions. A unit is determined by what the character that runs the scene wants. So the opening unit of *Some Explicit Polaroids* could be called 'Nick wants to befriend Helen'. Nick has just been let out of prison after a long sentence for a politically motivated kidnapping and assault. He is desperate to get a place to stay and some dry clothes. An action is the tactic the protagonist takes to achieve that objective, and it has to be described with a transitive verb. Nick's first line in the play is 'Hello Helen'. Clearly a pretty neutral line, but in the context of the situation where Helen is shocked to find her old boyfriend on her doorstep after years in prison the action is probably 'steadies' or possibly 'befriends'. Helen then responds 'Fucking hell', which is 'resists' or 'reprimands', and Nick's second line is 'I tried to ring you', which is 'reassures'. And so on. It's a method which places analysis before instinct but is none the worse for that.

I had first met Lloyd Hutchinson when I was directing *A Jovial Crew* at Stratford, and he had also been in *Three Sisters* and Timberlake Wertenbaker's *The Break of Day* in 1995. Towards the end of the run of *Three Sisters*, I gave the script to Barnaby Kay, who was playing Tuzenbach and, without telling me, he gave it to Lloyd.

🔊 LLOYD HUTCHINSON: We read it, and we weren't turned on by it at all. We said, 'Oh God. This is weird.' Kate Ashfield liked it and wanted to do it. I ended up doing it when it went into the West End before a world tour, because there was an actor in the role I played who couldn't hack it. So Max phoned me up and the next day I was rehearsing.

The script we had read was very different to the way it ended up. I think Mark owes a huge debt to Max for *Shopping and Fucking* becoming the phenomenon it was. If anybody whipped Mark into shape, it was Max, who suggested a way the play could go. And that's kind of what can happen in rehearsals with Max. You'll be sitting there, and he'll say something like, 'Oh, I get it now. This is a play about . . .', and then he'll say a couple of weeks later, 'Yes, but it could be about . . .' So it's finding the meaning of the work . . . the meaning can change.

When the play went into the West End, it was absolutely brilliant. On Shaftesbury Avenue, *Shopping and Fucking* was next to Ben Elton's *Popcorn*. There I was shagging a guy up the arse in front of all these tourists. People had come to a West End show, a night out you know, and there's me. And it was hilarious and dangerous, the way theatre should be.

I had seen Ian Redford's work at the Royal Court but was to work with him for the first time on *Shopping and Fucking*.

◀) IAN REDFORD: The first thing I did with Max was a tour of *Shopping and Fucking*. It was being completely recast. Before that, I'd been up to see him for seven jobs. First thing to do was sit down and start actioning. And we started doing a few exercises, a few improvisations . . . Someone went off to research a rehab centre.

He likes to keep some distance. If you are sat at a table at lunch, he'll sit at another table. He prefers to worry on his own. There is that extraordinary balance he has between affection, loyalty and that distance, that detachment. He makes actors feel he respects them. I've never, ever felt that he's not been available. Sally Rogers [actor] said the worst you get from Max is, 'You're just not getting this, are you?'

THE REHEARSAL PERIOD

The international success of *Shopping and Fucking* coincided with the 'discovery' of new English theatre writing by colleagues abroad, and 'in-yer-face theatre' became a fashionable phenomenon. The pressure on Mark and the anticipation surrounding his work weren't entirely dispelled by the Actors Touring Company production of his next play, *Handbag*. We were due to start rehearsal on a brand new play by Mark at the end of June 1999, but he hadn't been well, and the delivery date was further postponed. The complex script was due at the end of December 1998, and by that point we had five scenes. By March 1999 the title had changed from *We're Happy Now* to *Some Explicit Polaroids*. At the end of April, Mark was ill again, and I've never seen a man more relieved when I suggested we postpone rehearsals in order to give him more writing time. We had to substitute another play and Graham Cowley, Out of Joint's Producer, had the difficult task of ringing the theatres where Out of Joint had been booked to explain that, instead of the eagerly awaited new play by the infamous Mark Ravenhill, Out of Joint would be substituting a first play, *Drummers*, by a completely unknown writer, Simon Bennett, who had done time for housebreaking. In addition Graham had to arrange a new tour for *Some Explicit Polaroids*, which would now begin rehearsal in three weeks, after *Drummers* had opened in Bury St Edmunds. It was a difficult situation, but, to their great credit, all the theatres that had booked *Some Explicit Polaroids* responded positively. They accepted our dilemma with great understanding.

🔊 MARK RAVENHILL: We did a workshop, and then I went away and did various bits of writing, none of which really amounted to a play. We actually started rehearsing with bits of stuff, but nothing much else. Whereas with *Shopping and Fucking* I had written about three drafts of the play, with *Polaroids* it was a very different process. We had a workshop based on no play. We began rehearsal still with no play.

During the technical rehearsal of *Drummers* in Cambridge the latest draft of *Some Explicit Polaroids* arrived. I read it between the end of the tech and the first performance. Stylistically it seemed a departure from any of the earlier drafts. Cambridge is one of those English towns that still doesn't have a decent hotel. Later that night in the discomfort of a bleak bed and breakfast, after the first preview of *Drummers* had fallen apart in front of a handful of puzzled punters, I wrote, 'This is not going to be a particularly easy one either. The writing is more fantasy-driven and more gothic than previous drafts. There's good stuff in both, but welding the two together will be hard.'

Part of the problem was that Mark's rewriting had embarked on an entirely different and fresh direction taking little account of any previous back-story. On the first day of rehearsals for *Some Explicit Polaroids* we read the two different drafts of the material Mark had written. David Sibley was alarmed to find that his character didn't exist at all in the second of the two versions.

Like *Shopping and Fucking*, *Some Explicit Polaroids* is an urban fairy tale. The plot concerns Nick, who has been in prison for twenty years for kidnapping and assault. On his release, he attempts to pick up the relationship with his radical girlfriend Helen, but in the intervening time she has become a Labour councillor committed to overhauling deregulated bus timetables rather than overthrowing the government. This Rip Van Winkle device of transporting the revolutionary hero, Nick, through a time lapse into the middle of Blair's second term gave the play a strong political context. Nick became an Innocent Hero blundering through the blunted Britain of Blair's second term and finding that there was not much occasion or demand for his radicalisation and rage. In a parallel plot, Tim, who is HIV positive, orders a Russian sex slave, Victor, from the Internet. Both are resolute that their relationship should remain on a level of total superficiality and are deter-mined they will never have any deeper feeling for each other. In contrast, Tim's New Agey friend, Nadia, has deep feelings for everybody. The characters are completed with Jonathan, the victim of Nick's kidnapping attempt, who is now a Soros-type multi-millionaire. He has learned that Nick is out of prison and is determined to find him.

Most classical drama is concerned with the crisis in the life of a single protagonist, say, Hamlet. Or at most, two protagonists like Romeo and Juliet. Peter Stein says that the real significance of Chekhov is that 'He has released us from Shakespeare's "terrible tyranny of hierarchy".' After Chekhov, theatre was able to concern itself with the scrutiny of a group of people rather than with a single hero. The problem with the group play is principally in sustaining and developing the lives of all the characters, and that became our task with *Some Explicit Polaroids*. Mark had defined the characters very clearly, and they had a strong starting point to their journeys. In rehearsal we set out to define the detail of each character.

✍ *23 Aug   SexPol* begins. Fritha [Goodey, playing Nadia] does a very good neurotic. She seems excellent. So do the whole cast. Keeping personal and political together. Is Nick the central character? Does he run-through the whole play? Whose story is it? Scene 2: Nick and Helen might be better in the old draft. Miss the scene where Victor and Tim go off to bed in Nadia's flat. Helen blaming Nick for split-up has gone in new version . . . Not a bad first day. Read through first two scenes swapping material about.

So at the end of the day we had Scene 1 from Draft 1 and Scene 2 from Draft 2. No wonder my Diary recorded ruefully:

> Editing is very elusive. The different versions skid about. Mark has till Monday to sort it out. We get Tuesday to work on the script and Wednesday (a.m.) to read it again, before I'm into the *Drummers* tech in the afternoon.

In the same week that we started rehearsal for *Some Explicit Polaroids*, *Drummers* had finished a regional tour and was opening at the Ambassadors.

✍ *24 Aug*   Talking to Joe [White, Assistant Director] about the 1983 Miners' Strike. Remembering how political people were and how wide-ranging discussions had become. I know we mustn't panic in the face of bits of play, but panicking anyway. Conversation with Mark: find out through-line and where scenes will fit in. Should it end with a violent confrontation between Jonathan the capitalist and Nick the ex-revolutionary? Maybe we have to accept that although capitalism throws up huge injustices, it's the big survivor . . . a bitter-sweet ending. The characters put the lid back on their lives. How did Nadia get New Agey? When did Victor arrive at the airport? How many of these questions do we really need to answer? Formidable amount of work to do, but Mark seems in good heart. *Afternoon*: We improvise story of Nick's kidnapping of Jonathan, and his relationship with Helen. Not very detailed, but still it gives us something to go on.

25 Aug   In Mark's mind Nick had kidnapped and assaulted Jonathan. The detail of how the attack had been planned, whether Nick had devised it on his own, how long he had been sentenced for and what life was like in prison were not of great interest to Mark, nor would they ever be included in the plot, but it was important for the actors and for me to grasp details as a starting point. Still no movement at the Ambassadors box office for either *Drummers* or *SexPol*. What can you expect? It's August . . . people are on holiday. But it's hard to keep your nerve. Idea of Helen pursuing Nick through the play. Nick pursuing Nadia, and Jonathan pursuing Nick. Final scene should be Nick and Helen at last together . . . a few compromises . . . watching the telly . . . a Millamant and Mirabell contrast, says Mark. [In Congreve's *The Way of*

The World (1700), Millamant and Mirabell agree to live together but, famously, draw up a contract of conditions. *Some Explicit Polaroids* was to end with Nick and Helen also agreeing on a *modus vivendi*. They arrived at a working relationship but with some sense of loss.]

26 Aug   A session this a.m., pinning up the scenes in order and locating those that need work.

This storyboard dominated the rehearsal room and became the map of our world. It helped us to plan the journey of the play and to pinpoint the missing scenes that would complete the story. But my Diary records the panic and confusion:

✍ *28 Aug*   Conversation with Mark: Scene 1 is now Nick and Helen again! First of all, he returns from prison to his old girlfriend. Then Tim brings Victor back from the airport to Nadia's. New Scene 2. Then Scene 3 could be Jonathan and Helen, and Scene 4 would be the old Scene 1 – Nadia bringing Nick back to her flat after she's been beaten up. Then hospital scene. No, before that would be the old Scene 2 . . . Blimey . . . I can't fucking make head or tail of it. The better scenes tend to be the older ones that Mark has worked on for a while. Given he's been working on it for a year without reaching the end, it's a fantasy to imagine that he can finish it all off in the next three weeks. He goes away to write in the afternoon.

Later: Spoke to Mark on the phone. He now wants to change Scene 1 again, and have Nick meeting Nadia at the club as the first scene. Of course that would be great, but I fear it's baby and bathwater time. The opening scene with Helen and Nick works well. Mark has to have a proper go at those scenes which don't work! However, Jonathan as Soros, who is funding the AIDS ward where Tim is being treated, is a good development and brings those two story-lines together.

In a later conversation, Mark explained that all his plays to date had headed towards a major climactic moment – Gary being buggered in *Shopping and Fucking*, a child having its body burned with cigarettes in *Handbag*. He felt uncertain about a sad and pragmatic realism. I suggested that a compromise ending was perhaps more appropriate to where we were. But was I saying the right thing?

✍ *31 Aug*   New read through. Some mysteries are revealed. What does Tim do? This is the character that Russell Barr plays who picks up Victor via the Internet. He appears to have enough money. As ever I'm determined to uncover the background of the characters, but it's not always that interesting to Mark.

2 Sept   (*Drummers*) Pretty good first preview last night at the Ambassadors Theatre and it sustained itself on a continuum of rage. [Our hasty reprogramming meant that *Drummers* and *Some Explicit Polaroids* were playing one after the other at the New Ambassadors Theatre.] (*SexPol*) Recut and hacked about Scene 5. Mark very good at rethinking on his feet. A new chilly scene between Nadia and Jonathan resurfaced. A bit weird. As he says, Mark moves towards violent confrontation given half a chance.

3 Sept   Rehearsal trundling along. Even though we don't have all the script, we keep actioning away. Unless he writes a lot more, I can't start staging it till after the weekend.

4 Sept   I watch *Drummers*, give notes, stagger home. *SexPol* looks as if it's going to be twelve scenes. We have seven complete scenes, plus three prototypes with bits of scene to come, plus two missing scenes yet to be written. It has a winning air but still much to be done. The good scenes *much* better than the next best.

6 Sept   Third week of rehearsal. Spent most of the day actioning. In the afternoon, Mark arrived with the new Scene 5 and we made some progress with that. In fact, we got through half the scene, breaking it down into units and doing actions. Cast buoyant. Writing lively if erratic. It appears to have been a good first night for *Drummers* at the Ambassadors and a very pleasant party afterwards.

Because of these changes in schedule and because it was still the summer holiday, the advance bookings were poor. When I had been at the Royal Court, I had had no time, or indeed inclination, to become involved in workshops for schools, but with Out of Joint they were set to become an increasingly important part of our programme. Over the years of Out of

Joint's existence, Theatre Studies had become a major growth industry and young theatregoers were both more informed and more sophisticated.

✍ *7 Sept*   Schools' mailout fucked because it was put in wrong envelopes. Cross after all the time I've taken with it. I have to do it again in the evening. Topping and tailing letters and stuffing envelopes isn't the best use of my time at the moment. Mark has finally delivered Scene 6. It's brief: three pages. It's taken him all day. Goodish work this morning, and we've now actioned all the script we've got. It's time to start moving things, even though I think we're a few sandwiches short of a major repast.

8 Sept   Surprisingly easy day. Beginning to move a couple of scenes which flowed well after all the editing and messing about. Julian's set lends itself more easily to the public scenes – airport, House of Commons – than it does to the private scene in somebody's flat, but that's okay. Three scenes short now. Alarming that Mark wants to go to Manchester on Saturday night for somebody's party. We must have one more scene if not two by the start of next week. The problem is that with all this writing, Mark isn't in rehearsals much. Pity, because he's very lively when he is.

On the morning of 9 September my mother rang at about 8 a.m. My much loved father had died. I went down to Brighton at once, and over the next few days funeral arrangements and obituaries took over the moment I left rehearsal. The cast were very supportive.

✍ *10 Sept*   Mark presented a version of the penultimate scene (Scene 10). It concludes their stories, but the end of Helen's story is missing and Jonathan is missing too. Mark wants to have another go at getting them both into this scene so there's one great big scene before the coda with Nick and Helen. So it's eleven scenes. Makes sense. But, later we reconsider; Jonathan won't go into the big scene, so there are two final codas. One will be the long-awaited meeting between Jonathan, the capitalist, and Nick, his kidnapper, and finally a scene which sees the relationship between Nick and Helen moving on to a more comfortable partnership.

Maggie McCarthy has the measure of Donal McCann in *The Steward of Christendom*.

Russell Barr is the proud owner of Matthew Wait in *Some Explicit Polaroids*.

Danny Sapani is Macbeth.

Max Stafford-Clark.

13 Sept   I realise that at the moment there are two consecutive scenes which feature Nadia having been beaten up by her violent offstage boyfriend Simon. We need a scene in between. Mark sees the problem and a scene between Nick and Helen is improvised. Mark will write a scene which will show Nick desperate to fit in to Helen's domestic arrangements. However, her objective is to get Nick to agree to meet Jonathan. What a relief it is to be in rehearsal. Heaviness descends the moment I get out. Still way behind with the script, but we're getting there.

14 Sept   Seemed to make progress this morning with the scene where Nick comes round to Nadia's flat and is faced with the banal but determinedly hedonistic philosophy of Tim and his Russian rent-boy, Victor. But in the afternoon we moved on to Scene 9. This takes place in the mortuary. Tim has died of AIDS, but, in one of Mark's characteristically outrageous touches, he emerges in the scene as a ghost and orders Victor to masturbate him. Victor does so at the same time protesting: 'There's got to be more than this. What is there? This is . . . animals. What makes us better than animals? Revolution never saved us. Money never saved us. No love. I want more than this.' Trouble is much of the debate seems similar to an earlier scene. How is it different? How have things progressed? Well . . . Victor's position has changed, but otherwise I came up with no answers. An arid afternoon.

15 Sept   The opening scene looks excellent . . . very witty. Then we look at the end of the play again. Helen, who is a Labour Councillor when the play begins, is set to become an MP and goes up before a selection committee. Sally Rogers has met Rima, a Labour Councillor, and has done some excellent research on the hazards facing prospective MPs. Trouble is I've not allowed the research enough time to filter down, and there aren't enough specific lines in the scene to make it clear just how difficult it is to become an MP. But then Mark has barely been in rehearsal because he is writing.

I wouldn't normally advocate a read through at the end of the fourth week of rehearsal, but we were becoming so involved in the detail of each character's story that it seemed a good idea to try and gain a more global view before the final week's rehearsal.

✍ *17 Sept*   Read through. Reveals the play has bounding energy and great wit. Mark thought Scene 6 wasn't sufficiently pivotal. This is the scene where Helen justifies her political position. Her drive is to make things better bit by bit. Mark thinks it should be rooted in something biographical, like her mum was mugged three times or whatever. I think that will be good. Mark always comes slowly towards realism. His style is much more at a tangent and much more interesting.

That night Mark wrote this speech for Helen: 'My mum. Living up here. Half the time the lift doesn't work. Which in some ways is a blessing. They stink of piss and there are needles on the floor. So she takes the stairs. Seventy-five and she's climbing fifteen flights of stairs. You don't know who's there. Muggers. Dealers. You take your life in your hands. Year before she died she was mugged three times. That finished her off.' It made the argument personal.

✍ *Sat 18 Sept*   The play read for one hour twenty-eight minutes yesterday, and I reckon will play for one hour thirty-five, so Mark and I agree we won't have an interval. Did good work in the morning on a couple of the earlier scenes. A pretty solid week despite the emotional toll. I'm reluctant to let rehearsal end, as a dull despondency takes over as soon as my mind is not engaged. At the end of the session we do Nadia's journey through the play . . . in five minutes.

Again this was an exercise designed to give each actor an overall view of the progress of their character. Thus we ran through the whole play in a condensed and speedy version lasting five minutes. This was entirely from Nadia's point of view, with Fritha as Nadia selecting key lines and pushing any particular emotion to extremes. We then chose a single verb to describe Nadia's state at the beginning of each scene and another word at the end. Thus in Scene 2 Nadia starts 'delighted' and ends 'excluded'. She goes to the airport with Tim in order to meet the Russian boyfriend he has ordered over the Internet, but ends up having an argument with Tim. She cannot accept that he doesn't wish to have any 'feelings' at all for his 'sex slave' Victor. It clarifies the progression of each character's journey.

✍ *19 Sept*   Down to Brighton again and conversations about a memorial service.

20 Sept   Further sorting of the script, particularly with regard to the last three scenes. Nick is still running after Nadia in Scene 9, but since we now know that he finishes up with Helen in Scene 12 we have to bring the pursuit of Nadia to a credible conclusion. I think we manage it, but it involves quite a lot of reshifting speeches. Confusing for the actors with only one week's rehearsal to go. 'Would you say that's it?' asked Nick Dunning hopefully, after yet one more change. A formidable amount of work still to do.

The work was not simply in getting the script right and concluding the story-lines; there was a considerable level of emotion to attain which had become neglected.

✍ *21 Sept*   We began the day with a ten-minute run-through. It's hilarious and it helps to clarify the shape of the whole play. Spent most of the afternoon jacking up the energy and obsession levels. Mark writes about obsession very clearly. Thus Nick starts with a fixation about the necessity for revolutionary action, but by Scene 6 all this energy has been invested into being a house-husband and looking after Helen. Nick and Helen are like Beatrice and Benedick – splitting apart from each other to come together again in the middle, split up once more, and then come together again at the end. All three of the love stories have an emotional depth certainly not present in *Shopping and Fucking*. Nick loves Nadia, but also loves Helen. Victor loves Tim so five of the six characters are emotionally linked.

22 Sept   Good purposeful day. We cracked on, got the end of the play right at least once and realised how hard the middle scene with Nick and Helen is to pull off. There are even more emotional levels than I had realised. *Afternoon*: Mark exhausted and falls asleep in the green room.

23 Sept   Worked on scenes during the day and finally ran the play in the evening. It lasted 1 hour 34 minutes. The acting seemed excellent, but I was too tired to spot any weaknesses in the structure. Mark says he thought Scene 10 was a bit static. I attributed it to the continued presence of Tim's ghost, who is still hanging around. I say I think he's had his moment of theatrical impact, and what's more we're trying to bring the stories to a conclusion for each character . . . not seeking to prolong them. Mark is getting a bit chilly with me, and I honestly don't know why . . . Is he focused on the play and can't find a conclusion? Or is he just exhausted?

24 Sept   A happier Mark arrives with a new scene from which the ghost has been exorcised. I'll do another run through tomorrow but will probably spend Monday doing scenes and won't do a third run-through until the Dress next Thursday in Bury St Edmunds. Yikes!

In fact the ghost of Tim did make a touching reappearance. After Tim's death, Victor is leaving to go to Japan. Nadia takes a farewell Polaroid of him and the ghost appears at the last minute at the edge of the photograph. The unexpected appearance of Russell Barr (playing Tim) now with ghostly white make-up, and in a white suit, always caused a shiver to run-through the audience. The white suit took a heavy toll on the costume budget, but I reckon it was worth it.

✍ *Sat 25 Sept*   Run through. In notes I define the three different stages of the play as Chaos, Demolition and Reconstruction. Whereas on Thursday the Chaos of actors doing the very first run-through led naturally to that section being instinctive and triumphant, today the final three scenes, Reconstruction, were much more carefully placed. Demolition, the dark heart of the play, is very powerful. Certainly, I've never heard a response to AIDS debated so candidly or seen a corpse wanked off on stage ere now. I've been pretty beady about punctuation. Because the actors are most at home with naturalism, they don't follow the short sentences, so when there are two actions on one line, it tends to become condensed into one. Jeremy James, the choreographer, and his partner, Sonia, arrive to choreograph the dance at the end . . . Once we define that we want cheesy they crack into it. It's very pragmatic. She dances a few steps. He changes it, and then they teach it to Fritha and Matthew. It's a finale worthy of Torvill and Dean. Fritha drapes herself like dying swan over Matthew. Very tacky – very Mark Ravenhill.

On the final Monday before going up to Bury St Edmunds, where we were to open the play, I did some final work on the backgrounds and the backstories of the characters. This has been neglected while we wrestled with the structure.

✍ *27 Sept*   We decide: that Tim (Russell Barr) has been HIV positive since he was nineteen. He's now twenty-five. Nadia is an only child. Her dad was something like chairman of Allied Dunbar. She had a nanny. In passing, she says in the script that her dad was a paedophile. Is this true? Yes. How does that affect her? Makes you search for 'proper' love, makes you promiscuous . . . sent to boarding school. In her scene with Jonathan (Scene 8) it is the first time she articulates her fragility and despair. Victor: became gay very late. Studied mineralogy. Met wife. Collapse of Soviet Union. Worked as a cab driver. Took western businessmen to go-go club. Thought it was an easier way to make money. Good day's rehearsal. Decide not to run it again. After all, anything we gain from that will happen anyway over the next few days.

To the National in the evening for the Platform NT 2000 reading of *Top Girls*. Amazingly, the National has assembled the entire original cast, seventeen years on. Joan Bakewell chairs the discussion. Caryl (Churchill) herself lingers anonymously in the wings . . . Joan Bakewell asked if I was aware at the time that I was reading 'a significant and major script' (i.e. *Top Girls*). I explain that I received the script piecemeal, and that it wasn't quite like that. Actually it's never like that. It's always like *Some Explicit Polaroids*. You're attempting to orchestrate chaos on a daily basis. 'Triumph and disaster' hover like vultures over the whole journey. Only at the very end does one of those bastards sheer away. Is *Some Explicit Polaroids* 'a significant and major script'? I hope so. I am the only man on the Platform. Carole [Hayman: Dull Gret and Angie in the original production of *Top Girls*] says she remembers that I directed the first scene so that it was miserable whereas she says it should be a celebration of women's achievements. Carole is reconstructing history in public according to feminist doctrine. It should be a deft balance of celebration and regret. Celebration, but each of the protagonists had lost children, some of them have been through enormous pain and sacrifice. I end the Platform feeling cross and ungracious. How silly of me. Still: it's hard to celebrate the past when you're struggling so hard with the present.

28 Sept   Manage to tech four scenes before we finish at 10.30 p.m. Julian McGowan's set looks good, but the acting disappears in a welter of costumes. Nadia disappears inside a Michelin Man's coat that makes acting both difficult and noisy. It will have to go, stylish though it is.

There's no entry in my Diary for September 29, but we must have finished the tech and done a dress rehearsal. I expect I was too fraught to write anything.

✍ *30 Sept*   First night in Bury St Edmunds goes well. General approval, but a feeling of lack of substance is there. I think it could be played with more gravitas, and that we probably do need more weight in the playing of the last two scenes. In the writing of the final scene. At the moment the play seems to stop rather than conclude.

After the first preview, Mark added some lines to the final scene. In themselves they were banal enough . . . about it raining and Helen's anxiety over whether Nick would get to the polling station in time. But, once again, they served to place the scene and set it in a mundane but moving domestic context. After the big ideas Nick and Helen were getting on with their lives.

✍ *8 Oct*   The play still needs work. Have I left enough time for it? The anxiety when you have a show up and running is always that it will settle and jell before vital changes can be perceived and made.

After a week in Bury St Edmunds and a week in the studio at Sheffield, we opened our London run at the Ambassadors Theatre. This had been freshly vacated by the Royal Court who, under the direction of Stephen Daldry, had moved back to the beautifully renovated theatre in Sloane Square. Both *Drummers* and *Some Explicit Polaroids* were, in effect, presented by Out of Joint acting as a commercial management for the London run and raising money. The financial terms were risky, but we hoped that the close presence to the Royal Court's season would help at the box office. It didn't.

✍ *12 Oct*   London tech (at the Ambassadors) goes smoothly. I go down to the Duke of York's for lunch with Royal Court's staff. I'm greeted with embarrassment and welcome both, like the Ghost of

Christmas Past . . . Very good first preview. Audience responsive, but young people a bit over-enthusiastic at any smut. Actors beginning to have more authority and to know where to change gear, to change from comic expectation to dramatic.

At the same time as *Some Explicit Polaroids* was previewing at the Ambassadors, *Drummers* was opening in Colchester.

✍ *13 Oct*   Not a terribly interesting preview [of *SexPol*]. Two student parties meant it was hard for the actors to keep their shape. To Colchester in the afternoon for the tech of *Drummers*. Back in the evening for the performance of *SexPol*. Wally Shawn was in the audience and, as always, was positive and polite. But the performance was lacking in sophistication because the audience pushed it somewhere else. If one hundred kids implode every time the word 'cock' is mentioned, where can you go? A long, long day.

14 Oct   Royal Court script meeting. My first for some time. Quite dull. We discuss *4:48 Psychosis*, Sarah Kane's final prose poem / play that preceded her suicide. Ironically, I find it much more theatrical and more vivid than her plays. First night at the Ambassadors – warm feelings at the post-show party. It seems to have gone well.

I still attended Royal Court script meetings and observed Stephen Daldry's decisions about the plays with interest, but no longer with the agony of responsibility. I could make little sense of Sarah Kane's early work and must confess that, had I still been running the Royal Court, I would have offered little enthusiasm. On the other hand, Stephen had been notably unenthusiastic about *The Weir*. I had supported it, but the decision to programme it must have been marginal. It turned out to be a long-running hit that made Conor McPherson's career and which owed everything to Ian Rickson's enthusiasm in backing it. Selecting 'significant and major scripts' was, it seemed, as hazardous and random as ever.

✍ *15 Oct*   The reviews begin to trickle in; they're pretty tepid. 'We've seen it before and Mark can't shock us this time' sort of stuff. Certainly no raves. This may be a reaction to *Shopping and Fucking*, but even the bad reviews make it sound pretty lively. Reviews in the *Independent* and *Guardian* have appeared in some editions but not in all.

I'm furious at allowing critics to review overnight. Inevitably it leads to shoddy writing and snap judgements.

18 Oct   Coffee with Sonia. She has offered me a production of [David Mamet's] *Speed-the-Plow*, and we discuss how it would be possible to direct that and revive *Our Lady of Sligo* in New York. The project came to Sonia via Patrick Marber, and he is to act in it with Mark Strong. I don't see how I can do that and revive *Our Lady of Sligo* in New York . . . To the Ambassadors where a packed house for *SexPol* appears to be having a terrific time. Later, Patrick Marber rings to say it was a storming show . . . I talk to him, and we conclude that it's unlikely that I am going to be able to do the Mamet. He suggested that Joe Penhall, whose idea it was, should act as assistant. It would certainly be a way to get to know two good new writers, but I feel drawn to New York.

26 Oct   Dinner with Mel [Kenyon, Ravenhill's agent]. I say how fond I have become of Mark and how panicked I believe him to have been both at the point when I took the decision to swap plays, and, understandably, somewhere in week four of rehearsal. We agree the critics have under-estimated *SexPol,* but then we would.

27 Oct   At the end of the Ambassadors run there was a further two weeks tour and then a date in Oporto. Mark offers to include an interactive element – other travellers at the airport; maybe another dancer, friend of Victor, in the club scene. These will be cast locally and played in the local language. I'd better tell Portugal.

SexPol played at the Oporto Festival on 8–9 December 1999. Ravenhill wrote a sequence which was added to Scene 2 for the international tour of his play. Actors from the host country played the sequence in their own language.

✍ *14 Nov*   I see Mark, who tells me that the new character will be a mother and her daughter in the airport scene and one older man in the nightclub scene who will take Victor off to Japan.

19 Nov   Audience clearly had a good time, judging by the response.

The play had a further life after its initial run. Early the next year, 2000, it was revived to complete some English touring dates and to play in Paris. It was revived a second time a couple of months later. Eventually the 'inter-active' element was played in Portuguese, German, Lithuanian and French. Tricia Kelly took over the role of Helen. She remembers:

🔊 TRICIA KELLY: Max had never seen me for anything, and then I got this phone call to go and meet him and Mark for a reading of *Polaroids*. So I just went round and read, and it was stuff I knew about. I'd been there in various ways, so it was right . . . Mark was lovely, a sweetheart. I don't know what I expected. I suppose I expected someone much more in-yer-face, and shocking, and challenging, and he was just the most delightful, friendly, interesting, middle-class boy.

It was a slightly different situation, because it was a show Max had already done, but what was very good was that Ian [Redford, who replaced Nick Dunning as Nick] and I were allowed to go through the whole process. So we actioned and re-actioned and read, and Max would check, because he had a note of what the original actions were and how we were differing, but that was fine . . . That was a process that both Ian and I knew about. It was through Joint Stock that I learned about actioning, and had done it ever since [Tricia Kelly played in *Fen* for Joint Stock in 1983, directed by Les Waters]. What Max and other Royal Court people trained by him do is a sort of abbreviated version of that. You break the text into units of actions, all active rather than passive . . . It was fantastic to have a means of being very specific. It doesn't mean you can't change things. I have never found it rigid. For example, the last scene: Max had said he never thought they had got it right because the play was written on the hoof, as it were, and that last scene was really interesting because it concludes Helen and Nick's relationship and did keep changing. It changed its mood, really. It could be optimistic or it could be played so it pointed to a rather dull future together, and Max was very receptive to that and very interested. If he sensed it was changing, he'd want to work on it and make sure it was then named and clear.

Re-reading the reviews today I still feel the play was underestimated by the critics. In London, *Shopping and Fucking* had four separate runs. In total it must have been seen by over 70,000 people. Probably 7,000 or so saw *Some Explicit Polaroids* in the London run. But in Germany the two plays are regarded equally and get the same number of revivals . . . often with *Some Explicit Polaroids* in the main theatre and *Shopping and Fucking* in the studio.

It was great to get *Some Explicit Polaroids* to the stage, but the combination of August and an unfamiliar West End banjaxed the impact of a fine play. It's one of Mark's most significant plays and it continues to be underestimated.

Case Study

MACBETH
William Shakespeare

Rehearsal: from 2 August 2004

First Performance: 9 September 2004, Batley Red Brick Mill

Cast: Kwaku Ankoma, Jotham Annan, Nicole Charles, Sidney Cole, Monica Dolan, Kevin Harvey, Chu Omambala, Ben Onwukwe, Chris Ryman, Susan Salmon, Danny Sapani

---

If it takes thirty-five seconds to have a good idea, there are others that swim around year after year without resolution or fruition. *Macbeth* was one of these. I'm amazed when I look back at the Diaries to find just how long I had been thinking about it. Of course there are plenty of reasons why a touring company committed to the production of new work shouldn't do *Macbeth*. One of the drawbacks of undertaking much-loved popular classics is that they are performed with alarming regularity. In the early days of Out of Joint I had planned a production of *Hedda Gabler* and had even commissioned April De Angelis to undertake a translation, but then two other fine productions had come along and taken the shine off the venture. I didn't feel I had much to add.

My experience of Shakespeare was limited to the production of *King Lear* I had done at the end of my time at the Court (1993). I had learned a lot from a stellar cast which had included Tom Wilkinson, Philip Jackson, Hugh Ross, Adrian Dunbar, Iain Glen, Andy Serkis, Lia Williams and Saskia Reeves. Tom Wilkinson had played Lear as a red-faced and bewhiskered Edwardian squire. Andy Serkis was a bitter fool in drag, who indulged Lear with spanking games and who in essence became the naughty daughter that the others were not allowed to be. Deliberately transgressive, the production began in the Gents' toilet, where the discussion between Kent and Gloucester about the King's likely mood and Edmund's bastardy took place over male bonding and a gentlemanly pee. As the play progressed, the time-scale moved closer to our own period and refugees with shopping trolleys full of possessions fled in front of the invading French army. If you are able to unlock and release even some of the scenes in a great play, it gives a glow that infuses the scenes around it. I now look back on the opening scene with the choleric Lear dividing his kingdom in front of an intimidated court with great affection, but I don't think I brought much to the storm scene.

However, it was extraordinary to experience at first hand how clearly one could perceive some of the most appalling moments of our own times through Shakespeare's great tragedies. I had been brought up to believe that the Holocaust was the disgrace of the twentieth century, an unparalleled event that would never be repeated. Yet the fleeing refugees in my *King Lear* had in part been prompted by images of Muslim refugees in Serbia, while within a year of the Royal Court production of *King Lear* the massacre in Rwanda took place.

From time to time over the next decade I picked up *Macbeth*:

   🖎 *2 Jan 2000*   Reading *Macbeth* again. I can sort of see how to do most of it site-specific in that deserted primary school . . . But I'm scared of it I guess.

Macbeth had been listed as a possible Out of Joint project in Board Meeting minutes as early as 1996 but what had prompted this particular rereading was a site-specific show staged next door to Out of Joint's old premises in Eden Grove by our fellow tenants, Theatre de Complicite. We shared offices that had once been the yard and headquarters of a trucking firm. Earmarked for demolition as part of the expansion of the new Arsenal stadium, the building was eccentric and pleasant enough in summer, but became a freezing and insanitary health hazard in winter. Next door was a derelict primary school that also awaited redevelopment, and it fuelled ideas for a possible production.

   🖎 *3 Jan 2000*   No more than fifty or sixty people [maximum audience size]. Like going into a foreign country, your passport stamped, guards take you into this lift, doors shut, enclosed, claustrophobic, witches appear. Then audience are released into what would have been the school playground at the back. It's now a wasteland with discarded desks, old rubber tyres and long grass. It's a battleground steaming with corpses. People groaning, being taken off on stretchers. Conduct the audience through that. Some scenes played out there in the open air. If it's raining, it's raining. Then into the school building. Different classrooms will host different scenes. The school hall could be where the banquet is held. It had a glass roof so the ghost of Banquo can appear hanging by his feet through a pane in the roof or alternatively will be visible with his faced pressed to the glass.

I'm surprised to find how many of these ideas stayed in my head and were eventually used. I clearly envisaged a very intense, small-scale production where there was chaos and broken glass and where the re-examination of the play was conducted simply in terms of proximity and by overturning the expectations of the audience with the promenade elements. But a day later I was going off the idea.

   ✏ *4 Jan*   I talk about *Macbeth* and find it quite exciting, but there's no doubt that Out of Joint had its revenue grant increased substantially because we tour *new* work.

(For the year 2000/2001 Out Of Joint's Arts Council grant was increased by a hefty 50 per cent. It went from £280,000 to £420,000. This was a welcome sign of approval. For the first four years of the company's life we had existed on project grants; we had to apply afresh for each production we undertook.)

Intellectually I believe it's essential for an organisation involved with new writing to challenge itself with the occasional production of a classic. Lindsay Anderson's famous dictum was that the Royal Court did new plays like classics and classics like new plays, but at the same time there has to be a compelling rationale for a 'new writing' theatre to displace a living writer from the schedule. Out of Joint only does two productions a year, but we guarantee a minimum income of £17,500 to each writer if a commissioned play goes forward to performance. In practice a successful production can often earn a playwright double or treble that sum, as the combination of a tour and a London run means they earn royalties for upwards of fifteen or sixteen weeks. In the event I was given a perfect excuse for postponement:

✍ *20 Jan 2000*   Long-awaited dinner with Ken Stott. He's lovely.
Our thinking on *Macbeth* harmonises. He's not averse to a promenade or
intimate performance at all. We agree on Katrin Cartlidge* . . . He
hasn't even heard that Tony Sher and Harriet Walter are doing it, and
isn't fazed. That's the upside. The downside is that he hasn't got time to
do it for two years. So we're talking about 2002.

And then somehow the idea got dropped altogether.

But in April 2003 I was directing David Hare's two-handed play *The Breath of
Life* at the Sydney Theatre Company. It was the first job I had taken without
Out of Joint's involvement in ten years. I had two superb actresses, Robyn
Nevin and Noni Hazlehurst, but Robyn was also Artistic Director of the
Sydney Theatre Company, and she would appear for rehearsals having already
put in two hours' hard work in the office. It became clear there would be no
question of rehearsing on Saturday mornings, and once again the rhythm of
life changed.

In Sydney, I had an apartment in Kings Cross and, wandering past the porn
shops towards Potts Point and Woolloomooloo, I came across an excellent
bookshop. I picked up *Emma's War* by Deborah Scroggins. It was the story of
Emma McCune, a young woman who leaves Oxford Brookes and goes to
Africa to find a job as an aid worker. She falls in love with an African warlord,
Riek Machar, who is the leader of a South Sudanese Christian militia. Against
all expectation and the advice of her friends she marries him. The photos
show a handsome tall girl with dark hair and a winning smile. The warlord
has a sly grin and looks as if he cannot believe his luck. I couldn't believe
mine either when on page 157 Emma's friends began referring to her as
Lady Macbeth. (Emma became so ferociously loyal to Riek that some Operation Lifeline types began repeat whispering, 'Out damned spot, out I say'
behind her back when she stopped by UN headquarters in Nairobi to argue
for more aid.) She appeared oblivious to the fact that her husband was
apparently using the schools she had helped establish in the bush to train
child soldiers.

This much I learned from skimming in the bookshop. I bought the book,
walked down Woolloomooloo steps, past Harry's Café de Wheels, the famous
diner outside the gates of the Navy Yard, and into the Botanic Gardens. I sat

* Katrin's tragic death in 2002 robbed the stage of one of its most luminous talents. We
had had several conversations about *Macbeth*.

reading under a Moreton Bay fig and by the time the fruit bats made their squeaking ascent into the darkening sky I had read about Emma's troubled home life, her growing passion for Africa, and her complex relationship with Riek. She was, wrote her biographer, 'determined to bring a code of conduct for Riek's men, to prevent some of the more barbaric practices such as rape, pillage and the recruitment of child soldiers'. It became clear that Emma was in above her head, involved in a bloody tribal war. 'Declaring, "I understand nothing", and closing her eyes to the details of what was going on, she preferred not to know. People all around her were being killed and mutilated. Women were brutalised, children kidnapped, old men murdered.' Emma McCune wasn't really much like Lady Macbeth, but her story gave me the beginning of a parallel journey. It was a possible back-story for the Macbeths' relationship and for a *Macbeth* with an African setting.

For some time I had been seeking to commission a play about Africa and had talked to a number of African writers, including Biyi Bandele, but he had both feet in the film world; the black British writers I talked to knew no more about Africa than I did. Back with Out of Joint I began to accumulate a thick file of images about conflict in Africa from magazines and newspapers. There were two which had immediate relevance. One was an ordinary picture of a white Toyota pick-up spattered with red earth. In the back are eight young men, five of them with AK47s. The bonnet is festooned with camouflage netting and branches, and two soft mannequins are tied to the front bumper. They could be from *Sesame Street*, but in this context they have a totemic and magical significance. A second photo shows a group of young men festooned with branches and leaves filing along a jungle path: over their shoulders they carry a selection of AK47s and RPGs: Birnam Wood coming to Dunsinane indeed. There are plenty of pictures of child soldiers: one shows a young man, aged about fourteen, his mouth fixed open in a rictus of concentration, aiming his AK47 straight at the camera. He has a white teddy-bear knapsack on his back. Another shows a young man with slitted eyes advancing with his AK47. He wears a maroon T-shirt cut off at the shoulders and neatly knotted around his bare neck is a smart businessman's tie. He is about nine years old.

Naomi Jones, my assistant, found a picture of Idi Amin in a Glengarry bonnet. He had been a boy soldier with the King's African Rifles, whose officers had all been Scottish. He was fatherless, and his warm feelings towards these paternal Scottish figures went some way to explaining his lifelong passion for all things Caledonian. In Giles Foden's wonderful novel, *The Last King of Scotland*, Amin equips a whole unit of the Ugandan Army with kilts and bag-pipes. Then there's a photo of a burly young man in a skin-tight, blue T-shirt with an AK47 balanced on one hip . . . nothing remarkable there except he is wearing a mauve fright-wig with the curls cascading down his shoulders. Magic beliefs recorded in Zimbabwe during the 1890s held that cross-dressing had the power to turn bullets into water. Warriors hurled them-selves into battle shouting, 'Water, water.' In Liberia Charles Taylor's militia looted wedding shops and went into battle in wedding dresses, wearing long white gloves and feather boas. Like Macbeth they believed they could not be harmed.

Two further photographs have to be drawn from the bulging folder. One is a picture of unbelievable horror. It is a Ugandan Tutsi woman of fourteen, who has been raped and has had her eyes burned out. Her red-veined eyeballs stare out from her face. Where else does one find such images of horror? Well, in Shakespeare of course. The term 'genocide'* is a twentieth-century invention, but that is what Shakespeare describes in the fourth act of *Macbeth*. One of the intriguing problems of the play is that the central char-acter disappears for almost the entire act. After his second encounter with the witches, Macbeth is offstage until the advancing English army has nearly reached Dunsinane. (Intriguingly, in the opening scene the witches accost Macbeth on his way back from the battle. In the second witches' scene he seeks them out. Does he have an appointment? Does he pay them a surprise visit? How does he know where to find them? Does he pay them?) What is he doing? Well, he declares his purpose at the end of the disastrous banquet:

> I am in blood
> Stepp'd in so far that, should I wade no more
> Returning were as tedious as go o'er:
> Strange things I have in head that will to hand;
> Which must be acted ere they may be scann'd.   (*Act 3, Sc. 4*)

Subsequent horrors are described by Macduff:

> Each new morn
> New widows howl, new orphans cry, new sorrows

---

* First coined in 1944 by jurist Raphael Lemkin in his work *Axis Rule in Occupied Europe*, it literally means 'killing a tribe'.

Strike heaven on the face that it resounds
As if it felt with Scotland. (*Act 4, Sc. 3*)

The new arrival, Ross, is asked 'Stands Scotland where it did?' He replies:

Alas, poor country,
Almost afraid to know itself . . .
. . . where nothing
But who knows nothing is once seen to smile;
Where sighs and groans and shrieks that rend the air
Are made, not mark'd; where violent sorrow seems
A modern ecstasy . . .
and good men's lives
Expire before the flowers in their caps,
Dying or ere they sicken. (*Act 4, Sc. 3*)

And finally there's a photograph published in the *Independent* on 10 February 2004. Not Africa this time, but Haiti. It shows jubilant rebels grinning and waving cutlasses as they trot towards the camera. One has a blue handkerchief tied round his head, and another with glasses and Hawaiian shirt is triumphantly brandishing a pole. Nailed to the top there appears to be a tattered black and pink pennant. Only on very close inspection can you make out that it is a severed penis. The detail is small; I don't think the *Independent*'s picture editor can have spotted it, and there's no reference to it at all in the caption. I recall a similar image of mutilation from Zola's *Germinal*.

I've sometimes been accused of ignoring the visual side of theatre. It's true that I often come to the images in a play very late in the process, whereas Stephen Daldry, for example, describes a project he is about to undertake solely in terms of the stage pictures he intends to realise. In fact he told me once that he couldn't start a project unless he could see it first. My starting point is usually the story. Not so with *Macbeth*. The images and photographs helped create a very clear setting that provided a tangible and graspable alternative to Shakespeare's medieval Scotland.

And there were books too: Paul Theroux is a gloomy companion these days, but his book *Dark Star Safari* (2003) is an account of a journey across Africa which gives a vivid picture of the botched models of European democracy or Russian socialism that have been foisted on different African countries.

I read a biography of Livingstone, a Scot who, with generations of Scottish engineers, Scottish district commissioners, Scottish businessmen and Scottish schoolteachers, had imposed an eccentric sense of Scottishness on the dark continent. *Soldiers of Light* by Daniel Bergner (2005) contains a fascinating account of a witch doctor making himself bulletproof, and *A Sunday at the Pool in Kigali* (2003) is a guilt-ridden novel set at the beginning of the massacre in Rwanda. I also struggled to understand *Guns and Rain* (1985), David Lan's fascinating academic book about his two years in Zimbabwe studying spirit doctors and possession ceremonies. I began to understand the social position filled by the witch doctor, and to see him as a skilled craftsman essential to the community.

I was gathering confidence as well as information, but it was still one of several possible projects that I outlined to an Out of Joint Board meeting in early 2004. Thankfully Out of Joint Board meetings are low-profile, informal affairs useful as a sounding board for ideas. Council meetings at the Royal Court were often composed of onerous self-justification, but even they were as nothing to the terrifying Board meetings at the Traverse, which had been chaired by the eminent and eccentric Scottish criminal lawyer and MP, Nicholas Fairburn. His mode of chairmanship was aggressive and forensic cross-examination. It was hilarious and entertaining if, say, it was the chairman of the finance sub-committee, but less so if your own shortcomings were being exposed. As the Out of Joint Board Meeting wound down, it was Stephen Jeffreys who said I had to do *Macbeth*. The ideas were in place; it was a good moment for Out of Joint to undertake a classic; it was time that I stopped flirting and got on with it.

THE REHEARSAL PERIOD

The play was cast by the end of May 2004, and we started rehearsals on 2 August 2004. Danny Sapani was Macbeth, and Monica Dolan, who had been in *Sliding with Suzanne* and *A Laughing Matter/She Stoops to Conquer*, was to be Lady Macbeth. Some decisions had been taken before rehearsals began, always something I find a bit nerve-racking, although probably essential if you undertake a major classic. Firstly of course Monica was white; the remainder of the cast were black, and so we were already in some measure shadowing the story of Emma McCune. The witches were to speak French – they could be refugees from a neighbouring French-speaking country: Benin, Chad, Mali, Rwanda – which got us away from the wearisome 'Double, double, toil and trouble', the cause of such mirth to generations of school kids. Justification? French is the second most widely spoken language on the African continent, and having the witches speak it goes some way to making them at once alluring and mysterious.

I had also talked to composer Felix Cross about music that might end the play: usually it concludes with Malcolm's rather dreary speech. I was after something that would be celebratory, sinister and stirring all at once. The show would end with a version of 'Scotland the Brave'; Felix was to arrange it for a mixture of pipes and African drums. This idea for the end came from a moment in the Edinburgh Festival some years before that I had filed away. As part of the Fringe Festival I had seen a sort of military band outside St Giles Cathedral; their faces were covered with *Braveheart* blue paint. There were three pipers, two side-drummers, two flautists and one guy beating the shit out of a huge bass drum. The noise they were making was both stirring and alarming. Felix undertook to transform 'Scotland the Brave' into an African/British anthem. He explained how much each culture had influenced the other: apparently the leopardskin worn by the bass drummer in military bands had come from regiments serving in Africa, while bagpipes had been co-opted into much African music.

✍ *2 Aug* Read through. Accents could be a problem. Some actors adopt an African accent, and that makes it hard for the emotion to come through. Would that be true with any accent? The French is pretty dodgy. It's obviously even less well-taught now than it was in my day.

David Lan was known to the actors as the distinguished Artistic Director of the Young Vic, but he had also studied as an anthropologist at the LSE. Years before at the Court, I had directed his play *Sergeant Ola and His Followers*, which was set amidst the cargo cults of Papua New Guinea. He came to talk to us on the second day of rehearsal.

✏ *3 Aug*   David: 'You've got to come at witches from a funny angle. Basic ideas of witchcraft are similar throughout Africa. In Zimbabwe in 1980 the guerrillas fighting against Ian Smith found inspiration from spiritualism and possession.' Witch doctors authenticated their possession of the land. 'The actual spirit medium is called a Mondoro' (it means lion-spirited), and his assistants, who act like agents prompting him and arranging appointments, are 'Vtapi'. David is fascinating and authoritative. Four important things. He says, '1. Most people are illiterate . . . so history is what is remembered. 2. No electricity, so people feel very vulnerable at night. 3. No access to info about other societies. 4. No antibiotics, so life is hard. The world of evil is very close to the surface, and it is nuanced, inflected and subtle.'

Violence can break out: if people believe their child is dying they kill the witch. Going into battle they disassociate themselves from women (could this be why Lady Macbeth is left so isolated in the second half?). Warriors perform rituals which purify themselves from women. Red is associated with menstrual blood, so you must never wear red at any witchcraft ceremony. David relates having to take his socks off because they were red. Black and white: the Mondoro wears half-black and half-white because he has authority over both day and night. At twilight drumming starts. Often kids start the drumming before it's handed over to the experts. Social event. Women dance till they are exhausted. So on his visit (second witches scene) Macbeth would bring a symbolic gift but also cash. David explains that people stay up all night to meet spirits but could then go straight to church next morning. If you go to market you could probably buy eye of newt by the ounce. Bush-meat and weird ingredients are available at any African market. When possessed the mediums speak in a much deeper voice. Speaking is ritual and response.

Felix Cross then takes a music session. It's clear we should start with dancing and a possession ceremony; I've asked him to select some simple lyrics from the French translation of the witches. He chooses 'Le monde est beau. Le beau immonde.' The music sounds powerful and entrancing.

4 Aug   Very hot and sticky arvo, but I actioned four or five pages, and we worked out the geography of the battle. I got Kevin [Harvey] to begin to see Ross as a trimmer. It appears Duncan is facing a double threat: the merciless Macdonwald is invading from the Western Isles while the King of Norway aided by the traitor Cawdor has invaded the East Coast. It seems Cawdor has been Duncan's main man and is probably set to be the new king if the invasion is successful. Duncan can't believe the treachery:

> There's no art
> To find the mind's construction in the face.
> He was a gentleman on whom I built
> An absolute trust.   (Act 1, Sc. 4)

Against the odds Macbeth's extraordinary prowess in the field has won the day . . . He should first appear with blood streaming from a cut on his arm – no wonder Duncan is so abjectly grateful: 'I have begun to plant thee, and will labour / To make thee full of growing,' he promises.

Recent African history is full of examples of internal rebellions supported by foreign powers. Four different militia factions invaded Sierra Leone, one of which was supported by neighbouring Liberia and one, EKIMOG, by Nigeria.

✒ 5 Aug   Another good day. Did murder scene in the morning. In afternoon got the actors in a circle and made them stand behind the character they admired most and on whom they were most dependent. Remember Peter Brook telling me that, working at the RSC with a mere ten weeks' rehearsal or whatever he had, he was only able to work with the principal characters and the smaller roles got ignored. This exercise ensures that there's some relationship to draw on when, for example, the Gentlewoman speaks to Lady Macbeth. Because Lady Macbeth is white she is by definition an outsider, which makes the relationship interesting. Monica Dolan and Nicole Charles (Gentlewoman) imagine Nicole is from the country. She admires her mistress, thinks she's extraordinary and unconventional. She wants her to give Macbeth sons. Her status has gone up as she has learned English, and Lady Macbeth has given her money for clothes. We then do the brief scene where she tells Lady Macbeth: 'The king comes here tonight.' The scene is immediately richer. She is the friendly but respectful bearer of thrilling news and gossip:

Our thane is coming:
One of my fellows had the speed of him,
Who, almost dead for breath, had scarcely more
Than would make up his message.   (*Act 1, Sc. 5*)

9 Aug   Janette Nelson came in the arvo and did some very necessary
RSC emphasis on accent work. Makes me realise how far we have to go.
I made rather heavy weather of the banquet scene. Slight disagreement
as to what level of hysteria Macbeth should start the scene at. Had a drink
after rehearsal, and Danny (Macbeth) talked warmly about performing
at the Globe and how liberating it was to be in such close contact with
the audience.

I think Danny was reassuring me. I had explained to the actors that the
audience, limited initially to one hundred and twenty people a night, would
be led into a separate room for the banquet and that some would be ushered
to seats round the long banqueting table itself, where they would be served
wine and canapés. Macbeth would seek refuge in the surrounding crowd
when he saw the ghost of Banquo. And on the third occasion the vision
appears Banquo would actually erupt through the table like a shark leaping
out of the water. Es Devlin, the designer, assured me that a hole in the table
and an elasticated slit in the tablecloth would do the job. And so it proved. I
always looked forward to the shock and terror on the faces of the audience
sitting at the table itself. It took the banqueting scene into the realms of
fairground horror, but I didn't think that was inappropriate.

I usually avoid a read through on the first day because it's so random, but I
do one at the start of the second week, which is the first time the rest of the
creative team hears the play. Of course there are scenes which haven't been
rehearsed at all, but there are also bits where the actors have a fairly clear
idea what they are doing.

✍ *10 Aug*   Jo [Town, lighting designer] says all lighting will be built
onto the set which means we will be self-contained even when we play
in non-theatre spaces.

At the Oxford Playhouse the audience and the actors were on stage and the
show began in the theatre paintshop next door. We played in a mill in Batley,
another mill in Bolton, a factory in Manchester and a deserted stately home
in the Welsh Marches.

✍ Wow . . . I grasp that Macbeth is absent for fifteen pages . . . No wonder the play is hard to focus. In this version Danny becomes more dependent on 'bush magic' as he draws away from Lady Macbeth. Es tells me that the overall concept is so bold that there can be no half measures. You can't have one foot in an African Shakespeare and one foot in *The Bill*. You can't be half-hog: it's not just a bit black . . . it's very black: Macbeth as an African dictator is so strong, she says, there's no option but to go along with it. The witches don't sound very French yet . . . You can't be a bit French either. From now on we call ourselves Whole Hog Productions.

11 Aug   Did some status games. Nigeria is very status aware, Kwaku Ankoma tells me (he plays Lennox). 'Lower-status people are bossed around relentlessly. The King would have a chair brought for him.' We do an improvisation: backstage the cast are meeting Prince Charles after a performance. Most people nod with a reasonable display of deference: a couple of girls sketch a bit of curtsey. I then transfer the scene to West Africa and immediately it's joyfully obsequious: people rush to bring chairs, to fetch drinks and to display respect. Good fun applying this to the moment of discovery of Duncan's body. People in shock, women running about, men keening loudly, women and young ones being ushered out of the room. The picture was of a society that displayed its grief quite openly. Then got stuck on the England scene. We have decided that Malcolm has been at Sandhurst for a year so he has a rather plummy English accent, but at the moment neither this nor the actions are helping him much.

The England scene, when the exiled Malcolm suspects the loyalty of Macduff, is notoriously difficult. Everyone advocates cutting it severely. Malcolm tempts Macduff. He outlines plans for steaming lechery and unfettered avarice. Macduff goes along with it in queasy fashion only to be told that Malcolm doesn't really mean it. He's just testing.

✍ *12 Aug*   We essay the England scene again. I decided to try and make it as conversational as possible. Things become marginally better. After an hour, take decision to cut all the redemptive lines from Malcolm. It becomes much more cynical. He really intends to fuck a lot of women and get a shedload of money . . . And much more true to the reality of Africa where, vampire-like, leader after leader has preyed on their own people.

13 Aug   Production meeting. Graham [Cowley, Producer], trying to cut costs and the stage-management team getting a bit stroppy: 'Well, we haven't been given a budget so far.' Can they find a jeep? 'Absolutely bloody not.' The side drum and bass drum for the music at the end comes to £273 for the run. Is this a good deal or a ludicrous extravagance? I haven't a clue. Stage management not on board, Jon [Bradfield, Publicity Manager] going on holiday next week and even the trusty Graham has one foot out of the boat as he's also producing anti-war plays at the Southwark Playhouse. We're not playing in theatres and don't have the use of their production staff, so we need more support not less!

I was beginning to panic: not without some justification. We were always understaffed and overstretched. Because of the promenade element we had to create our own horseshoe-shaped auditorium wherever we went out of assorted chairs randomly painted in bold colours by Es. When we got to the Arcola in Dalston in East London, there was an afternoon when both Graham and I were lugging about huge chunks of rough-hewn rostra. It was exhausting. We're both old men – well, nearly – and Gary Beestone, the Production Manager, was concerned about Health and Safety. Health and Safety is the new political correctness. I soon worked it out. I would approach a particularly malignant and evil piece of rostra, bend down, lift it an inch off the ground, groan and Gary would immediately dispatch two hulking lads to move it.

Out of Joint's HQ is in a mews off the Seven Sisters Road appropriately named Thane Works. We have a modest-sized rehearsal room under the office. It's pleasant to have the operation under one small roof. The downside is that Thane Works is also by way of being a small industrial estate. Over the four years we've been there it's become more gentrified. The sweatshop that finishes clothes shipped from Romania is still there, but the small ironworks opposite (ornamental gates a speciality) has been succeeded by a Yogic Massage Centre, while a Cookery School has replaced the Dispatch Centre that made parking such a nightmare. Vans still whiz in and out all day, and when Islington Council are collecting the bins, or when the Mencap van is delivering (the silencer is shot and it needs a new cylinder head), then rehearsal has to be suspended. Saturday mornings are really quiet because nobody else is working.

✍ *Sat 14 Aug*   It didn't fall completely apart as we moved the opening scenes up and down the empty Thane Works, but open-air performances demand energy, and energy veers towards comedy if you're not sure what you're doing. Ben (Duncan) and Kevin (Ross) have to be steered back to the gravitas of the rehearsal room. The idea is that the show will begin with the audience filing into a space where the witches' possession ceremony is starting. Kids are trying out the drums, and dancers are warming up. Before entering, the audience will be challenged by guards on the gate wielding AK47s. It should be an arbitrary provocation. Some are let through; some have to pay a bribe. No political correctness either. Attractive girls are harassed and mobile phones confiscated. Trouble is we can't rehearse much of this till we get an audience . . . but the Bloody Sergeant does arrive in a wheelie bin pushed by nurses, and the public nature of Duncan's speeches and his heartfelt embrace of Macbeth and Banquo, who have saved the day, is clear. We certainly command the attention of the staff at the Apollo Restaurant opposite, who stop preparing lunch and come out of the kitchen to watch. Kwaku (Lennox) is great at keeping the play firmly in West Africa. He points out that there would be real excitement at the arrival of the king. It's kind of indicated in the text (a general cry of 'God save the king'), but Kwaku translates it into Twi, and there are stirring cries of 'Oba' as Duncan appears.

I had already done a preliminary two-week workshop for *Talking to Terrorists*, and there was a certain crossover between the material I had encountered there and *Macbeth*. Sarah Uppard from Save the Children had told us about the etiquette of the roadblock. She recounted how she had been held up by a drunk fourteen-year-old who had pointed an AK47 at her head. 'What do you do?' we asked. 'Well, persuading him to put the gun down is a good start,' she said dryly. In another incident her car had been held up by a mob of six- and seven-year-olds that had draped a piece of string across the road. Unsure whether their elder brothers might be in the bush, Sarah had stopped, but had no money to give. 'Give us that, give us that,' cried the kids, pointing at two unused Kleenex that sat folded on the dashboard – and jumped up and down with excitement when they were handed over.

Extraordinarily enough, Shakespeare writes about child soldiers. In our version Lennox refers to Macbeth's army being full of 'many unrough youths that even now protest their first of manhood'. We had chosen to emphasise the amount of young people in Macbeth: there are Donalbain, Fleance, the Macduff children, and there's also a possibility that Lady Macbeth has a child too. She very clearly says:

> I have given suck, and know
> How tender 'tis to love the babe that milks me.   *(Act 1, Sc. 7)*

Yet Macduff contemplating revenge in Act 4, Scene 3 says of Macbeth: 'He has no children.' We opted to make sense of this conundrum by giving Lady Macbeth a little white boy (or girl depending on local casting) from a previous relationship. The child was to bring the bad news that the English horde was approaching in Act 5 Scene 3, when Macbeth says:

> Go prick thy face and over-red thy fear,
> Thou lily-livered boy. What soldiers, patch?
> Death of thy soul! Those linen cheeks of thine
> Are counsellors to fear. What soldiers, whey-face?

The lines have particular resonance if a big black geezer is shouting them at a little white kid whose mum is on her deathbed. But the logistics were made even more complicated by having to cast them from four local kids, one white and three black, wherever we were playing.

✍ *16 Aug*   Put the children into Duncan's arrival at Chateau Macbeth (Act 1, Sc. 6), and it certainly makes the scene a lot clearer. The invasion and the civil war are over. The men have been three months in the field, and so it is a joyful reunion. Fleance should run across the stage and fling himself into Banquo's arms, the Macduffs are reunited, and even little Angus (Lady Macbeth's child) is led forward by his nanny (Gentlewoman) to present Duncan with an extempore bouquet. It places the scene emotionally. Monica takes up time, reviewing decisions, disputing moments already arrived at. I take up time too; unable to stage things as immediately as I would wish. In fact, it's humbling for all of us working on a great play. You imagine it in your head, do the actions, stage it: some of it looks good, but you are constantly thinking, 'Is that it? . . . What more could I be doing?'

18 Aug Act 2, Sc. 4. How does the court realign itself after Duncan's death? Who suspects Macbeth has done it? Who opts to befriend the incoming regime despite their reservations? Each character takes a decision at some point to flee the country. Macduff straight away; Ross in Act 4, Sc. 3; Lennox in Act 5, Sc. 2; and in our version, at the last, Seyton himself will desert to save his own life. He will take Siward's lines in Act 5, Sc. 9: 'This way my lord, the castle's gently render'd'. And he ingratiatingly offers Malcolm the keys. By that time Macbeth has alienated everybody and rages: 'Then fly, false thanes . . . Bring me no more reports; let them fly.' In the scene under examination, Ross, who has been absent from court, is wondering which way to jump: 'Then 'tis most like the sovereignty will fall upon Macbeth,' he muses. But it already has. Who voted for him? Was it an open election? Did Banquo vote for him? Probably – 'There's not a one of them but in his house / I keep a servant fee'd'. Who is the servant in your house? How did Ross miss out on voting?

Improvisation: the actors are given numbered cards to determine their enthusiasm for the new regime. A ten means they are passionate about the opportunities provided by a new king. A two or three means they have to flee the country without getting killed, i.e. they have to get to the car park at the end of Thane Works. Danny (Macbeth) gets a brief opportunity to talk to each of them before selecting a cabinet. Monica (Lady Macbeth) flees the country immediately. Ben (Duncan) and Chris (Seyton) get killed. Susan (Lady Macduff) escapes but only after bribing Kwaku (Lennox) with promises of sex. Kwaku leads a successful life as a double agent. Nicole (Third Witch) is wrongly accused of being a traitor. She protests her innocence but is killed anyway. After this expedition into paranoia, we did the scene where Macbeth briefs the two murderers, and it got much better. Macbeth gets very chummy with them and gives them a Fanta each. Making good progress, not going too fast. Monica and Danny are both doing brilliantly, and yet the play is so good it dwarfs our efforts. In five weeks' rehearsal we will probably get to rehearse each scene three times . . . Enough to be good but not definitive.

I was overly pessimistic. We were actually able to rehearse each scene five or six times.

✍ *20 Aug*   Event of the day was visit of Peter Badejo. Introduced by
Ben Onwukwe, he is an expert in Possession Ceremonies and West
African dances. A small, jovial guy in a baseball cap, he takes charge
immediately. He made the actors reach up to the spirits with their left
hand while they are dancing. 'The good thing about being a witch is you
can be what you want to be,' he says. 'Witches are a bit arrogant. Of
course. They know what is going to happen tomorrow.' To the villagers
he says, 'You have to know something may happen . . . Today is not an
ordinary market day.' He approves of the arrangement we have made:
Sid (Sidney Cole) is the spirit medium (the Mondoro). The other two
witches (Susan and Nicole) are Vtapi. They are responsible for creating
the right mood for the dance at the beginning and for the financial
arrangements. In the second witches scene, Susan takes charge of the
cash that Macbeth proffers. To the women Peter says, 'Your movement
must be much stronger than the men. Because you give power to the
men.' To Sid he says, 'Smile. You are the most blessed man here' . . .
and to the villagers he says, 'You must rest when you dance. It is like
speaking . . . If you speak all the time it is like, blah, blah, blah, blah,
blah, and the spirits will get bored of you. You must rest. You must have
a silence'.

21 Aug   A sunny Sat. morning, and, with the alleyway free, I run most
of the first act. It's a strange and uncertain mixture of improvisation (the
road block), apparently spontaneous music and dance (opening witches
scene), energised outside encounters straight from the battlefield,
thoughtful monologue (Lady Macbeth), intense plotting (the Macbeths)
and a group scene (Duncan's arrival). Moving from the energy outside
to the focus needed inside has its difficulties, but it's certainly a vigorous
and lively mixture.

Kwaku left me with a magazine called *Ovations* for the weekend. It was
a Nigerian version of *Hello* and showed various Nigerian millionaires at
different social gatherings. One gent was in his mid-sixties with his three
wives; one was about his age, one was in her late thirties, and one was about
twenty-two. All wore identical flowing dresses. They all looked very happy.
Well, why wouldn't they be? His fortune was estimated at £15 million, and
he also has a mansion outside Edinburgh on the Firth of Forth. The sofa is
white, embossed with gilt . . . and lots of cocktail cabinets. It gives us an idea
of what Macbeth's house might look like.

Over that weekend I also looked up 'paranoia' in my Dad's medical text-book, *Psychiatry for Students* by David Stafford-Clark.

'Feelings of persecution . . . may occur in people who have experienced radical life changes.' Maybe Macbeth has risen from the ranks like Idi Amin. 'There are usually no other symptoms of mental illness apart from occasional hallucinations. In time however, the anger, suspicion and social isolation may become severe.'

Thanks, Dad. And I turned to 'night terror' for Lady Macbeth: 'May show distress or cry out . . . Likely to be associated with an anxiety disorder . . . Sufferers wake up screaming in a semi-conscious state and remain frightened for some minutes . . . They usually cannot be comforted.'

✍ *23 Aug*   Got stuck on Act 5, Sc. 3 . . . 'Bring me no more reports.' Or rather Danny got stuck and didn't see why he had to be so forceful. We look at the scene again. Well . . . Macbeth is angry, isolated and frightened. He believes in the immunity the witches have given him. 'I cannot taint with fear,' he tells Seyton, but the next minute he confides: 'I am sick at heart . . . I have liv'd long enough,' and contemplates a horrible death. 'I'll fight till from my bones my flesh be hacked.' In Act 5, Sc. 5 it's in a spirit of desperate defiance that he makes a crazy and rash tactical error, quitting the safety of Dunsinane ('Our castle's strength will laugh a siege to scorn') to confront the enemy head on ('Arm, arm and out . . . Ring the alarum bell! Blow wind! Come, wrack! At least we'll die with harness on our back'). We talk through all this and then do the scene again. Now Danny loses his temper and shouts at the terrified Chris (Seyton) . . . only to befriend him again the next minute. It's a ghastly but convincing picture of a man veering out of control.

It's astonishing how pervasive are the images of fear that run-through the play. Macbeth's big fear is fear itself . . . and perhaps his superobjective is to prove himself a man. In the battle that opens the play he has shown reckless and ridiculous bravery. The Bloody Sergeant reports:

For brave Macbeth — well he deserves that name!
Disdaining fortune with his brandish'd steel
Which smoked with bloody execution,
. . . Carv'd out his passage . . .

So they doubly redoubled strokes upon the foe:
Except they meant to bathe in reeking wounds
Or memorise another Golgotha,
I cannot tell —   (*Act 1, Sc. 2*)

Lady Macbeth knows his weak spot too. She taunts:

> *. . .Wouldst thou have that*
> *Which thou esteem'st the ornament of life*
> *And live a coward in thine own esteem?*   (*Act 1, Sc. 7*)

'I dare do all that may become a man', he protests. 'When you durst do it, then you were a man,' she sneers back. But by the end of the play Macbeth looks back on his fears with nostalgia:

> *I have almost forgot the taste of fears.*
> *The time has been my sense would have cooled*
> *To hear a night-shriek . . .*   (*Act 5, Sc. 5*)

Shakespeare doesn't go in much for family biography or psychological profiles. King Lear gets one reference to his dead wife, and Lady Macbeth has one to her dad; 'Had he not resembled / My father as he slept, I had done't.' Macbeth is given no parents . . . Perhaps he was beaten by his father. The actors were talking one day about the responsibility African fathers feel to instil discipline into their kids. A spot check revealed that every one of the actors brought up in Africa had been beaten by their fathers with a stick. And later, when working on *Talking to Terrorists*, China Keteitsi, who had been a child soldier in Museveni's rebel army, told me that she had run away from home at the age of eight because her father beat her so severely: 'He jammed my head between his legs, gripped tight, couldn't breathe, beating me, beating me . . . my stepmother moving the chairs so he could beat me more easily . . . my brothers and sisters screaming, "Stop, stop . . . Father, you're killing her . . . stop, stop . . .". When my father finished, I was full of blood.'

✍ *24 Aug*   When people who work in the theatre know you're doing *Macbeth* they say two things: the first is 'Are you going to cut the England scene?' and the second is 'What are you going to do about Act 5?' Well I *have* cut the England scene, but I think the fifth act could be terrific. It's different. Short scenes mirror Macbeth's own disintegration. It is necessarily fragmentary, so there's a particular requirement to locate and place the back-story. In the brief Act 5 Sc. 2, Lennox has a rendezvous with Ross and is clearly changing sides. We've made it tangible with Lennox discarding various fetishes and his orange fright wig while Ross provides him with a flak jacket and a pale blue UN beret.

25 Aug   As we go through the Macbeth/Lady Macbeth relationship again, Danny and Monica alike have second thoughts. Problem is these second thoughts are nowhere near as good as their first . . . Inevitably it means going back to the actions and re-finding what it was we originally discovered.

26 Aug   Conversation with Es [Designer], Jo [Lighting Designer] and Emma [Costumes] about the nature of what we are up to. 'A bastardised Scottish world': yes, but is it posh like *Ovations* suggests, or is it a refugee camp? I say we are drawing on both sources. Hmmm. We discuss lighting. We are not in a theatre . . . so are we in an industrial space? Does Jo use sodium lights or flares? Apparently she wants to use 'caged builders' festoons'. Or do we want some moments to be theatrically lit? Like Banquo's eruption into the banquet. And there are many references to it getting dark:

> *Come, seeling night,*
> *Scarf up the tender eye of pitiful day . . .*

Or . . .

> *Light thickens, and the crow*
> *Makes wing to th' rooky wood.*   (*Act 3, Sc. 2*)

But does it get darker? Probably not . . . especially during a Saturday matinee at Red Brick Mill, Batley, where there's no way of blacking out the windows.

27 Aug   Am sort of within sight of the end of my ability and talent to take the Macbeths any further in terms of what I can do with the acting. Not so with the *mise en scène*, which is in my head but is difficult to realise in the rehearsal room. Begin to panic. Why haven't I done more research? Why haven't I made Monica examine sleep-walking in more detail? Or Danny research Stalin's massacres? Why don't I know where Burundi is? Of course it's impertinent to imagine that we can realise the experience of people who have been through horrors. How can I ask a little boy who has only acted in a school play to be a terrified child soldier? And how can I ask Susan (Lady Macduff) to pull her pants down and act having been raped, until the elements of a *mise en scène* are there which will place it in some sort of context and reassure her?

Terry King came in the morning to work on the fights. It's hard to make sense of soldiers toting AK47s when all the references are to swords and sharp blades. But here history is on our side: in Rwanda 800,000 Tutsis were killed within a time span of three months by Hutu militia armed with spades, hoes and machetes imported from China. The murder of Lady Macduff now seems sufficiently slow and horrible.

Seyton is the unidentified man who rushes in to warn Lady Macduff that she should flee: in a wordless sequence that follows the murder, and, in our version, the rape of Lady Macduff, Ross is led back by Macbeth, offered a machete, and forced to kill the Macduff's baby, whose crying can be heard from the next room.

✍ *28 Aug*   Jotham (Malcolm), at his own initiative, has arranged an interview at Sandhurst and went yesterday to meet Captain Gorman, who talked to him about the annual intake (three hundred) for the officers' course, which lasts forty-two weeks. Some overseas students return to their own countries where they may well be instantly promoted to Lieutenant Colonel and put in command of a battalion. Most British graduates become Second Lieutenants in the British Army. As Jotham impersonated Captain Gorman, he became more confident, easy and self-contained. Then we ran the play. First half held together very well. Second half, unsurprisingly, fell apart . . . Well, I've hardly touched it this week. Danny was very good and was, justifiably, pleased with his morning's work. He came into notes and whispered in my ear, 'We were all just saying what a clever bastard you were, guv.' I was pleased. And then Aisha Kosoko from Benin, who is helping with the French for the witches, said, 'It's such a difficult play. If you get only 50 per cent of it right you will have done very well . . .' Hmmm. There's a corrective.

It was a Bank Holiday weekend, but Jotham led an expedition to an African village in the middle of Hertfordshire about five minutes from Stansted

Airport. Largely funded by school visits, the African village offered authentic encounters with different tribal customs and dances.

✍ *31 Aug*   Jane Edwardes, theatre editor of *Time Out*, in rehearsal this arvo. We need some sort of publicity, but it's always hard to make a public event of a private matter.

Jotham, Danny, Monica, Nicole, Susan and Kwaku report back on their trip to the African village. They learnt how to shake hands with a King or Chief (your own left hand clasps your right forearm to show you have no concealed weapons). They learnt how important a symbol a fly whisk is, watched an African dance and watched the Olympic boxing on telly. The partner of the organiser is white and comes from Rochdale. Brilliant part for Monica. They improvise the encounter. Made more sense of the post-Duncan murder scene.

Worked on 3.6 with Ross and Lennox. Ross is dealing with text messages while Lennox is cleaning his AK47. The gossip about Macduff and his whereabouts is incendiary and dangerous. It must be whispered. A pretty stolid but unspectacular day. I have no idea if Jane was impressed. She said she couldn't understand some of the accents. Later Danny said, 'You were showboating, you only rehearsed scenes you knew we could do.' There was some small truth in this accusation.

3 Sept   Valuable input from Janette Nelson, Felix Cross and Terry King in the supplementary disciplines of dialects, music and martial arts. Actors' resolution to stick to the 'actions' is beginning to wimp, buckle and bend under the pressure of the imminent performance. Of course the play will develop in performance, but too often the actors don't realise that by adding energy they are changing intentions: animated conversations become arguments, arguments become steaming rows and rows become all-out fights. It's not always an improvement.

4 Sept   We run the play through in front of a small invited audience: Mark Ravenhill, Kitty my daughter, Fritha Goodey (invited by Monica) and a glam friend of Nicole's called Ashley. I send the audience down to the end of the mews so they can approach the road-block singly: situation is made more complex by the fact that Tricia (Graham Cowley's wife) is auditioning kids for the anti-war plays she is directing in a spare unit further down Thane Works. Some mums are understandably upset at being rudely challenged by a pair of brawny youths in fright-wigs brandishing AK47s on a Saturday morning. But the kids are delighted.

The run through went well, but it was important to note what went awry rather than what went right. We had set ourselves particular problems by including promenade elements where the audience were shepherded into different spaces. It was hard to pick up the energy anew when we moved from location to location. We were deliberately disrupting the spectacle, but it was essential that we should stay in charge and didn't permit the spectacle to disrupt us. I stopped the actors getting too chummy with the audience or improvising too much; the phrases used as they moved the audience were restricted to 'Come, you are my guest,' or 'Come quickly now.'

✍ *5 Sept*   Got some good notes from Mark (Ravenhill) this morning. He thought the narrative at the beginning and the story of the battle finishing could be helped by sound, blood and costumes. He liked Monica's performance a lot. I thought it had veered perilously close to Penelope Keith territory in 1.5 when she reads the letter from Macbeth. She had to wait while the audience filed into the main space, and during this time changed from wellies to sandals to indicate she had been gardening but the over-inventive use of an insect spray had had Mark laughing heartily. Ever anxious about the schoolkids at the matinee, I cut it immediately. Kitty thought it potentially terrif and particularly loved Chris Ryman's speech as the Porter.

Over the previous three years I had been collecting productions of *Macbeth* like an assiduous lepidopterist. I had seen five. In one of them (Dominic Cooke's production at the RSC) there had been one hearty laugh at the lugubrious and tedious wordplay of the Porter. It is an important moment because it immediately deflates the tension that has built from the beginning of the play to Duncan's murder. All the academics assure you how hilarious it must have been in Shakespeare's day, but I had seen enough of actors mugging themselves silly and had pointed Chris Ryman in a different direction. Immediately prior to rehearsal I had spent a week in Tokyo at a theatre conference. Trapped in my hotel room by the sweltering and humid weather I had spent most of the time fretting about *Macbeth* and wishing I was back in London. But there had been one curious encounter. A medical conference had also been taking place at the same hotel, and in the bar I had met a doctor from Nigeria. Dressed in vivid orange, her name was Zana, and she was a gynaecologist from the Muslim north. She drank orange juice while I drank beer, but I ran into her a couple of times. She told me of the problems pregnant women encountered by depending on native doctors. At the end of the week I told her I was leaving the next day. 'One minute,' she said, 'I have something for you.' She went up to her room and returned with a long list of medical text books. She wanted the books or the CD-ROMs sent to her in Nigeria. The total cost would have been about £250. I sent one of the books when I got back. I felt obliged. She had provided the starting point for Chris's speech. He explains that, though he is currently multi-tasking for – (and he nods in the direction of the Macbeth's bedroom), he is really studying to be a doctor.

Knock, Knock! . . . Knock, Knock! Here's a knocking indeed!

Listen my friends . . . can anyone lend me £5? I'm in need of money . . . Okay, maybe $5?

No . . . I thought so . . . this is the problem! I'm studying to be a doctor of tropical diseases, but I am in a lot of trouble, I cannot complete the course. I do not have the CD-ROMs. They are not working any more . . .

And so on. He concludes *'Please my friends, remember the porter; www.seyton.com.'*

One measure of his success is that by the end of the run Chris was regularly getting £5 a night and sometimes £10.

✍ 6 Sept   We run the play again at Out of Joint's rehearsal room. Not the best run in the world, but after a day off it remains pretty solid. Worked on getting Banquo and Macbeth to appear as real friends in the first scene, got Lady Macbeth to hit her opening scenes less hard. Made a sharper differentiation in the first act between public oration, private conversation and confidences played straight to the audience. I then tell the actors that we may have peaked already. Their performances are fine, but ahead lies a technical rehearsal on a disused floor of an old mill in Batley, Yorkshire, that is now a major Habitat outlet. We will be in a non-theatre, where the only blackout will be natural darkness, where there are no dressing rooms and where the nearest working toilet may be two floors away. I say a really bad time is available for all of us if we want to choose it. So it's no good saying, 'There's no proper light in my dressing room' . . . And if the toilet is blocked, then roll your sleeves up.

7 Sept   7.35 a.m. Yorkshire Pullman to Leeds calling at Stevenage and Wakefield. Then 10.41 a.m.: Arriva Trains Northern to Batley, having checked in at the Calls Hotel, Leeds. In Batley I walk down the hill past the site of the Station Hotel, where a plaque tells me that wool buyers from Russia used to stay amidst Edwardian opulence. There's a terrace of town houses that could be straight from Edinburgh's New Town except that half of them are boarded up. I can see my destination, the Red Brick Mill, in the distance towering over the valley. Down the hill out of Batley station to the Dewsbury Road, past the various motor outlets, an Indian restaurant and the Batley Working Men's Club that once hosted Frank Sinatra. Our space is a huge dusty floor above the Habitat store; one end has floor-to-ceiling windows which look over the car park to the hill on the other side of the valley. There I can see the floodlight pylons ringing the ground of the Batley Bulldogs, currently leaders of Rugby League's First Division. Turning this industrial wasteland into a theatre is a mammoth job.

Naomi Jones, my assistant, and I take it upon ourselves to build the auditorium. It's a hot and sweaty job. Nobody seems to be prioritising what should happen next. Es is busy painting chairs orange rather than supervising the creation of the inner room where the banquet will take place. The stage management seem to have disappeared in search of one swivel chair: hardly my priority . . . we have at least two already. Meanwhile there's no blood and no severed hand for the scene in the small inner room where, on payment of a small supplement, the audience may view the ravaged and murdered body of Lady Macduff. Everyone else is off for their dinner break: Batley being well north of the linguistic lunch–dinner divide. Phil the machete, Gary the table, stage management the blood. Sarah, the ASM, spends all arvo twisting ribbons round the hoe for the final dance. Richard and Naomi spend some time putting a filing cabinet together: it flops apart as soon as somebody touches it. Where's the blood?

Then the loyal and trusty Naomi deserts to go to Huddersfield to rehearse the kids. She asks if she can get a cab. 'No,' I say in a moment of ludicrous and inappropriate meanness in the middle of all this conspicuous expenditure. She goes. In the midst of this chaos sadly sits my mother's sofa. It is to form the centrepiece of the auditorium seating. A sort of Royal Box. I think that that would have pleased her, though she would be horrified to see the coils of cable and tools that have been dumped on it now. Downstairs Habitat bespeaks £1,000 glistening leather sofas and an order of harmony that seems a million miles away.

Later, a miracle. Everything ran to time. We started the tech more or less at seven as scheduled and went through till ten without stopping. A carpenter brought up from Putney (no expense spared there) had put the filing cabinet together, the blood arrived special delivery, and even the hoe looked presentable. We had nearly arrived at Dunsinane. Brisk fifteen-minute walk to Dewsbury Station, caught the 10.41 and, footsore, was in the Calls by 11.15. On the way from Leeds Station I was hailed by one of two weird sisters: 'Are you alright, darling?' she enquired. 'Do you want business?' I declined.

8 Sept   Monica phones distraught, to say that Fritha Goodey is dead. She has committed suicide. How can this be? She was at the run on Saturday. Monica and Fritha were in *She Stoops to Conquer/A Laughing Matter* together and have become very good friends. I phone Mark Ravenhill and Graham Cowley, but both have already heard the awful news. I go to Batley in a state of shock, but teching in daylight is no help to Jo Town and there's not much I can do, so I walk up to Batley Tops with Naomi. In the fields up behind the mills are a goat and two scrubby horses. Naomi reveals she was very depressed in her final year at university. What a strange profession: weeks of intimacy in rehearsal, where you get as close to people as you do to anyone in life, then, apart from the occasional party, you don't see them again for years. It makes me think perversely that there are actors that I love, but few of them that I know well.

Later: The kids are a handful. Donalbain, aged ten, is a great hunk of a child. No question of him jumping into anyone's arms. Es objects on aesthetic grounds and wants to graffiti the wall with 'Donalbain ate all the pies'. Of course they have mixed abilities, and there's a limit to their patience. Es's costume team of Penny and Emma are very strong.

Now we're moving through the play with some momentum they get a clear grasp of the particular aesthetic we're after and every costume reappears amended and improved.

The dress rehearsal and the first preview came and went in a welter of notes. My most memorable impression is that, in the battle between the play and the mill, the mill had been the clear winner. The floor creaked badly, and for the first few days we were kicking up dust that had accumulated through a century and a half of industrial use. The wardrobe mistress lasted a week and the company manager didn't last much longer. 'It just wasn't,' said the wardrobe mistress, 'the production of *Macbeth* I signed up for.' The actors grew more adept at crowd control and gradually we were able to impose the focus we had in rehearsal. I made last-minute improvements with the battle scene in the final act, which took place over the whole mill rather than just in front of the audience.

10 Sept   Third preview. Battle scene much more convincing. There were mistakes, and we still can't move the audience very quickly from the Witches' Wasteland (as it is known) to the main acting area. But tonight I thought we delivered the play for the first time. The triumph was that not one person laughed when Danny put on the pink fright wig. Lots of stuff in the paper about Fritha, an obituary and a big picture in the *Guardian*, something in the *Metro*; and the *Mail* have been on the phone too. Apparently she 'was on the brink of stardom'. The horrible irony and the awful question is: would she have done it if she had realised how warmly so many people feel about her? To the techies' hotel for drinks after the performance. Very pleasant and well managed by Graham. I order a cab, and when I left there was a warm and spontaneous round of applause from the actors. Earlier Nicole had asked me how I managed to cast such a harmonious group of actors. Humph. It's early days and it's clear she hasn't done much touring. In the cab back to Leeds the driver, who has a Batley Bulldogs pennant on the dashboard, tells me that he comes from a particular group of Gujarati Christians, and now there are more of them in Batley than remain in India. 'The first grave in Batley Cemetery with my name on dates from 1953,' he says proudly.

Over the next few days colleagues and friends who ventured up from London were impressed, as was the Leeds *Metro*, which gave us five stars. There were to be many more good reviews but none more timely or more heartening. Danny and Monica went on to give terrific performances. I have fond memories of Batley because the production came together there for the first time, but the most unforgettable night was in the Black Mountains of Wales. The demands of the production made it hard to find suitable venues, but Theatr Brycheiniog of Brecon had found us a beautiful but derelict home in the Welsh Marches. It had a gate-tower, an inner courtyard and a timber gallery running round two sides of the curtain wall. There were certain rooms we couldn't use because of load-bearing restrictions, and in one instance because a rare colony of bats had made their home in the fireplace. The opening scene with the witches took place in the courtyard; the original courtroom was used for the main action, while the banqueting scene took place in the old banqueting hall.

Our first performance there was on a damp evening in early October. It had been raining all day and I feared for the promenade elements of the play, but the rain held off. The atmosphere was appropriate, and the actors were coping admirably with the strange geography of the exotic venue. In the scene before the banquet the turmoil in Macbeth's mind boils over, and Danny gave great agony and weight to the line, 'O, full of scorpions is my mind, dear wife!' Disturbed by the noise, two curious bats flew in from the neighbouring room and completed two circuits by the time Danny had arrived at:

> Then be thou jocund: ere the bat hath flown
> His cloister'd flight, ere to black Hecate's summons
> The shard-borne beetle with his drowsy hums
> Hath rung night's yawning peal, there shall be done
> A deed of dreadful note. (*Act 3, Sc. 3*)

A light drizzle came on again towards the end of the play, but once again held off as the battle for Dunsinane raged round the castle walls. Danny slipped on the wet grass during the fight with Macduff, but our final rendition of 'Scotland the Brave' thundered boldly round the enclosed walls of the courtyard. It finished on a crescendo of drums and at that moment two RAF Harriers practising low night-flying screamed overhead at a height of a hundred feet. The fly-past was a fitting salute to a magical evening.

There is a postscript to *Macbeth*. Success brings its own obligations in the theatre, and although the limited audience meant it was always going to cost money, there were two further runs of *Macbeth*. The first, in January 2005, was five weeks at Wilton's Music Hall. The second began re-rehearsal in August 2005 and, following a two-week return run at the Arcola, toured to Pilsen in the Czech Republic, Minneapolis, Guanajuato in Mexico, Edinburgh, Bury St Edmunds, the Hague and, finally, courtesy of the British Council, to Lagos and Abuja in Nigeria. My Diary picks up events in Holland:

✎ *11 Nov*   Exhausted. It's the morning after a generous first-night party from our Dutch hosts. I crave the Dutch experience, i.e., ham and eggs on two slices of white bread. Last night, I met this elderly British party. When asked what he did in the Hague, he replied 'Acksee inder brishamshare.' 'I didn't quite catch that.' 'Actually, I'm the British Ambassador,' he repeated. He had three Dutch policemen as security guards, who had been alarmed by our cross-dressed child soldiers at the start of *Macbeth*. He told me that the American Ambassador has five guards, and the Israeli Ambassador never goes out. Back to the hotel to find that our flight to Lagos has been cancelled. Apparently, the international runway at Lagos has been out of action for over a year, so KLM has been landing on the domestic runway, and one of its planes was damaged by scrunching over loose tarmac. The Nigerians responded by limiting the weight of all aircraft. This in turn means that KLM has to refuel elsewhere or cut back the payload of passengers. KLM has responded by suspending flights. Oh, the joys of touring.

12 Nov   Amsterdam: because of yesterday's cancellation, the flight is jam-packed. There is a queue to get into the departure lounge; a queue to get on the plane; and a queue, once on the plane, to get seated. The overhead lockers are overflowing. But it's all very amiable, because people are going home. The inflight film is *Charlie and the Chocolate Factory*. It has absolutely no cultural connection with anybody on board.

Later: chaos at Lagos Airport. The baggage carousel spews out faxing systems, air-conditioning units, expensive toys, and a Toyota carburettor.

13 Nov   Slept like a dead one from midnight to nine in the morning. 'Good morning, suh, you are welcome,' says the security guard. The language of Shakespeare is peppered with 'Worthy thane', and 'My noble lord'. Here also, pleasure is taken in deferential language. At breakfast, I note the butter is from Normandy, the jam from Holland. The security guard's gun is from the Czech Republic.

The performance is to be in the open air, and the set is being built on the tennis court. Though the day is overcast, it's incredibly hot. Gary, the production manager, is supervising the Nigerian crew, who will stay with us throughout. Naomi, my assistant, is rehearsing the children. Children here will not call adults by their Christian names. Naomi's options are Miss, Sister, or Auntie. She opts for Auntie. The manhole covers are from Birmingham, the security system is from the USA, and the cars are from Japan. The Deputy General explains that there used to be a thriving local agricultural economy, but oil prices raised the value of the currency, and it became easier to import. He says corruption is openly admired. The Governor of Bayelsa State had one million in cash and ten million in his bank account when he was arrested in London. News on the damaged runway front. The contractor arrived to do the job, but there was no money. It had been siphoned off at a higher level.

15 Nov Do the technical rehearsal in blinding heat. Go back to the hotel for a shower, but traffic over the lagoon is at a standstill. This transforms the area into a market. Salesmen weave between the cars offering everything from lottery tickets to jewellery. A girl presses herself against my car window. She winks and lolls her tongue suggestively. She's about ten.

Later: A mighty strange evening.

Our performance is to celebrate the opening of the spanking new British Council building. The Council's Director General, the Governor of Lagos State, and the British High Commissioner all make speeches. It goes on for some time. We are assured that everything will overrun, but in fact there's an hour to kill before the performance at 7.30. Panic. I hear the Director General say to the Governor, 'Well, I do hope you will be able to stay for at least some of the performance, sir.' Six security guards, and three protocol officers flank the Governor and his beautiful wife. We rate somewhere below the catering, and on a par with the drivers. We're asked to bring our performance forward by half an hour, but the actors haven't begun their warm-up. We decline. In the event, the Governor is tired and leaves. His wife stays.

The witches' encounter with Macbeth is staged under a huge banyan tree. There is no seating. Again. Panic. The Governor's wife rates a special seat. One is brought, but unfortunately placed in a position where she will see nothing. I approach to suggest she moves, but six security men step forward, and an iron arm prevents my approach. She sits politely through the scene, seeing nothing, and then she and her party withdraw. It's a relief, but the evening doesn't get much easier. The audience is infinitely more amused by its own cleverness and wit than anything that Shakespeare or the actors can come up with. 'Oh, now they are serving us Banquo's blood,' says Chief Segun Sithole, as he is offered a glass of red wine. A chief's wife queues to view the corpse of the raped and murdered Lady Macduff. A cash supplement is demanded, but she has no change. 'Oh, they don't take Mastercard', she quips amid much hilarity. Phone conversations bubble through the performance, including one actually between two members of the audience. One man makes a phone call, and walks across the stage in mid-conversation. We have all the ingredients of a Restoration theatre audience: ageing beauties, distinguished members of the aristocracy, wits, bankers, and armed members of the public. It makes for a difficult evening, but the play still works its magic, and the response at the end is warm.

16 Nov   Workshop in the morning at Terra Kulture. At ten o'clock, there are four smartly dressed girls in high heels, and three guys in ties and jackets, all sitting in ranked chairs. It looks like a Bible class. I'm impatient of latecomers, but in Lagos there's plenty of excuse. I start with seven actors and, two hours later, end with twenty. They are inventive with improvisations, but find the text work harder. One man who runs a children's theatre explains bitterly that there is no professional structure to theatre in Nigeria, and that as soon as people leave school they want to make music videos. He says that though he is grateful to the British Council, this is just charity. Back to the British Council compound where an Afro Fusion dance band is playing. The dancing is sensational. The booty-action is plentiful. Backsides shake like blancmange. I find myself awake all of a sudden.

As for *Macbeth* – people still flick through their mobiles, but the performance is much more resolute and controlled. We cut six minutes. The students from the morning workshop are very enthusiastic. We are beginning to get the hang of outdoor performance. In a theatre, a pause makes energy flow towards you. Outside, it flows away, and becomes an opportunity to check your phone messages.

There is supposed to be a post-show discussion, but the audience is alarmed at staying any later. Travel after 9.30 without an armed guard is dangerous.

18 Nov   Abuja. A late arrival means an even later dinner with the British Council last night. I sit next to the lady in charge of the Kano office. She's a former schoolmistress. She tells me she has two gardeners, a cook, a driver, an indoor maid, and six security guards. From a schoolteacher in Slough to a duchess in Abuja. Shakespeare, Farquhar and Oscar Wilde are peopled with servants, but it's no longer a world we have any experience of. The security all seems rather excessive. Both British Council compounds are like small fortresses. The former teacher tells me that two weeks before we arrived, Patience, in charge of the Port Harcourt office, had her car hijacked. The driver was shot and is still in hospital. This has been kept from us so as not to cause undue alarm. 'All the security seems unnecessary,' she says, 'until the day you need it.'

19 Nov   Abuja is the federal capital of Nigeria and, like Canberra or Brasilia, it's comparatively spacious and quiet. We are staying in the capacious and marbled Nicon Hilton. A kind of *faux* Egyptian palace. The play is staged in a garden and the floor is grass. I decide to water it amidst a spectacular African sunset. An hour later, *Macbeth* begins. There is a smell of cooking fires and, as the evening cools, the grass releases a sweet scent. The best performance in Nigeria yet.

20 Nov   The British Council Toyota Prada has random lime-green panels in order to avoid robbery. The thinking behind this is that it looks so vile that robbers won't bother. Another workshop. This time with an acting group from Kos. They are clever and anarchic. I do a status game with them using playing cards. The higher the card, the higher the status, and vice-versa. I tell the group that each actor has to find a partner of the same status and 'marry' them. Johnson, who is a ten, pairs off with Daughter (her Christian name), who is a six. I question this decision. 'Oh, suh,' he giggles, 'I felt sorry for my poor sister, so I thought I would make her very happy.' It seems an excellent re-definition of the exercise.

Our last performance. It's a beautiful night. Rather cooler. A final panic. One of the mothers explains that her daughter (playing Lady Macduff's child) cannot take part in the opening scene. It contains witchcraft. I point out that Lady Macduff is raped and murdered, and the daughter herself is killed in a later scene. 'Oh, yes,' says the mother sternly. 'We know about these things. It is the witchcraft that is dangerous. There will be trouble if my husband finds out that I have let my daughter take part.'

It's a terrific performance, and the audience is on its feet at the end. I am delighted, particularly for our colleagues at the British Council, who have worked for over a year to make this happen.

21 Nov　　There is a ten-hour wait for the plane in Lagos, so I hole up at the Sheraton until evening. At seven, my armoured car with driver plus a guard with an AK47 arrives. No more giggling. It no longer seems such a luxury. Later, the KLM McDonnell Tri-Star pounds along the runway, tyres thumping. Overhead lockers fly open, luggage spills out, and a galley unit breaks loose from its fittings and slides across the deck. It is the roughest take-off I have ever experienced. Out of the window, I see the gleaming yellow tarmac-laying equipment parked on the international runway. Unused. We nose up into the hot velvet night and point northwards over the Sahara towards Europe.

Afterword

The dedication of this book is to Bill Gaskill, one of the great theatre directors of the second half of the last century. Bill exemplifies the traditions of the Royal Court as expressed by its first Artistic Director, George Devine. When he inherited Devine's job, he took the disciplines of that theatre forward for seven years. As he was doing that, from 1965 to 1972, Max Stafford-Clark was developing his own production values in Edinburgh from the mid-sixties. As this book chronicles, the two directors came together to form a unique partnership with Joint Stock.

Subsequently, in inheriting the Artistic Directorship of the Royal Court, Stafford-Clark (the first Court Director not to have met Devine) imported both his own methods, and also what he had learned from Gaskill. Thus, two Artistic Directors of the Court, one past, one future, worked together in the seventies, and then Stafford-Clark faced the turbulence and the excitement of the eighties.

Surviving that was a major feat. Going on then to establish Out of Joint with Sonia Friedman shows a stamina and belief possessed by few artists. And the story continues. To date, Stafford-Clark has been responsible for directing all the plays produced by Out of Joint since it began in 1993. The company rightly enjoys an international reputation – and shows no sign of flagging.

Philip Roberts
November 2006

Appendix

PLAYS DIRECTED BY MAX STAFFORD-CLARK, 1965–2006

Traverse Theatre, Edinburgh

1965

Dublin Fair (Mike Jones/Mike Newling)
Dublin University Players in association
with the Traverse. Reworked and
revived as *Stewed Irish*, 1965
Transferred to Arts Theatre, London
Oh Gloria (Robert Shure)

1966

The Paterson's Shortbread Show (Mike
Jones/Mike Newling)
Double Double (James Saunders)
The Man Outside (Wolfgang Borchert)
The Dancers (David Cregan) Co-directed
with Gordon McDougall
Caledonian 6895 (Mike Jones/Mike Newling)

1967

The Recluse/Balls/Hurrah for the Bridge (Paul
Foster triple-bill) Transferred to Bristol
Arts Centre
An Expedition to Pick Mushrooms (Ranald
Graham)/*The King* (Steward Conn)
Cover Story (Michael Jones)/*Freddy* (Patsy
Southgate)/*Geoffrey* (Stanley Eveling)/
The Sword (Steward Conn) Revived,
Mickery Theatre, Amsterdam
Come and Be Killed (Stanley Eveling)
Transferred to New York Arts Centre
Trio (James Saunders)/*The Gymnasium*
(Olwen Wymark)/*Natural Causes* (Ellen
Dryden)/*Twenty-Six Efforts at Pornography*
(Carey Harrison) A bill of mini plays,
which transferred to Mickery Theatre,
Amsterdam, touring to Groningen and
Rotterdam
The Inert (Brian McMaster)

1968

Comings and Goings (Megan Terry) Trans-
ferred to Mickery Theatre, Amsterdam
*The Lunatic, the Secret Sportsman and the
Woman Next Door* (Stanley Eveling)
Transferred to Spingold Theater,
Brandeis University Interact Festival,
Boston; thence to Mickery; finally to
the Open Space, London
Anna-Luse (David Mowat) Transferred to
the Mickery
The Line of Least Existence (Rosalyn Drexler)
Revived at Liverpool University Arts
Festival, 1969; transferred to Stables
Theatre Club, Manchester

1969

Dracula (John Downie) Transferred to
Close Theatre Club, Glasgow; thence to
the Mickery Theatre
Another Town (Leo Lehmann)/*Play* (Samuel
Beckett)
Dear Janet Rosenberg, Dear Mr Kooning
(Stanley Eveling) Transferred to Royal
Court Theatre Upstairs Toured to
Mickery Theatre and Denmark
Sawney Bean (Robert Nye/Bill Watson)
Transferred to New Theatre

Traverse Workshop Company

1970

Ultramarine (David Brett)/*Mother Earth*
(David McNiven)

1971

Oh Starlings / Sweet Alice (Stanley Eveling) /
   Amaryllis (David McNiven and the
   Traverse Workshop)
Our Sunday Times (Stanley Eveling)
In the Heart of the British Museum (John
   Spurling)
Blubber (John Grillo)
For the Royal Court: Slag (David Hare)

1972

Hitler Dances (Howard Brenton)
Amalfi (David Mowat)

Freelance

1973

Trelawny of the 'Wells' (Arthur Wing Pinero)
   Long Wharf Theater, New Haven
The Royal Hunt of the Sun (Peter Shaffer)
   Palace Theatre, Watford
Come (David Mowat) Soho Poly
Magnificence (Howard Brenton) Royal Court

Joint Stock Theatre Group

1974

The Speakers (adapted from the book by
   Heathcote Williams) Co-directed with
   William Gaskill, Birmingham Repertory
   Studio and ICA, London
Shivvers (Stanley Eveling) Traverse Theatre
   and Royal Court Theatre Upstairs
X (Barry Reckord) Theatre Upstairs
Fourth Day Like Four Long Months Of Absence
   (Colin Bennett) Traverse Theatre and
   Theatre Upstairs

1975

Fanshen (David Hare, based on the book by
   William Hinton) Crucible Studio
   Theatre, Sheffield and ICA, London Co-
   directed with William Gaskill

The End Of Me Old Cigar (John Osborne)
   Greenwich Theatre [Freelance]
The Beggar's Opera (John Gay) Nottingham
   Playhouse [Freelance]

1976

Yesterday's News (The company and Jeremy
   Seabrook) West End Centre, Aldershot
   and Theatre Upstairs Directed by
   Gaskill and Stafford-Clark
Light Shining in Buckinghamshire (Caryl
   Churchill) Traverse Theatre and Theatre
   Upstairs
The Speakers (Revival) BITEF Festival,
   Belgrade; Hamburg; Dublin Theatre
   Festival; British Tour
Better Days Better Knights (Stanley Eveling)
   Traverse Theatre
Tea and Sex and Shakespeare (Thomas Kilroy)
   Abbey Theatre, Dublin

1977

A Thought in Three Parts (Wallace Shawn)
   ICA, London
A Mad World, My Masters (Barrie Keeffe)
   Young Vic Theatre and the Roundhouse
   Co-directed with William Gaskill
Epsom Downs (Howard Brenton) The
   Roundhouse
Fanshen (Revival) University of East Anglia
   and the Oval House, London
A Bit of Rough (Gilly Fraser) Soho Poly

The Royal Court

1978

The Glad Hand (Snoo Wilson) Joint Stock at
   the Royal Court
Prayer for my Daughter (Thomas Babe)
Wheelchair Willie (Alan Brown)

1979

Cloud Nine (Caryl Churchill) Joint Stock at
   the Royal Court
Sergeant Ola and his Followers (David Lan)

1980

The Arbor (Andrea Dunbar)
Cloud Nine (Revival) Co-directed with
    Les Waters

1981

The Seagull (version by Thomas Kilroy)
Borderline (Hanif Kureishi)

1982

Operation Bad Apple (G.F. Newman)
Top Girls (Caryl Churchill)
Rita, Sue and Bob Too (Andrea Dunbar)

1983

Top Girls (Revival, and to the Public
    Theatre, New York)
Falkland Sound (devised piece)
The Grass Widow (Snoo Wilson)

1984

Tom and Viv (Michael Hastings)
Rat in the Skull (Ron Hutchinson)
An Honourable Trade (G.F. Newman)
The Pope's Wedding (Edward Bond)

1985

Tom and Viv (Revival, and to New York)
Rat in the Skull (Revival, and to New York)
Aunt Dan and Lemon (Wallace Shawn)

1986

Prarie du Chien (David Mamet)
A Colder Climate (Karim Alrawi)

1987

Serious Money (Caryl Churchill) Transferred
    to Wyndhams, and to New York

1988

Bloody Poetry (Howard Brenton)
The Recruiting Officer (George Farquhar)
Our Country's Good (Timberlake Wertenbaker)

1989

Icecream (Caryl Churchill)
The Recruiting Officer / Our Country's Good
    (Revival) Garrick Theatre, and to
    Australia

1990

My Heart's a Suitcase (Clare McIntyre)
Maydays (Julie Burchill)
Etta Jenks (Marlane Meyer)

1991

All Things Nice (Sharman Macdonald)
Top Girls (Revival)
Three Birds Alighting on a Field (Timberlake
    Wertenbaker)

1992

A Jovial Crew (Richard Brome) Royal
    Shakespeare Company [Freelance]
Hush (April De Angelis)
Three Birds Alighting on a Field (Revival)

1993

King Lear
Three Birds Alighting on a Field (New York)
The Country Wife (William Wycherley) Royal
    Shakespeare Company [Freelance]

Out of Joint Theatre Company

1994

The Queen and I (Sue Townsend)
    Haymarket, Leicester; Royal Court;
    Vaudeville
Road (Jim Cartwright) Haymarket
    Leicester
The Wives' Excuse (Thomas Southerne) Royal
    Shakespeare Company
The Libertine (Stephen Jeffreys) Royal Court
The Man of Mode (George Etherege) Royal
    Court

1995

The Steward of Christendom (Sebastian Barry) Theatre Upstairs
Three Sisters (Chekhov) Bristol Old Vic and India
The Break of Day (Timberlake Wertenbaker) Bristol Old Vic

1996

The Steward of Christendom (Revival: Australia; New Zealand; Dublin)
Shopping and Fucking (Mark Ravenhill) Theatre Upstairs; Transferred to Gielgud Theatre

1997

The Positive Hour (April De Angelis) Hampstead Theatre
Blue Heart (Caryl Churchill) Theatre Royal, Bury St Edmunds; Royal Court
The Steward of Christendom (Revival: New York)
Shopping and Fucking (Revival: West End; Australia; New Zealand)

1998

Our Lady of Sligo (Sebastian Barry) Oxford Playhouse; Royal Court
Our Country's Good (Revival: Theatre Royal, Bath)
Shopping and Fucking (Revival: Tour; New York)
Blue Heart (Revival: Tour)

1999

Drummers (Simon Bennett) Cambridge Arts Theatre; New Ambassadors
Some Explicit Polaroids (Mark Ravenhill) Theatre Royal, Bury St Edmunds; New Ambassadors
Our Country's Good (Revival: Tour)
Blue Heart (Revival: New York)

2000

Rita, Sue and Bob Too (Revival: Everyman Theatre, Liverpool)
A State Affair (Robin Soans) Everyman Theatre, Liverpool
Some Explicit Polaroids (Revival: Tour)
Our Lady of Sligo (Revival: New York)

2001

Feelgood (Alistair Beaton) Hampstead Theatre; Transferred to Garrick Theatre
Sliding with Suzanne (Judy Upton) Theatre Upstairs
Rita, Sue and Bob Too (Revival: New Zealand)

2002

Hinterland (Sebastian Barry) Octagon Theatre, Bolton; Royal National Theatre
A Laughing Matter (April De Angelis) Oxford Playhouse; National Theatre
She Stoops to Conquer (Goldsmith) Oxford Playhouse; National Theatre

2003

The Breath of Life (David Hare) Sydney Theatre Company
Duck (Stella Feehily) Traverse Theatre; Tour
The Permanent Way (David Hare) Theatre Royal, York; Tour; National Theatre

2004

Macbeth Red Brick Mill, Batley; Tour; Arcola Theatre, London; International Tour, 2005

2005

Talking to Terrorists (Robin Soans) Theatre Royal, Bury St Edmunds; Tour; Royal Court

2006

O Go My Man (Stella Feehily) Royal Court
The Overwhelming (J.T. Rogers) National Theatre

Select Bibliography

PRIMARY SOURCES

Institutional Archives

Papers of Neville Blond; Stuart Burge;
William Gaskill; Earl of Harewood;
Donald Howarth; Greville Poke; Rob
Ritchie; Joint Stock Theatre Group;
Royal Court archive (Brotherton
Library, Special Collections, University
of Leeds). Papers of Max Stafford-Clark
(British Library). David Hare Archive
(Harry Ransom Humanities Research
Center, University of Texas, Austin).
Traverse Theatre Archive (National
Library of Scotland). Papers of
Matthew Evans (Faber and Faber).
Minutes of the Board of Out of Joint
Theatre Company.

Taped Interviews with Philip Roberts

April De Angelis, 8 Nov. 2002
Stuart Burge, 9 July and 14 Aug. 1996
Ron Cook, 3 April 2001
Graham Cowley, 8 Nov. 2002
Stephen Daldry, 4 Feb. 1998
Matthew Evans, 16 Jan. 1997
Sonia Friedman, 25 Oct. 2002
William Gaskill, 15 April 2003
Lloyd Hutchinson, 10 Aug. 2001
Stephen Jeffreys, 31 Aug. 2001
Tricia Kelly, 2 July 2001
Lesley Manville, 17 Sept. 2001
Mark Ravenhill, 20 Oct. 2002
Ian Redford, 31 Jan. 2002
Rob Ritchie, 21 Aug. 2003
Max Stafford-Clark 21 Feb. 1985; 19 May
1995; 13 Dec. 1996; 7 May 1997;
15 June 10 Aug. 17 Sept. 2001; 25 Jan.
18 May 19 Sept. 2002
Nigel Terry, 1 May 2001
Timberlake Wertenbaker, 24 April 2001

Letters

Caryl Churchill to Matthew Evans, 7 March
1987; 3 Nov. 1989 (Evans archive,
Faber and Faber)
Stanley Eveling to Philip Roberts, 27 Sept.
1999 (author's possession)
Paul Foster to Stafford-Clark, 28 Jan.
1967; Gordon McDougal, 8 April 1967
(Traverse archive)
Jocelyn Herbert to Stafford-Clark, 4 Feb.
1998 (author's possession)
Max Stafford-Clark to: Lynn Dearth, 14
August 1982 (Diary); Matthew Evans, 6
Aug. 1986 and 14 Nov. 1987 (Evans
archive, Faber and Faber); William
Gaskill, 23 April 1987 (Faber); David
Hare, 27 Sept. 1981, 11 April and May
1984, 21 May and 22 Oct. 1992
(Ransom); Jocelyn Herbert, 28 Jan. and
23 March 1998 (author's possession);
Sir Brian Rix, 10 Feb. and 2 March
1989 (Brotherton Library); Philip
Roberts, 15, 20 May, 10 June and 21
Sept. 2002 (author's possession);
Michael Rudman, 28 Sept. 1971
(Traverse archive, as also 2 undated
letters to Rudman, c. late 1971); Ellen
Stewart, June 1967 (Traverse archive);
Arts Editor, The Times, 30 April 1968;
The Times, 1 Sept. 1984

SECONDARY SOURCES

Sebastian Barry, *The Steward of Christendom,*
Methuen, 1995

Howard Brenton, *Epsom Downs* in *Plays 1,*
Methuen, 1986; *Hot Irons,* Nick Hern
Books, 1995

Caryl Churchill, *Sunday Times Magazine,*
2 March, 1980; *Cloud Nine,* Nick Hern
Books, 1989; *Serious Money* in *Plays 2,*
Methuen, 1990

Brian Cox, *Plays International,* Aug. 1983

Andrea Dunbar, *Rita, Sue and Bob Too*
with *The Arbor* and *Shirley,* Introduction
by Rob Ritchie, Methuen, 1988

Stanley Eveling, *Guardian,* 16 April 1974

William Gaskill, 'Introduction to *The
Speakers'*, *Gambit,* vol.7, no. 25, 1974;
A Sense of Direction, Faber, 1988

David Haig, *Guardian,* 17 Jan. 1988

David Hare, *Fanshen* in *Plays 2,* Faber, 1997;
*The Permanent Way. A National Theatre
Workpack,* www.nationaltheatre.org.uk

Robert Hughes, *The Fatal Shore: a history of
the transportation of convicts to Australia,
1787–1868,* Collins Harvill, 1987

Suzie Mackenzie, 'Intrigue at Court', *GQ
Magazine,* March, 1992

Cordelia Oliver, *Guardian,* 3 Aug. 1970

John Osborne, 'Why I am angry today',
Sunday Telegraph, 10 Feb. 1980

'The Prudential Awards for the Arts',
Stage, 6 Nov. 1997

Mark Ravenhill, *Some Explicit Polaroids,*
Methuen, 1999

Rob Ritchie (Edited and Introduced), *The
Joint Stock Book: the Making of a Theatre
Collective,* Methuen, 1987

Philip Roberts, *The Royal Court Theatre and
the Modern Stage,* CUP, 1999

Tony Rohr, *Plays and Players,* Feb. 1982

David Stafford-Clark, *Psychiatry for Students,*
Allen and Unwin, 1964

Max Stafford-Clark, *The Times,* 30 April,
1968; 1 Sept., 1984; *Plays and
Players,* June, 1971; Jan. 1974;
Jan. 1983; March, 1989; *Sunday
Telegraph,* 17 Feb., 1980; *Letters to
George,* Nick Hern Books, 1989; The
Theatre Shop, Tenth Anniversary
Conference, Dublin, 3 Oct. 2003—
(Stafford-Clark interview).
www.theatreshop.ie

William Watson, *Scotsman,* 8 Aug. 1970

Timberlake Wertenbaker, *Our Country's
Good,* Methuen, 1991

Index